Neronians and Flavians

Greek and Latin Studies
Classical Literature and its Influence

Editors

D. R. Dudley and T. A. Dorey

Greek and Latin Studies
Classical Literature and its Influence

Neronians and Flavians
Silver Latin I

Edited by
D. R. DUDLEY

Routledge & Kegan Paul: LONDON AND BOSTON

First published 1972
by Routledge & Kegan Paul Ltd
Broadway House, 68–74 Carter Lane,
London EC4V 5EL
and 9 Park Street,
Boston, Mass. 02108 U.S.A.
Printed in Great Britain by
William Clowes & Sons, Limited
London, Beccles and Colchester

ISBN 0 7100 7273 2

Contents

Editors' Foreword

This is the first of two volumes on Latin Literature of the Silver Age. It contains chapters on Seneca, Lucan, Persius, Petronius, Statius, and Martial; the companion volume will add the names of Velleius Paterculus, Valerius Maximus, Pliny the elder, Pliny the younger, Quintilian and the writers of Panegyric.

These will be the tenth and eleventh volumes to be published in the series, and with their appearance the responsibilities of the present editors will come to an end. The series will be edited in future by Mr C. D. N. Costa and Dr J. W. Binns, also of the Latin Department of the University of Birmingham. Its scope is to be enlarged to include Greek literature as well as Latin. The new editors will announce their aims and programme in due course. We wish them well, and are glad to know that they intend to follow our original objectives in bringing in scholars from other disciplines, encouraging classicists to write for a wider audience, and stressing the influence of classical literature in later times.

T. A. Dorey
D. R. Dudley

Introduction

'Silver Latin', 'Silver Age'—the terms have probably taken root too deeply to be shifted. It is useful to have a group label for the Latin authors of the period from Tiberius to Hadrian: 'Early Empire' is too vague: 'Julio-Claudian and Flavian' is clumsy and falls short in time. But if the term 'Silver' is to be used, its limitations must be kept in mind. A degree of inferiority is implied: a silver coin is less valuable than one of gold: the 'silver age' of mythology is a degeneration from the age of gold. Roman society and culture in this age were not, in general, inferior to those of the late republic. In some respects, as in architecture, they were much in advance. And if the term is confined, as it should be, to literature, no general inferiority can be allowed. Tacitus, Juvenal and Petronius, three of the greatest and most original of Latin authors, are proof to the contrary. But silversmiths are understood to work in a valuable metal whose qualities determine their art. The analogy may be helpful for a critical understanding of the Silver Age of Latin literature.

Whether these authors wrote in prose or verse, common factors were at work on them all. They were the product of the rhetorical schools, accepting the modes and outlook there in vogue. They had to live under an imperial autocracy, abrasive under Tiberius, light under Trajan, but always unchallengeable. As a guide to morals, there was little but the form of Stoicism which Panaetius and Posidonius had restyled for the Roman market, and which was further adapted by Seneca, Cornutus, Musonius Rufus and Epictetus. All were conscious that Latin literature had already passed its high pinnacle of achievement. Several genres had run out. There was no more to be done in erotic or lyric poetry. In epic the mighty name of Virgil was a spur to emulation but a barrier to success. History too was felt to involve more danger for less ample themes. Political eloquence—the highest form—had died with the republic. The authors of the Silver Age had either to strike out anew, or work in the shadow of established reputations.

Four of the six authors in this volume lived under Nero. They knew the hothouse atmosphere of the Neronian court, and saw the metamorphosis of a gifted young prince into a fickle and criminal tyrant. Seneca was Nero's tutor, Lucan (for a time) his friend, Petronius the chosen companion of his pleasures. All were driven to suicide by this fatal intimacy. Fortune granted Persius the boon of an early death. Statius and Martial worked under the autocracy of Domitian, but from a safer distance and were better adapted for survival. Content with patronage, they did not aspire to friendship: when adulation was called for, they had ample reserves on which to draw. Martial, like Tacitus and the younger Pliny, lived on into the happier times of Nerva and Trajan, when men felt free to speak their minds, especially if they chose to vilify the dead tyrant.

The first two chapters examine Seneca as a man and as a philosopher, subjects on which a wide range of views has been expressed. To what extent is there a consonance? Or was there a basic flaw in Seneca's character which makes him unacceptable—even intolerable—as a moralist? If Diogenes is to leave his tub, it should not be for a palace. Professor Ferguson has some telling modern parallels of men who could not endure success, among them the Nigerian statesman whose life ended as starkly as that of Seneca. Roman philosophical writing is not much esteemed nowadays—witness the eclipse of the writings of Cicero—but Mr Currie shows that there is more vigour and originality in Seneca than is commonly allowed.

Professor Dilke contributes two chapters on Lucan. In the first, he shows how Lucan's political views of the Caesars must be seen in the light of the contemporary Stoic 'opposition', which went far beyond a dislike of the personal excesses of Nero to a reasoned hostility to the principate. The leading personages of the Civil Wars had been refurbished into political exemplars—as have, in our own times, those of the Irish struggles for independence of fifty years ago. Lucan's poem accepted these portrayals, and gave them a new vitality. Proof of this is the long, if discontinuous, influence Lucan has had in English literature. To have provided the prototype for the antihero of *Paradise Lost* might be thought enough. But, as Professor Dilke shows, Lucan has influenced English poets from Chaucer to Robert Graves, not invariably as admirers.

For both Lucan and Seneca as a field of maximum force one should look to Spain. For centuries they have been regarded as Spanish authors, who happened to live in classical times and to write in Latin. The bi-millenary of Seneca in 1966 was (appropriately enough) celebrated in Cordova: he was treated as one of the greatest thinkers in the Western tradition. As for Lucan, the *Pharsalia* has littered a copious Spanish prodigy, not least among them a Lucanian epic on the Araucanian War, composed in the early stages of the Spanish conquest of the New World.

Detailed analysis is used by Miss Grimes to establish the main features of Persius' style, and to show how its effects are achieved. Dense and self-sufficient, as she rightly calls it, it is also highly individual, scarcely less so than that of Tacitus, even if more limited in range. There is something almost frightening about the intensity of the moral feeling it contains, a reminder of what Marcus Aurelius has to say about his own Stoic tutors.

Of our six authors, Petronius is certainly strongest in contemporary appeal. In content, style and outlook, the *Satyricon* is congenial to our times. There have been several recent translations and it has been adapted for the cinema and the radio. Mr J. F. Sullivan, whose own translation has been so well received, writes on the problems a translator of Petronius must face. He must avoid an overly seductive modernity, the price of which could be that his version would quickly date. He must be aware of Petronius' own quick changes of style, as he passes from narrative or verbal imitation to parody and mock epic. Petronius could let his characters speak for themselves, as in the *Cena Trimalchionis*; the translator must be sure that he conveys the right effect. Right or wrong, that effect can be potent. For example, in 1948 the Third Programme of the BBC broadcast a version of the *Cena Trimalchionis* by Louis MacNeice. Regional accents—Cockney, Yorkshire, Irish, Welsh—were used to distinguish the guests. No more was needed. The Welsh accent was contributed by the poet Dylan Thomas, then a frequent reader for the BBC. The *Cena* was again broadcast in 1951. In the years 1952 and 1953 Dylan Thomas was at work, 'slowly and sporadically', as his biographer says, on a radio drama of his own. The result was the poem *Under*

Milk Wood, which was first read by the author to audiences in Boston and New York in 1953. He was not the man to waste ideas—whether his own or another's. A link Petronius–MacNeice–Dylan Thomas is perhaps not so odd as it sounds.

Dr Gossage's appraisal of Statius comes when that poet is, and has long been, in almost total eclipse. Poems from the *Silvae* appear in anthologies, but one does not turn to Statius for the Theban legend or the tale of Achilles, as men did in the Middle Ages. As Dr Gossage shows, Statius did not use the *Thebaid* as an exercise in escapism, but rather to probe the problem of evil, of human cruelty and of the atrocities of war. On such topics we are no doubt better informed. Martial, as Professor Carrington shows, is another matter. He knew his limits, and directed a minor talent to achieve perfection in a narrow range. The only demand that his poetry makes is that one should enjoy it.

Note

I should like to record my thanks to the editorial department of the publishers, who saw this volume through the press at a time when illness made it impossible for me to do so.

D. R. D.

Abbreviations

AJPhil	*American Journal of Philology*
BAGB	*Bulletin de l'Association Guillaume Budé*
CJ	*Classical Journal*
CPhil	*Classical Philology*
CQ	*Classical Quarterly*
CR	*Classical Review*
J. Engl. & Germanic Phil.	*Journal of English and Germanic Philology*
J. Hist. Ideas	*Journal of the History of Ideas*
Mod. Lang. Notes	*Modern Language Notes*
Mod. Lang. Rev.	*Modern Language Review*
Mus. Belge	*Musée Belge*
Mus. Helv.	*Museum Helveticum*
Neue Jahrb.	*Neue Jahrbucher fur d. klassische Altertum*
PBA	*Proceedings of the British Academy*
PP	*La Parola del Passato*
PQ	*Philological Quarterly*
Rev. Arch.	*Revue Archéologique*
Rev. Ét. Anc.	*Revue des Études Anciennes*
Rev. Ét. Lat.	*Revue des Études Latines*
RES	*Review of English Studies*
Stud. Eng. Lit.	*Studies in English Literature*
Stud. in Phil.	*Studies in Philology*
TAPA	*Transactions of the American Philological Association*
Trans. Royal Soc. Canada	*Transactions of the Royal Society of Canada*

I

Seneca the Man

JOHN FERGUSON

'Notable Seneca', wrote Thomas Carlyle in his essay on Diderot, 'so wistfully desirous to stand well with Truth and yet not ill with Nero, is and remains only our perhaps niceliest proportioned half-and-half, the plausiblest Plausible on record; no great man, no true man, no man at all.' A few months earlier, on 10 August 1832, he had written his opinion of Seneca in his diary.

> He is father of all that work in sentimentality, and, by fine speaking and decent behaviour, study to serve God and mammon, to stand well with philosophy and not ill with Nero. His *force* had mostly oozed out of him, or corrupted itself into *benevolence*, virtue, sensibility. Oh! the everlasting clatter about virtue! virtue!! In the Devil's name be virtuous and no more about it.

Carlyle's was not the only voice to be eloquently raised last century in prosecution of Seneca. Macaulay turned to the attack in his essay on Bacon. He was contrasting the Baconian doctrine of Utility and Progress with the Stoic philosophy which 'disdained to be useful and was content to be stationary'. Seneca stands in the frontline of attack. Posidonius had taken an almost Marxist view of technological progress; Seneca scorned this imputation that philosophy might raise the material standards of the human race (*Ep.*, 90). 'We shall next be told', he wrote as a knockdown blow, 'that the first shoemaker was a philosopher.' 'For our own part,' commented Macaulay, 'if we are forced to make our choice between the first shoemaker and the author of the three books *On Anger*, we pronounce for the shoemaker. It may be worse to be angry than to be wet. But shoes have kept millions from being wet; and we doubt whether Seneca ever kept anyone from being angry.' Macaulay goes on:

It is very reluctantly that Seneca can be brought to confess that any philosopher had ever paid the smallest attention to anything that could possibly promote what vulgar people would consider as the well-being of mankind. He labours to clear Democritus from the disgraceful imputation of having made the first arch, and Anacharsis from the charge of having contrived the potter's wheel. He is forced to own that such a thing might happen; and it may also happen, he tells us, that a philosopher may be swift of foot. But it is not in his character of philosopher that he either wins a race or invents a machine. No, to be sure. The business of a philosopher was to declaim in praise of poverty, with two millions sterling out at usury, to meditate epigrammatic conceits about the evils of luxury, in gardens which moved the envy of sovereigns, to rant about liberty, while fawning on the insolent and pampered freedmen of a tyrant, to celebrate the divine beauty of virtue with the same pen which had just before written a defence of the murder of a mother by a son.

In their essence these moral criticisms of Seneca go back to the unsavoury P. Suillius in A.D. 58. The burden of Suillius' attack is recorded by Dio Cassius (61.10). After charging Seneca with adultery with Agrippina he goes on:

This was only one of several instances where his behaviour was diametrically opposed to his professions. He preached against tyranny, and tutored a tyrant. He ran down the hangers-on of those who held power, but he was never far from the palace. He condemned flattery, but was for ever currying favour with Messalina and Claudius' freedmen; he actually sent them an adulatory book from Corsica, though a guilty conscience led him later to suppress it. He became a millionaire while castigating the possession of wealth. He attacked luxury in others while himself possessing five hundred identical tables with cedarwood tops and ivory legs for his banquets. To say this is to imply the rest. He had no morals. He contracted a brilliant marriage; at the same time he was indulging himself with boys past their prime, and teaching Nero to do the same.

Tacitus (*Ann.*, 13.42) adds a little:

... Senecam increpans infensum amicis Claudii, sub quo
iustissimum exilium pertulisset. simul studiis inertibus et
iuvenum imperitiae suetum livere iis, qui vividam et incor-
ruptam eloquentiam tuendis civibus exercerent. se quaestorem
Germanici, illum domus eius adulterum fuisse. an gravius
aestimandum sponte litigatoris praemium honestae operae
adsequi quam corrumpere cubicula principum feminarum?
qua sapientia, quibus philosophorum praeceptis intra
quadriennium regiae amicitiae ter miliens sestertium para-
visset? Romae testamenta et orbos velut indagine eius capi,
Italiam et provincias immenso faenore hauriri: at sibi labore
quaesitam et modicam pecuniam esse. crimen, periculum,
omnia potius toleraturum, quam veterem ac domi partam
dignationem subitae felicitati submitteret.

(Seneca received his deserts in exile under Claudius; no friend
of Claudius is a friend of his. His experience lies in cloistered
scholarship, with inexperienced young men; he casts a
jaundiced eye on those whose eloquence is alive and
unspoiled and used to defend their fellow-citizens. When I,
said Suillius, was quaestor to Germanicus, he was an
adulterer in his home. Which is a more serious crime—to
receive for honourable service a gift freely given by a client,
or to violate the bed of women of the imperial house? What
wisdom, what philosophical precepts made him a millionaire
within four years of the emperor's favour? In Rome his nets
spread for childless testators; his rates of interest are in process of milking Italy and the provinces dry; I have a modest,
hard-earned competence. But I will face a criminal charge—
anything rather than allow an honour which I have long won
by my efforts to succumb before a prosperity so newly
gained.)

Yet this is the man whom the Christian Tertullian claims as
'often one of us' (*De An.*, 20.1), who was spuriously supposed
to have conducted a correspondence with Paul of Tarsus, and
whom the Council of Trent quote as an acknowledged father of
the Church. There is a dichotomy somewhere, between words

and works, language and living. His brother told him so in his lifetime (*D.*, 7.18.1; 7.20.1). He himself said that there are two factors in right living—knowledge and practice (*Ep.*, 94.49). Precisely.

Seneca was born at Cordoba in Spain, probably shortly before the Christian era. He was a sickly child, with a sickliness which extended into adult life: Caligula refrained from executing him on the grounds that he would die a natural death any minute. He appears to have been consumptive; he was asthmatic all through his life (*Ep.*, 54); later he suffered from gout (*D.*, 7.17.4). Endowed with material goods, he still felt deprived and insecure, and from that sense of deprivation and insecurity came the drive to economic and political power. He had to compensate for his physical deficiencies. There is a passage of autobiography at the beginning of one of the letters:

vexari te distillationibus crebris ac febriculis, quae longas distillationes et in consuetudinem adductas sequuntur, eo molestius mihi est, quia expertus sum hoc genus valitudinis, quod inter initia contempsi: poterat adhuc adulescentia iniurias ferre et se adversus morbos contumaciter gerere. deinde subcubui et eo perductus sum, ut ipse distillarem ad summam maciem deductus. saepe impetum cepi abrumpendae vitae; patris me indulgentissimi senectus retinuit.

(I'm sorry to hear that you suffer from frequent colds, and the high temperatures that attend that chronic complaint when you can't get rid of it. I sympathize; I used to suffer the same way myself. At first I didn't take it seriously. Before we're grown up we can stand things going wrong. We're plucky enough when we fall ill. Later I succumbed. I reached the point when I was so thin that my flesh was running like my nose! Time and again I felt the impulse to cut my life short; it was my dear father's age which stopped me.) (*Ep.*, 78.1)

The references to suicide in the letters show that he had come to a balanced Stoic view: 'I shall not abandon old age, if old age keeps me complete—at any rate complete in the part that matters. If old age begins to weaken my intellect and pull its faculties to pieces, leaving me breathing but not living, then I shall leap out of a building which is in danger of collapsing' (*Ep.*, 58.35). But while they show that he had arrived at a committed position, they also show that he continued to brood on the theme. Even at the end of his life he has a long, depressed discussion of suicide, whose most optimistic note is 'Life has one entrance but many exits' (*Ep.*, 70.15). He had in fact strong neurotic tendencies from an early stage, which may be seen in a different form in the Sotion episode; he was seeking salvation in theosophy and an exotic asceticism, and gave it up at his father's request owing to political scandal; we can date the episode accurately to the years A.D. 15–19, when Seneca was in his teens or early twenties (*Ep.*, 108.17–22). His ready impulse towards the occult and his equally ready abandonment of it alike show a certain instability of character. Later we see a different aspect of the same tendency: in the third book *De ira* there is a really nasty brooding on scenes of torture, a deep spiritual sadism; his nephew Lucan shared the same proclivity. Of course he himself knew that the personality has its irrational side, if only from Plato and the textbooks (*Ep.*, 92.8).

As he grew up, there were five great influences on his life. The first was his father, a rich man of the upper middle class, born about 55 B.C., who lived through till about A.D. 40, a Spaniard who returned from Rome to Spain either to an administrative post or with business interests or both, a man of letters, something of a historian, a notable writer on rhetoric, nothing of a philosopher. Seneca's attitude to his eminent father is marked by a strong sense of duty. It was his father who directed him to the Bar, where he practised with skill but without enthusiasm; it is significant that he ceased to practise after his father's death. It was his father's displeasure which pulled him back from an un-Roman asceticism; he returned to a vegetarian diet and water-drinking, though not till twenty years after his father's death. It was the thought of his father which restrained him from suicide during his deepest depression. His attitude to his father is classically ambivalent—obedience and conflict. For he espoused the philosophy which his father despised. The mixture of respect and revolt recalls Edmund Gosse's *Father and Son*. Or, to take a more recent example, Seneca in his youth was not so different from the modern hippies who are in revolt against the generation of their fathers. The establishment soon recaptured him; it is not unfair to call him 'the half-hearted hippie'. His father's influence held him from beyond the grave (*fr.* 98).

The second influence was his mother, Helvia. We know little about her, except what we can glean from a letter of consolation which Seneca wrote to her during his later exile. This is a tender letter, and contains two particularly revealing passages. From one it appears that Helvia was interested in the study of philosophy, but Seneca's father deterred her (*D.*, 12.17.4); there is a wealth of suggestion about the triangular relationship in that simple fact. The other is a passage in which he lays before his mother the ideal of Rutilia who followed her son Cotta into exile (*D.*, 12.16.7). Apart from the fact that Helvia was in Spain not Rome (*D.*, 12.18.9), this is such an odd thing to write that it can have arisen only from a deep sense of need. It looks as though Seneca missed his mother; she had not been with him when he first moved to Rome, and after her husband's death she had returned to Spain. Seneca craved for dependence, and independence was thrust upon him.

As a mother-substitute he had his aunt, wife of Vetrasius Pollio who governed Egypt for sixteen years. As climax to his letter of consolation he commends Helvia to her, the mother to the mother-figure (*D.*, 12.19). She was a woman of the old-fashioned sort, self-effacing and devoted. Seneca writes of her with unaffected warmth:

> She always shares your emotions; but where I am concerned her sympathy is not just for you. It was in her hands that I travelled to Rome; she nursed me devotedly back to health, like a mother, through a long illness; she used her influence to support me when I stood for the office of quaestor. She was usually too shy to make conversation or greet anyone except in an undertone, but, where I was involved, affection overcame shyness.

There is something here which Seneca would like to have been, but he was a man and a Roman, and it was not for him.

The fourth great influence was his elder brother; again we sense a mood of dependence. M. Annaeus Novatus was a young man of public promise who attracted the attention of the distinguished rhetorician L. Junius Gallio, who adopted him under the name of L. Junius Annaeus Gallio. We know little about his career; he was an *amicus* of Claudius; he served as governor of Achaea, when the incident recorded in Acts 18:12–17 took place. At some point he was consul, perhaps suffect consul with A. Marcellus. He was executed under Nero the year after Seneca. Seneca has a most attractive character-study of him (*Nat. Quaest.* 4 pref. 9–11) in which he praises his intelligence, speaks of him as utterly free from vices and as abominating flattery, and particularly commends his companionableness and his lack of interest in money. In one of the letters he actually calls him 'my master' (*Ep.*, 104.1). Seneca also addressed to him the treatise *De ira*, which was written at his brother's request and is one of Seneca's earliest works, as it antedates his brother's adoption by Gallio, the fragmentary work *De remediis fortunae*, and the later treatise *De vita beata.* I have argued elsewhere (*Palaeologia* 7, 1958, 111ff) that Seneca's brother was an Epicurean, and that this explains the detailed and sympathetic knowledge of Epicurus shown by Seneca throughout his life. The brother escaped the father's leading-strings; Seneca did not.

Finally there is Attalus. We know of three of Seneca's teachers. Sotion was a flash in the pan (*Ep.*, 108–17ff). Fabianus Papirius was perhaps an intellectual rather than a personal influence (*Ep.*, 100). But Attalus is the subject of unrestrained tribute (*Ep.*, 108, 3ff, 13ff). Attalus was a magnetic teacher, accessible to his students. Seneca laid siege to him, was the first to arrive and last to leave, and was persistent in questioning. Attalus stressed discipline of the body and independence of character. He called himself, in Stoic phrase, a king; Seneca thought him the judge of kings. The young man was caught up in his enthusiasms. Did he praise poverty? If Seneca's wealth had been in the classroom he would have given it all away. Did he denounce luxury and extol sobriety? Seneca said to himself, 'I resolve to limit my food and drink.' 'And', he commented whimsically many years after, 'some of it has stuck.' There is something a little hothouse, a little unhealthy about Seneca's enthusiasm, which tended to catch a chill outside the classroom. But his self-knowledge is delightfully honest.

He first appears in public before our eyes in the later years of Tiberius' reign; his quaestorship must have fallen in the early thirties and he gives a first-hand picture of the frenzied accusations which were bandied about during the years after Sejanus' fall (*De ben.*, 3.26.1). He was married at about this time, but we

7

know little about the marriage. A child died in infancy. His writing attracted the attention of Caligula, who described his style, scathingly but not wholly unjustly, as 'sand without lime' (Suet., *Cal.*, 53). We may assume that from this period date the lost works listed by Quintilian (10.1.129) and the tragedies, which allowed an emotional outlet in an age of tyranny without committing their author (cf. *Thy.*, 446; 600). More dangerous was the emperor's jealousy of his brilliance at the Bar. For the moment Seneca's ill-health saved him. When Cassius Chaerea assassinated Caligula, the senate, with the sententious lawyer present but without much influence, debated restoring the republic; the praetorian guard was busy enthroning Claudius. The new regime brought disaster to Seneca. Julia Livilla, the emperor's niece, was recalled from the exile to which she had been consigned by Caligula. Within a year she was in exile again; so was Seneca; the charge was adultery. It is impossible at this distance to know whether it was true; Diderot thought it was. To his mother Seneca naturally implies his innocence (*D.*, 12.13.3); to Polybius he enters no such plea. Seneca's sexual life was suspect, but such charges, from the time of Augustus himself, were a convenient way to break up political conspiracies, and Julia's husband, M. Vinicius, had been canvassed as a possible successor to Caligula (Jos., *Ant. Iud.*, 19.251). There is one curious aspect of the episode. The force behind the condemnation was the empress Messalina, but Seneca never mentions her, though her career offered obvious moral lessons for the preacher. Claudius intervened for clemency, and had an original sentence of death commuted to one of banishment (*D.*, 11.13.2), yet Seneca harried Claudius with his pen after the emperor's death (*De ben.*, 4.32.3, and the lost *Apocolocyntosis*).

Seneca spent nearly eight years in exile in Corsica. They were years of self-pity. He did not live by the principles he later laid down: 'I may become an exile. I will act like a native of the place where I am sent' (*Ep.*, 24.17). (Two paragraphs later he says, 'It is dishonourable to write one thing and mean another.') From this period we have two letters, one to his mother, the other to the emperor's freedman and adviser Polybius. The letter to Helvia, though over-rhetorical, is not ignoble, and the Stoic clichés about independence of circumstances ring with a certain dignity from a man who has actually been deprived of his homeland.

Even here, he pretends to be sustaining a poverty which *relegatio* did not involve (*D.*, 12.10.1). The letter to Polybius is utterly deplorable and contains the most nauseating flattery of the emperor 'under whose rule exiles live more peaceably than did princes under Gaius'. 'Lift yourself up. When tears well into your eyes, fix your gaze on Caesar; the spectacle of his great and glorious divinity will dry them' (*D.*, 11.12.3ff). There is no more persuasive evidence that Seneca lacked greatness of character.

Agrippina saw through him. Once Messalina was out of the way she had him recalled, and advanced to the praetorship. Seneca was a popular writer, and she thought that the move would enhance her popularity; she also wanted to use his advice in furthering her plans for the succession of Nero, knowing that Seneca would be hostile to Claudius and would favour her (Tac., *Ann.*, 12.8). Even as a preacher to royalty, Seneca failed, and Renan in *L'Antichrist* went so far as to lay the monstrosities of Nero at the door of Seneca. For Seneca, who warned Lucilius against letting *philosophia* degenerate into *philologia*, himself played with words. The habit of using words to serve the cleverness of the moment is empty in the pulpit, fatal in the political arena. At the outset of Nero's reign, Seneca confronted him with the image of absolute power, in order to reinforce his sense of responsibility; it was the awareness of absolute power that remained. A philosophy which puts all good in the will and none in the act is not a philosophy of politics. What is more, rightness of will is caught, rather than taught, and Seneca, who combined strong professions with a weak will, was hardly the person to catch it from; indeed, as we are told that Agrippina did not let Nero study philosophy (Suet., *Nero*, 52), Nero had from Seneca words without substance, instruction in language and respectable friendliness (Tac., *Ann.*, 13.2).

In A.D. 54 Claudius was removed by means of poisoned mushrooms, and Nero succeeded. There is no evidence that Seneca was party to the murder, or to the subsequent murder of Britannicus, but it does not seem that he protested overmuch. He wrote Nero's speeches, and Tacitus comments maliciously that there was something in Seneca's way of thought which satisfied contemporary taste (*Ann.*, 13.3). Seneca tried to call the tune of the new reign in his treatise *De clementia*; the note is sounded by Calpurnius Siculus also (1, 58–9). It is a frightening document.

Nero is to say to himself: 'I have been selected to perform on earth the office of the gods, I am lord of life, death and destiny. But I bear the sword of severity sheathed, and wear instead the breastplate of Clemency' (1.1.1–4). Clemency is the attribute of an absolute monarch. The theme is decked round with obnoxious flattery (1.8.4.). Nero is the sun; he does not appear in public, he rises. For a time all seemed well. Seneca, with Burrus, the praetorian prefect, controlled policy. Tacitus (*Ann.*, 13.11) suggests that he was inclined to self-advertisement, but the state was at least stable. There was some revival of senatorial activity. The picture of general prosperity in the provinces must be offset by the exploitation of Britain by Seneca's own agents (D.C., 62.2.1), but on the whole the empire stood firm. But there is little sign of Stoic concern being transmuted into legislation. Seneca might preach against the gladiatorial shows (*Ep.*, 7.2ff), but they continued in practice, though there was an attempt to reduce the killings (Suet., *Nero*, 12.1). More serious is the matter of slavery. Seneca took a genuinely enlightened view on the subject, and was rare, if not unique, among Romans of his time in taking meals with his slaves (*Ep.*, 47; cf. *De clem.*, 1.18; *De ira*, 3.35; *De ben.*, 3.18.28). But there is no trace in Nero's reign of the humane legislation which graced the reigns of Claudius, Vespasian and Hadrian, and an incidental reference in the treatise *De clementia* (1.24.1) shows a fear of slaves as a body. In A.D. 61, after the murder of Pedanius Secundus, C. Cassius put the case for the mass-execution of his slaves. Neither Seneca nor anyone else demurred, and four hundred men, women and children were killed. Nero meantime was indulging his calf-love for Acte, with the encouragement of Seneca, who was fully prepared to cover up for him (Tac., *Ann.*, 13.13; 14.2). The Suillius episode took place in A.D. 58. Seneca, who could preach in the noblest language the doctrine of turning the other cheek (*De ira*, 2.34.5), when he was struck, struck back hard, and Suillius fell.

But now Nero could no longer be restrained. Agrippina was murdered. Seneca wrote and presented the letter justifying this to the senate. 'Perhaps to judge him fairly,' wrote Glover with a deal of charity, 'one would need to have been a Prime Minister.' Seneca's fellow-Stoic, Thrasea Paetus, a man of very different fibre, walked pointedly from the senate-house. Seneca was at the height of his power, and it turned to ashes in his grasp; as Pliny the elder put it, the power itself overwhelmed him (*N.H.*, 14.4.51). 'There are many', wrote Seneca with characteristic self-awareness to the Epicurean Serenus, who by his very profession renounced power and ambition, 'who are compelled to cling to their pinnacle; they cannot come down except by falling' (*D*, 9.10.6). Serenus might legitimately answer that no one compelled him to ascend in the first place. Seneca tried to climb down (Tac., *Ann.*, 14.52) with flattery as unctuous and odious as he directed towards Claudius, but his respectability was too useful to Nero, and he was not allowed to retire. He banished the crowds of courtiers who waited upon him; they were now dangerous. What is significant is the cult of expediency in this man of principle. He did not disdain the crowds when his power was secure, and he dismissed them not because they were unworthy of his Stoic professions, but because they were politically perilous. Even now he dealt with his enemies in no spirit of philosophic detachment. In A.D. 62 Romanus attacked him and Seneca struck down his attacker (Tac., *Ann.*, 14.65). He tried to use nervous debility as an excuse for retirement; Tacitus says that it was feigned, but though he may have exaggerated it, its basis was real enough (Tac., *Ann.*, 15.45). This is the period of the letters to Lucilius; he worked very hard; he wrote for future generations; he had diagnosed his own disease and wished others to have his prescription (*Ep.*, 8.1–2). We need not doubt the sincerity of this. The end came with Piso's conspiracy. There is no evidence that Seneca was implicated; his mood of weary resignation suggests the opposite; but he may well have been scheduled to replace the mountebank; the suspicion was enough to bring his death. He had at some point married again; his young wife Paulina wanted to die with him, but Nero would not let her. Seneca was no feminist (even in his praise of women: *D.*, 2.1.1.; 5.24.3; 6.16.1; *De clem.*, 1.5.5.) despite his great assertion that if a wife should not have a lover a husband should not have a mistress (*Ep.*, 94.26), and Paulina's devotion is a large item to his credit.

We happen to have a portrait of Seneca in his prime; it is perhaps needful to stress that the old fisherman, long identified as Seneca, and used as a model by Rubens and others, is not Seneca at all. The authentic portrait shows neither the young weakling nor the elderly ascetic. It is of a middle-aged man, balding about the forehead, clean-shaven, with a full face, large eyes *à fleur de tête* (like those of Socrates), large close-set ears, a straight nose, fleshy neck, treble chin, full lips and weak mouth. It fits all too well with what we know of Seneca during his years of power, wealth and indulgence. The face is humourless, and one of Seneca's most depressing traits is his lack of a sense of humour. Aulus Gellius (12.2) quotes two alleged jokes, but they are not very funny; through all his writings Seneca has point without wit.

Seneca was, as Quintilian put it, a notable castigator of vice (10.1.129). It is notorious that we castigate most strongly the offences to which we are most prone; this proneness may be an inclination of our inner selves which we have suppressed, a side of our private behaviour which we wish to pretend to others or to ourselves does not exist, or an aspect of our lives of which we and others are well aware but which our better self would wish otherwise. At the beginning of the work *De beneficiis* there is an impassioned account of the vices of the day; it is important to realize that this was almost certainly written during Nero's golden quinquennium, when Seneca himself was virtually regent. He starts from sexual immorality—the only wife anyone takes is someone else's (1.9.4)—and political corruption: attractive subjects, as he says. Of course every generation tells the same story: morals have gone to the dogs, wickedness is in control, man is going down the drain, crime is gaining momentum (1.10.1). 'Mankind', said Josh Billings, 'wuz made a little lower than the angels and has been gitting a little lower ever since.' Mr Punch's answer to the grouse, 'Things aren't what they were', is apposite: 'They never were.' Seneca breathlessly identifies the sins he sees coming to the fore: sexual misbehaviour, luxury, cruelty, political revolution and drunkenness. The fact is, he says, we are wicked, always have been wicked, and I regret to say, always will be wicked.

If we may take this as a guide, Seneca's greatest temptation was the pursuit of power through wealth; indeed it was his capacity for accumulating riches that most struck Juvenal about him (10.15–18). His obsession with this is well seen in his collection of Greek quotations on the vanity of riches (*Ep.*, 115.14). In his *Naturales Quaestiones* a reference to mirrors plunges him into the praise of poverty (1.17.9). This is typical of the treatise. In one of the letters he claims that Roman greatness was founded on poverty and wealth has been its corruption (*Ep.*, 87.41). He states over and over again that riches may hamper the pursuit of wisdom but that poverty never did (*Ep.*, 17.3), that riches arise from greed (*Ep.*, 87.22) and father pride (*Ep.*, 87.31). He repeatedly asserts the familiar commonplace of Nature hiding silver and gold (*Ep.*, 94.57; 110.10). 'To how many are riches a burden' he wrote (*D.*, 10.2.4), and 'Money never made anyone rich; it infects everyone with a passion for itself' (*Ep.*, 119.9). In between penning these two passages he became a multi-millionaire. The riches of nature should be enough for any of us. He said it *ad nauseam*, but he did not live by it. How did Seneca dare to attack the rich tables which he himself possessed (*De ben.*, 7.9.2), or to commend Democritus for renouncing riches (*D.*, 1.6.2)? When he tells Lucilius that the way to avoid envy is to know how to enjoy possessions privately without flaunting them, we see the inadequacy of his position (*Ep.*, 105.3). He knows it, and suggests that people will attack philosophy by asking him why he talks more courageously than he lives, why he licks the boots of his superiors, why he can't do without money, why he is emotional at the death of others, why he is concerned about his reputation, why his estates are bigger than nature requires, why his dinners are extravagant, his furniture luxurious, his wine vintage, and so on. He turns the criticism by anticipating it, by an expression of humility which is demonstrative but not necessarily insincere (*D.*, 7.17.1ff). He knows how much comes from the desire to 'keep up with the Joneses'. We are moulded to the pattern of others (*Ep.*, 123.6); the example of others is our ruin (*D.*, 7.1.4). Once or twice he tried to rationalize his own possession of wealth. Negatively, wealth is in good Stoic doctrine a thing of indifference (*Ep.*, 17.12). He puts this most strongly in his treatise *De vita beata*, where he lays before himself the ideal of despising riches whether he has them or not. 'So stop forbidding philosophers to own money. No one has condemned wisdom to poverty. The philosopher will own plenty of wealth' (*D.*, 7.23.1). He goes on to define the conditions. The wealth must not be obtained by murder or illegal action against others; honestly acquired; honourably used. That said, the philosopher will not refuse to accept the generosity of Fortune; it is nothing either to blush about or to boast over. Furthermore—and this is scarcely Stoic—the wise man finds a greater opportunity for the display of virtue in riches than in poverty (*D.*, 7.22.1). To this he adds the sentiment that where you are dealing with an autocrat, you must accept what you cannot refuse (*De ben.*, 2.18.6–7). It sounds reasonable, and few Christians ('Woe to you rich!') can throw stones. But I do not know how far we can trust Seneca's financial honesty. There is a startling passage in the work *De beneficiis*, where he says that it was not worth breaking a promise for 500 denarii (4.39.2).

There is something which does not ring true in Seneca's praise of the simple life. One is reminded of Chesterton's millionaire:

Mr. Mandragon, the Millionaire, he wouldn't have wine or
    wife,
He couldn't endure complexity; he lived the simple life.
He ordered his lunch by megaphone in manly, simple tones,
And used all his motors for canvassing voters, and twenty
    telephones;
Besides a dandy little machine,
Cunning and neat as ever was seen
With a hundred pulleys and cranks between,
Made of metal and kept quite clean,
To hoist him out of his healthful bed on every day of his life,
And wash him and brush him, and shave him and dress him
    to live the Simple Life.

One of Seneca's most—unintentionally—amusing letters is written in praise of the simple life. He goes for a brief camping holiday with a friend named Maximus. They sleep on the ground, with only a mattress and a couple of blankets each. They are accompanied by a very small number of slaves—only one wagon-load—and their very simple meal, so simple that it would be impossible to subtract anything from it, takes no more than an hour to prepare (*Ep.*, 87.2–3). Need one say more?

In the general tirade at the beginning of *De beneficiis* consideration of sexual morals forms a prominent part. They press equally strongly in the ninety-seventh letter. On the whole, however, Seneca is not a prurient preacher, and the theme of sex does not obtrude repressively. He suggests, following Panaetius, that the majority of us, who are not perfect, cannot be trusted to fall in love, and extends this promptly to the other emotions (*Ep.*, 116.5). That his attitude to sex was not wholly healthy may be seen in the sadistic dwelling on scenes of torture we have already noted; he was ambivalent, however, for he rejected the sadism of the gladiatorial shows. His advocacy of a single standard of morality for wife and husband is wholly commendable. There is, however, one passage which shows a perturbation. This is in *Phaedra*; the nurse in urging Hippolytus to take Phaedra urges him to *follow nature* (435ff; 481). One would almost think that this was a parody of the Stoics; it certainly suggests a way in which Seneca may have rationalized a measure of sexual promiscuity. I am not fully persuaded that we need reject as spurious the two homosexual poems attributed to him (*AL.*, 430; 439). There is no special reason to doubt that he sowed his wild oats, whether or not the charges of adultery with particular individuals can be sustained. He was a man and a Roman; later he may well have settled down. It does not seem that his behaviour in this regard was worse than average, and his professions are no more hypocritical than most.

Seneca's attitude to public life in his writings is of some interest. At the end of his life we find him advising Lucilius to retire from public activity (*Ep.*, 19; 22); he himself did not do so, or did so only partially, and even then only when his power was declining, and he never expresses to Lucilius regrets for having stayed. A bitter little letter deals with the Vanity Fair of politics, and the ignominy of canvassing (*Ep.*, 117). When Lucilius shows no intention of withdrawing, he gives him good, if sententious advice to let his life be open and aboveboard, and to be ruled by conscience (*Ep.*, 43). In fact this advocacy of withdrawal was not the considered conclusion of the philosopher at the end of a life of experience, but a mood which pursued him throughout. He gives the same advice to Paulinus in a treatise written ten or fifteen years before (*D.*, 10.18). In contrast, even in the letters to Lucilius he comments unfavourably on Vatia's evasion of public life (*Ep.*, 55.3-4), and remarks with some honesty of himself: 'People often think that I have gone into retirement in disgust with politics, finding my public position intolerably thankless. A combination of tiredness and fear drove me to take refuge, and in refuge I sometimes find my political ambition burgeoning again' (*Ep.*, 56.9). It is Seneca who gives us the distinction between Epicurus ('The wise man will engage in politics only in exceptional circumstances') and Zeno ('The wise man will refrain from politics only in exceptional circumstances') (D., 8.3[30].2). In one important letter (73) he examines the tensions of the political life, and the relationship of the philosopher to politics. It is typical of the presuppositions of the Roman aristocrat that he assumes that the man who becomes a philosopher will first have played his part in senate, lawcourt, and in all the affairs of state; he acknowledges also that the philosopher's power to retire depends on the fact that there are others continuing to bear political responsibility. This is an open and honest letter. In another (90) he dreams of a world in which there is no need for government, industry, or commerce; in the world as it is philosophy has one social function, to devise laws for the control of malefactors; its principal function remains to establish the individual on the path of his salvation. In another, very revealing, passage he says that everyone is worried by what happens to his neighbour, and the wise man gets out while the going is good (Ep., 74, 5–7).

Perhaps we are apt to underestimate the terror of the times. There is a mood of fear, of expectation of evil to which Seneca testifies even while rebutting it (Ep., 13.10–1). When he writes from exile to console Polybius on his brother's death, however ulterior his motive and overwritten his rhetoric, there seems to be sincerity in his picture of the insecurity of life, a sea, ebbing and flowing, surging and receding, shipwrecking some and causing fear to all. Life is a punishment (D., 11.9.6.). Man, he says pessimistically, is just a lump of matter in flux, on its way down exposed to influences of all sorts (Ep., 58.24). Happiness is a fragile support; Fortune is fickle, to bear and beware (Ep., 98). He gives a rather sad picture of the sage as the man who can stand up to the evils which sap the resolve of others (Ep., 71.26). One thing Seneca did not fear—death. Here at least he lived by his profession of constancy; the fragments of the treatise De remediis fortunae show a well worked-out position. There is nothing hysterical about his attitude; it is firm and clear (Epp., 24; 26; 30). He had no faith and little hope. His occasional description of the body as a prison and life as one long punishment (derived from Pythagoras and Plato) doubtless implies the expectation of something beyond; but his thought is focused on the character of this life, not the reality of the next (D., 6.20.2; 11.9.6.; Epp. 65.16; 120.14). To Marcia he does speak of the future life of her son among the Scipios and Catos before his soul is resolved into its primal elements in the great conflagration (*D.*, 6.25-6), but a man is not on oath in the peroration of a *consolatio*. Once in a letter he describes himself as surrendering himself to a belief in immortality when the arrival of a letter from Lucilius shattered his fantasy (*Ep.*, 102.2). His real belief was that death is non-existence (*Ep.*, 54.4); once he says that it is either an end or a new beginning (*D.*, 1.6.6). But this itself, Epicurean-wise, left him fearless, and when the summons came he met it with none of the craven cringing of his nephew Lucan, but with courage and with the only real joke of his life. The terror of the times is important. In the mid-eighteenth century Garat read Seneca and thought him a bore. But when the Revolution came and Garat was awaiting the guillotine, he found that the words sprang to life from the page: he was living in the atmosphere in which Seneca wrote, and the words took on existential truth.

Seneca has been compared with La Rochefoucauld. La Rochefoucauld, unlike Seneca, was born to greatness, but he was shy and sensitive, a dreamer of Arcadia. He was a young man of great promise; at fourteen, already married, he was in the army; he was a colonel within a year. He was immersed in public affairs. He was a lover; his mistresses included the Duchesse de Chereuse, the Duchesse de Longueville and Mme de LaFayette. Then came failure over the assassination of Retz, and disaster in fighting for Condé. Brooding on disappointment and failure he wrote his memoirs. He had lived in a noble world of falsity and he dissected it pitilessly. Mme de LaFayette, on reading the *Réflexions*, commented to Mme de Sablé: 'Ah, Madame, what corruption one must have in mind and heart to be able to imagine all that.' La Rochefoucauld was like Seneca in many ways, in his capacity for honest self-examination: 'Though we admit our faults, we are not entirely frank. We admit them, to counterbalance the harm they do by the impression of sincerity. But sincerity is not easy; we present our faults as we want to; we would rather say evil of ourselves than not talk at all.' As he looked into his own character, he saw, as did Retz, the fatal flaw of irresolution. Morris Bishop's comment on him could have been written of Seneca: 'He was not made to rule; he was made to look at the world and at himself, and to find his own little parcel of truth.' It was entirely appropriate that the first edition of La Rochefoucauld should have the bust of Seneca for its frontispiece.

17

Perhaps a personal reminiscence may be permitted here to obtrude. I came to understand Seneca through coming to understand Cosmo Gordon Lang, Archbishop of Canterbury from 1928 to 1942. I had known him as a radical with a deep sense of concern for the poor who became a proud prelate enjoying his involvement with the rich. I had disliked intensely his part in the Abdication Crisis, and still more his apparent unctuousness through it all. Then a close friend, in whose judgment I could have full confidence, went for ordination to Cuddesdon and wrote: 'The Archbishop was here this weekend; what a saint the man is!' I was puzzled, for the Lang I knew was no saint. Years later J. G. Lockhart's life of the Archbishop revealed the truth. Lang was a son of the manse, devoured by insatiable ambition; his curse through life was self-conceit and self-consciousness. In his youth he drew up prophetic entries for *Who's Who*: he would get a first at Glasgow and Oxford, be President of the Union, be called to the Bar, and end up as Prime Minister or Lord Chancellor. His innate ability and capacity for work set him on the road, though he missed his first at Oxford. Then an insistent voice within him began to cry: 'Why shouldn't you be ordained?' In an act of heroic renunciation he gave up all his ambitions to become a curate in Leeds; yet before long he was signing himself 'Cosmo Cantuar' to see what it looked like. He *was* a snob; he loved the company of kings and, next to that, of noblemen. But he knew himself; it was no mere snob who called his journey from one country house to another 'the Snob's Progress'. Lockhart wrote with compassionate understanding (p. 145):

> For him the social ascent was a necessary part in the play of the poor Scots boy who made good, of the drama—'From Woodlands Terrace to Lambeth Palace'—which one Lang was acting and the other Lang was watching. The contrast must be accentuated. The audience must be constantly reminded how strange and wonderful it was that an obscure youth from Glasgow should reach such remote and shining heights, should stay with Kings and Queens and call Earls and Countesses by their Christian names. The theatre made its demands and he complied.

For there was indeed the other side to Lang; he *was* my friend's saint. Every summer he retired to Scotland, first to Tavantaggart, and then to Ballure, simple homes far from the pomp of aristocratic London. There for a month, in the little room he had made into a chapel, he spent each morning on his knees, 'burdened with the thought of manifold failure'. 'It is here', he scribbled in a notebook 'that my real self—at least what ought to be my real self—lives' (p. 187). And from there he would return to Lambeth Palace, to luxury, to the Establishment. He was Archbishop of Canterbury; he could do no other. Lang was not a hypocrite; that is too facile an explanation. After his resignation, while at Cuddesdon (perhaps on the very occasion my friend encountered him—I do not recall), he wrote in a notebook:

> I see all along, so to say, two selves—the outer and the inner man, never wholly united. God knows the weakness and failure of the outer man—Priest, Bishop, Archbishop. Yet I cannot doubt that there has been all along the inner man, the man God meant me to be, deep down, often submerged, yet by God's grace kept alive, from time to time coming forth, as here or in the 'Cell' at Ballure. (p. 443)

Such, *mutatis mutandis*, was Seneca. The analogy is indeed very close. Seneca, like Lang, was proud of his *novitas* (Tac., *Ann.*, 14.52). Seneca, like Lang, was in revolt against his father; Lang moved from the manse to the Episcopal Church, Seneca from rhetoric to philosophy. Seneca, like Lang, joined the Establishment, and as Lang rejected Edward, Seneca rejected Coriolanus, Catiline, Marius, Sulla, Pompey, Caesar, and Antony (*De ben.*, 5.16). Seneca, like Lang, loved high society, yet could also espouse the simple life. Seneca, like Lang, could see the country-side as a means of escape from the temptations of the capital; faults, he remarks ruefully, depend on an audience (*Ep.*, 94.69). But retreat to the countryside would be escapism for a Stoic, who accepts his lot where God has placed him. Marcus Aurelius, addressing himself, puts it well:

> We seek out solitary retreats, cottages in the country, the seashore, mountains; like others, you enjoy dreaming of all this. How childish, when at any moment you can retire— into your own soul! There is no more peaceful retreat for a man, especially if within his soul are things which he can

contemplate and induce calmness. So learn to enjoy this
retreat, and to renew your strength there. (4.3.1)

Seneca stresses the inwardness of the mind. 'God is at hand for us
all wherever we are' (*Ep.*, 95.48); 'God comes to men; closer still,
He comes into men; without God no mind is good' (*Ep.*, 73.16);
'God is near you, with you, within you. Let me put it this way,
Lucilius: a holy spirit takes up his place within us, he watches our
actions, good and bad, he is our guardian' (*Ep.*, 41.2). So every
day, in bed, after the lights were out and, he says engagingly, 'my
wife has stopped talking', he practised self-examination (*D.*,
5.36.3). *Nosce te* meant something to him (*D.*, 6.11.2). Lang
seems to have found his deepest awareness of this only at Cuddesdon and Ballure, but he and Seneca alike rationalized their
continuance in society by the compulsions of duty. But Seneca,
like Lang, had real humility behind the mask of pride. They were
both, so to say, inverted Uriah Heeps. 'I am no saint; I'm not
even halfway there' (*Ep.*, 57.3), says Seneca, without affectation, to
Lucilius; and again, to his brother, 'I'm no ideal, and—to add fuel
to your reproaches—I never will be. So don't expect me to rival
the saints, only to be better than the sinners. I am quite satisfied
if each day I learn to criticize my mistakes and reduce my failings'
(*D.*, 7.17.3). Elsewhere he acknowledges that he is too sensitive
to his public image (*Ep.*, 87.5). He has many faults, but com-
placency is not among them; he never holds himself up as an
example to be emulated. On the contrary he is aware of the two
selves, as surely as Lang, as surely as Catullus, whose language he
seems almost to echo, or Blake or Yeats. 'Men love their sins
even while they hate them' (*Ep.*, 112.4).

A second comparison from personal experience is with the
late Prime Minister of Nigeria, Sir Abubakar Tafawa Balewa.
Tafawa Balewa was a *novus homo*, like Seneca: born of no princely
house, he came to power from the feudal north. God was central
to his life, as to Seneca's or Lang's; his religion was Islam, which
means resignation to the will of God, a resignation preached by
the Stoics. But this very resignation meant a tendency to accept
abuses rather than to correct them, and government was as
corrupt in independent Nigeria as ever in imperial Rome. It is
just to add that Tafawa Balewa never attained to Seneca's riches;
it was left to others to do that. He was a man with the desire to be

honest but without the courage to stand up to the dishonest. Hence his biggest impact on history was in Commonwealth affairs where his immediate involvement was less. His Nero was his party leader, the Premier of the Northern Region, the Sardauna of Sokoto, a man of dominant personality, a progressive in his youth, who combined implacable ambition with ruthless execution. A fraudulent election in the Western Region returned one of the Sardauna's political allies to power. Sir Abubakar had in his hands the evidence of fraudulence, but did nothing about it. This was for him what Agrippina's murder was for Seneca, the decisive compromise in a political career which was already compromised. For Sir Abubakar it was literally a fatal weakness. A group of army majors assassinated four leading politicians. Three were crooks; the fourth was the Prime Minister, who by his temporizing had associated himself irrevocably with the crooks. Yet I knew the man, liked him and in many ways respected him; it was impossible not to have compassion on him. A weak, good, eloquent man—I suddenly found I was describing Seneca.

Perhaps it is more dangerous to be weak and good than anything else. This was Seneca. Stoic philosophy did not help him in a world of power, any more than it helped poor Marcus Aurelius, another weak and good man. Epicureanism might have helped him, had he had the courage to put away ambition, but Roman Epicureanism had forgotten the prescription of salvation, and Epicureans in office had become as common a sight as Christians in the army were later to be. Epicureanism could change individuals but not societies; Stoicism, though its influence did slowly permeate the structure of Roman law, in its doctrine of indifference was not really interested in changing anything at all. Had Seneca been a stronger man, he would still have been hampered by his philosophy. But he was not a strong man. It is an error to write him off as a hypocrite; in him real goodness was sapped by inescapable weakness. The drive which came from physical deprivation dissipated itself in fantasy, intense preaching and uncertain action, and unwillingness to move in time of prosperity combined with acute depression in time of adversity. He deserves not condemnation but compassion.

BIBLIOGRAPHICAL NOTE

The main object of this paper is to examine the dichotomy between Seneca's life and writings in the light of the ancient evidence, and I have therefore been principally concerned with Seneca's own works, together with the evidence of Dio Cassius, Josephus, Pliny, Quintilian, Suetonius, Tacitus and the Juvenal scholia. I have also consulted the following:

ALBERTINI, E. *La Composition dans les ouvrages philosophiques de Sénèque*, Paris, 1923.

BAILLY, A. *La Vie et les pensées de Sénèque*, Paris, 1929.

BARKER, E. P. 'Seneca (2)', *Oxford Classical Dictionary*, Oxford, 1949, 827-8.

BERNOULLI, J. J. *Römische Ikonographie*, vol. i, Stuttgart, 1882.

BISHOP, M. *The Life and Adventures of La Rochefoucauld*, Ithaca, 1951.

CARLYLE, T. *Critical and Miscellaneous Essays*, London, 1839.

CHARLESWORTH, M. P. 'The virtues of a Roman emperor', *PBA*, 23 (1937), 105ff.

CHESTERTON, G. K. *Collected Poems*, London, 1927.

DIDEROT, D. *Essai sur les règnes de Claude et de Néron et sur les moeurs et les écrits de Sénèque*, Paris, 1779.

DILL, S. *Roman Society from Nero to Marcus Aurelius*, London, 1905.

FAIDER, P. *Études sur Sénèque*, Ghent, 1921.

—— 'Possédons-nous le portrait de Sénèque?' *Mus. Belge*, 18 (1920), 153ff.

FARRAR, F. W. *Seekers After God*, London, 1884.

FERGUSON, J. 'Was Gallio an Epicurean?' *Palaeologia*, 7 (1958), 111ff.

GERCKE, A. *Seneca-Studien*, Leipzig, 1895.

GLOVER, T. R. *The Conflict of Religions in the Early Roman Empire*, London, 1909.

GUMMERE, R. M. *Seneca the Philosopher and his Modern Message*, Boston, 1922.

HOLLAND, F. *Seneca*, London, 1920.

LA ROCHEFOUCAULD, F. *Oeuvres complètes*, Paris, 1950.

LOCKHART, J. G. *Cosmo Gordon Lang*, London, 1949.

MACAULAY, LORD *Works*, London, 1898.

MARCHESI, C. *Seneca*, Messina, 1920.

MARTHA, C. *Les Moralistes sous l'empire romain*, Paris, 1865.

MENDELL, C. W. *Our Seneca*, New Haven, 1941.

REINACH, S. 'Un portrait mystérieux', *Rév. Arch.* sér. v. 6 (1917), 357ff.

REINHARDT, T. F. G. *De L. Annaei Senecae Vita atque Scriptis*, Jena, 1816.

RENAN, E. *L'Antichrist*, Paris, 1899.

ROSSBACH, O. 'Annaeus (17)', *PW*, 1, 2240ff.

STELLA MARANCA, F. 'L. Anneo Seneca nel "Consilium Principis"', *Rendiconti Lincei*, ser. v. 32 (1923), 282ff.

WALTZ, R. *La Vie politique de Sénèque*, Paris, 1909.

WETMORE, J. H. L. *Seneca's Conception of the Stoic Sage as Shown in his Prose Works*, Alberta, 1936.

II

Seneca as Philosopher

H. MACL. CURRIE

The younger Seneca was a man of letters with a strong interest in philosophy who occupied an important position in high politics at Rome. The philosophical school to which he adhered was Stoicism, a system found peculiarly congenial on its moral side by many amongst the cultivated members of the Roman upper class when they made contact with it in the middle of the second century B.C. It was much in tune with the ideal of simplicity and frugality embodied in the typical hero of republican times. One could almost say that the Romans did not become Stoics but realized they were.

Stoicism was a closely-knit system with three main parts, physics, logic and ethics, the last of which formed its centre of gravity. As formulated by the founders of the school, the ethical teaching was rigid and very idealistic. Later, during its middle period when it had passed to and been widely embraced at Rome, the moral ideas, under the guidance of two very eminent Greek teachers working then, Panaetius and Posidonius, were subjected to a certain amount of revision, being brought more into line with the facts of ordinary human experience and common sense. The Romans were by nature disinclined to abstract speculation; they respected the actual and the practical—hence the liberalizing process. This was maintained in the school's later period, one of the chief personages in which was Lucius Annaeus Seneca.

In the Hellenistic world the primary question for philosophy was taken to be 'How ought we to live?' or, in other words, 'What is the right way to happiness?' The real business of philosophy was considered to be the provision of clear precepts to show people how to conduct themselves amidst the vicissitudes of life. Epicurus, the contemporary of Zeno who was the founder of Stoicism, saw mankind degraded by fear—of death and of the gods. Teaching a highly sublimated sensuality, he held that happiness was to be identified with pleasure, which was therefore man's proper goal; but, the doctrine continued, wisdom lay in the assessing of pleasures with regard to intensity and permanence, as a result of which it would be seen that the virtuous life was the pleasantest.

Stoicism developed alongside Epicureanism, but at Rome was much more widely accepted, becoming in the first and second centuries A.D. the predominating way of thought. The Stoic answer to the question of virtue and happiness was quite different from that presented by Epicurus. Writing with an evangelical zeal, Seneca produced a large number of works designed to explain and commend Stoic teaching on the good life. He was not rigorously sectarian as a moral teacher, borrowing when he liked whatever was useful to his purpose in other schools, Epicureanism included. The literary taste of the age demanded that style be richly rhetorical and epigrammatically arresting; pregnant phrases and allusive brevity were much admired. These qualities are strikingly present in Seneca's style, meeting the aesthetic expectations of the times, while his vocabulary and general procedure suggest the tone of easygoing conversation.[1] Philosophy for Seneca was an everyday matter, of importance to all; the writer had to make contact with people and maintain it. The cultivation of an informal manner with jokes, anecdotes, and all the other manoeuvres which help to create the atmosphere of friendly dialogue subserved his propagandist intention.

For all his readiness to quote aphorisms of other schools, Seneca was a firmly committed Stoic. Wherever we are in a position to judge, we see that his knowledge of, and loyalty to the fundamental teachings were sound. The first part of the treatise *De constantia sapientis*, for instance, subsists on the basis of Stoic logic and physics with their notion of the corporeality of essences and qualities, while in the second part Seneca turns to more 'popular' arguments.[2] In the *De vita beata* the various analyses offered of the *summum bonum* are rooted in Stoic psychological theories: pleasure cannot be accorded an absolute value, as the Epicureans claim, since the attendant feeling is a transitory experience in our conscious existence and waits upon acknowledgment by the will. Though Seneca always reserved the right to differ, he basically remained orthodox.

It is in the *Epistulae Morales* that he shows himself explicitly impatient of certain traditional Stoic attitudes or ideas. Of his works which have been preserved these are the last in date and they present his thought at its most mature. His powers of meditation on the great themes of the moral life and its practice have notably developed. He handles a wide range of topics, following the promptings of free association and enlarging on each with plentiful illustrative material. An ordinary or trivial event can be the highly suggestive beginning for a train of reflection—the annual Roman merrymaking or *Saturnalia* in December (*Ep.*, 18), a sea-trip (*Ep.*, 53), the arrival of mail-boats at Puteoli (*Ep.*, 77). This last letter turns into a discussion of suicide, the mention of boats naturally leading to talk of journeys which in turn suggests the journey of life. The emphasis in the letters, as elsewhere, is upon the problems of living and the Stoic answers. Considerations of logic or dialectic are introduced apologetically; Seneca is not happy about discoursing upon finicking distinctions and subtleties when much more pressing business is on hand. 'What has all this logical quibbling to do with living properly?' is his cry. Referring to syllogistic reasoning, he says (*Ep.*, 85.1): 'I declare again and again that I take no pleasure in such proofs. I feel ashamed to go down into the arena on behalf of gods and men armed only with an awl.' Similar strictures occur in *Ep.*, 82.22ff where, at section 30, he speaks of the *subula* or awl of logical niceties as a poor weapon against the lion of fear by which mankind is oppressed; *Ep.*, 45.5 where *verborum cavillatio* and *captiosae disputationes* are mentioned with disapproval; and *Ep.*, 117.25ff where, at section 30, the refined logical hair-splitting which was a mark of Stoicism is dismissed as being of no real help amid the stresses of ordinary existence. Seneca was convinced enough a Stoic to see the supporting value of the physical and metaphysical doctrines and he devoted a considerable amount of space throughout his works to one or other of their aspects, but nevertheless he wished it to be fully realized that they were merely ancillary.

The writings show moral philosophy to be Seneca's chief interest. Even the tragedies contribute to his programme. It has been rightly argued that they are not imitations of the Greek but a fresh treatment of old themes from the view-point of Stoic ethics and psychology.[3] Suffering and death and the way they are to be faced, and the effects of strong emotion form the essence of these pieces, while corresponding motifs run through the prose works—the wise man's fortitude in the midst of misfortune (*De constantia sapientis*, 6), violent passion (*De ira, passim*), death as a release (*Ep.*, 24.26; *Consolatio ad Marciam*, 20 etc.). In the same way, the *Naturales Quaestiones*[4] sets out to find in the study of natural phenomena the hand of God at work and to elicit from the study as much moral significance as possible. Thus, in the fifth book, which deals with the winds, the discussion, by a transition, becomes (at 18.4) a tirade against avarice which causes men to put to sea and brave the fury of these uncontrollable forces. Seneca advises Lucilius to apply at once everything he reads to morals, a policy he himself plainly follows (*Ep.*, 89.48).

For the Stoics logic (comprising theory of knowledge, logic, rhetoric) and physics (ontology, physics, theology) constituted the framework in which their system of ethics was set. To answer the question 'How do we know what we know?' they appealed to that materialism or corporeality which was basic to their teaching and always remained so. Only bodies, they held, could act and be causes, and it was only bodies that possessed a real, substantial existence. Thus, God and soul were bodies. Only four things were admitted as incorporeal—time, space and void (the *places* in which bodies are) and the things which could be said about bodies (*lekta*). Knowledge was conceived in terms of the effect produced upon one body, the soul, by other bodies. The usual channels of reception were the organs of sense, but other means were possible, though here too the same material process was operative. The object perceived made an impression on the soul. The soul responded by giving, rightly or wrongly, its assent to this impression; if rightly, it achieved 'comprehension' of the object—a firm, immediate, and certain mental grasp of it. For assent to be right it was necessary that the impression or image be an accurate representation of a real object. This the Stoics called a 'gripping representation' since it took hold of the mind, forcing it to give assent. Memory now came into play, creating a reservoir of experience to show that particular judgments were comparable with one another and that the same causes always brought about the same effects. And this could only be so if there was a single, rational will maintaining the coherence and permanence which was apprehended in the universe. Virtue, wisdom and all other qualities or general concepts were, with their opposites, specific bodies, separately recognized as individual instances of virtue, wisdom etc., just as each soul was a part of the universal soul. These general ideas, being animated and endowed with physical properties, were able to act upon persons and things.

The whole question of knowing was for the Stoics removed from the realm of the individual's consciousness to the cosmic plane. It was the duty of the devoted Stoic to put himself into harmonious relationship with this immanent power of reason in the universe and discover the laws of its working. The universe was the supremely intelligible entity, and universal reason and that of the individual were identical. As Seneca declared (*Ep.*, 66.12), 'Reason is nothing other than a part of the divine spirit set in a human body.'

Both body and soul were material, and the soul acted upon the body, as tears, blushing and the pallor of fear showed (cf. Seneca, *Ep.*, 106.1ff). The soul, defined as a particularly subtle, warm and living breath, was part of that *spiritus* (*pneuma* to the Greeks) or breath which was the soul of the universe. This divine breath was a continuous, non-molecular substance activated by a tension or indefinitely expansive force peculiar to it (cf. Seneca, *Nat. Quaest.* 2.6.2–4). It was by this substance that the cohesion of complex things, our bodies included, was maintained, and not least that of the whole complex organism which we call the universe.

We thus see that in the Stoic scheme physics, logic and morality were closely interconnected. Seneca was editing his notes for the *Naturales Quaestiones* at the time when he was also writing his *Epistulae Morales*, both works addressed to his friend Lucilius. In them he was tackling two sides of the same subject. When he wrote on the causes of thunder and lightning and earthquakes, or on comets and the different winds, and when in the middle of these discourses he stopped from time to time to draw out moral themes, he was not indulging in merely rhetorical displays but deliberately exemplifying Stoic principles. Philosophy was a comprehensive activity; the elements of man's moral life were to be considered against the background of the wonderful whole of which man was indissolubly part. The interwoven fabric of macrocosm and microcosm was the Stoic's proper study.

The conception of the earth as a living organism goes back as far as Empedocles,[5] and Posidonius[6] certainly stressed it as a fundamental point in his teaching. We find Seneca continuing the idea; in *Nat. Quaest.* 3.15.1ff we are told that the earth is governed by nature in the same way as the human body. We have veins and arteries, while the earth has channels and passages for the circulation of air and water.

The soul of the world totally pervaded it, and similarly the human soul pervaded and breathed through the whole body, instructing and directing it, and imparting to the individual his essential characteristic of rationality. 'The soul is our overlord. If it is safe, the other parts remain loyal and serve obediently; but if it loses its equilibrium a little, they too waver' (Seneca, *Ep.*, 114.23). There were eight parts to the soul—the 'principate' or rational, ruling part, the five senses, and the powers of speech and generation—but the various processes were regarded as functions of the governing part. The soul of man was a portion of the divine *spiritus* or vital breath containing an *impetus* (Seneca's word; Cicero used *appetitus*, while the Greek term was *hormē*) or impulse which was the prime mover or quickening influence for men and animate creatures at large. 'No action can take place without impulse' (Seneca, *Ep.*, 113.2). Mental processes were interpreted as opinions or judgments which were the individual's reaction when affected by a presented object. Awareness meant, as we have already seen, assent; but awareness also implied the adoption of some attitude, and from this point of view 'every phase of conation and emotion, whether desire, will or purpose, love or hate or fear, is but another interpretation of the judgment "This is A." '[7] The conative or emotional states, being the movement of the soul towards or away from the object, came under the general heading of impulse. Seneca, writing on this matter (*Ep.*, 113.18ff), supposes by way of example that he has to go for a walk; this obligation is an external stimulus to which the internal impulse reacts. The response, however, must wait for the judgment's ratification. In discussing the genesis of anger (*De ira*, 2.1ff), Seneca adheres to the same doctrine, showing that though anger is clearly aroused by the direct impression (*species*) of an injury, nevertheless it does not follow immediately upon this but requires the intervention of the consenting judgment.

The interaction of primary impulse and judgment was the foundation of knowledge for the Stoics. The deceptiveness of the senses was regarded as really false judgment, and could be avoided if care was exercised. In *Ep.*, 71.32ff Seneca describes virtue as the only good ('at least there is no good without virtue') and locates it in 'our nobler part, that is, the rational part'. He then goes on to define it as true and steady judgment, from which will spring all mental impulses and which will clarify any external appearance that stirs an answering *impetus*.

Clarity of perception being the sole criterion of truth, the proper end of mental activity was to analyse and reduce to clear images and conceptions the data of consciousness. The judgment's function was to discipline the feelings, to purify the subject from the evil of error and obscurity. The psychology of the Stoics was rationalist to its core.

The inherent rationality of every person's soul was, for the Stoics, exposed to corruption right from earliest infancy. Stoic thinkers from the time of Chrysippus[8] had studied the process of corruption with a view to devising a sound method of training. The baby, fresh from the womb, had been used there to warmth and comfort, qualities it associated with its preservation, and it went on seeking similarly pleasurable sensations. It thus confused pleasure and the highest good. As the child grew up the seductions of pride and ambition led to the acceptance of false standards, and money, honour and all other things which properly were 'indifferent'[9] (to use the Stoic expression) in the search for the good life were set up as idols. The rationality of the soul was perverted in these circumstances and men became almost indistinguishable from animals. The good, as Seneca demonstrated in *Ep.*, 124, had a rational character to which only the rational in man could respond.

But in human contacts there was a strong risk of demoralization, and the bigger the crowd the greater the danger—a theme handled by Seneca several times. In the *De otio* he considers the need for retirement from the world amongst like-minded friends if we are to preserve our moral integrity, while in *Epp.*, 7, 19 and 22 the same quietist idea is advanced. Deploring the cruelty of gladiatorial exhibitions (which attracted vast numbers of spectators) in *Ep.*, 7, he makes his point forcibly by the paradox that if ever he has attended he has come away more cruel and less human—because he has been amongst human beings. However, quietism was never an end in itself for the Stoics as it was for the Epicureans. The Stoics preached an active benevolence which was something different from uncritical sentimentality. They loved and helped people always with an eye to their rational capacity and development. They did not object to the punishment of wickedness and vice,[10] and they pointed to standards far removed from those of the mob.

The universe was held to be a rational substance and the aim for the Stoics was to achieve a harmonious relationship with it. By their watchword, 'follow Nature', they did not mean a return to primitive simplicity in any Cynic or Rousseau-like fashion. Diogenes the Cynic lived in a tub and scorned the conventions of polite society; Rousseau yearned romantically for a life freed from artificial constraints. To torture one's body with austere living, to be deliberately dirty, and to eat food which was not only plain but actually disgusting and off-putting, was not the Stoic way, said Seneca (*Ep.*, 5.4). The earliest form of existence was not necessarily the most perfect for man. The historical evolution of human society and that of virtue were separate. In works vindicating the claims of philosophy and encouraging people to take it up, it was apparently the custom to urge its great antiquity, with a statement of the various benefits it had conferred on mankind and the advances it had effected. According to Seneca (*Ep.*, 90), Posidonius was so eager to establish philosophy's position that he claimed early man as a philosopher with the invention of a number of trivial tools and implements to his credit. But Seneca showed independence and took issue with Posidonius: the self-sufficiency of the true philosopher who has no need of such inventions is, he said, set at naught by this teaching; early man was ignorant and therefore innocent, though his rude life possessed certain qualities akin to the major virtues. But virtue proper depends upon reason, and only voluntary acts attract praise and blame.[11]

Reason is man's generic mark, and if we are to live in accordance with nature it is our duty to foster it within ourselves as part of the rationality that is the essence of the universe (*Ep.*, 124.23–4). Reason, the source of perfection and the good, is the ordering power in the world, and we must submit to its dictates if we are to attain to the good.

In pursuing his ambition to reconcile the ways of God to man, Chrysippus had argued plausibly that natural evil was a thing indifferent—that even moral evil was necessary in the divine economy as a contrast to set off good (a line of thought which goes back to Heraclitus).[12] The really perplexing question why the unjust were allowed to flourish while the just suffered calamity he tried to answer in various ways: sometimes he alleged the forgetfulness of the higher powers; sometimes he would find such contrasts and bizarre passages unavoidable in the grim comedy of human existence. In *Ep.*, 82.10ff, Seneca discussed the Stoic teaching on things indifferent, as he did also in *Ep.*, 66.36–7, and *Ep.*, 109.12–13. But it was in his work *De providentia* that he gave it, rather optimistically perhaps, fullest treatment, with scattered references elsewhere: the wise man cannot really meet with misfortune, for all outward calamity is a divinely appointed means of training, exercising his power and showing the world the indifference of external conditions. The Stoic wise man is invulnerable within himself. The cruelly tortured Regulus and other such moral heroes find their reward in the glory their steadfastness will confer. Their vision of what is right carries them triumphantly through their tribulation, and death will release them at last to enjoy supreme happiness (*De providentia*, 3–4). While being roasted alive in the bronze bull of Phalaris (a common example amongst ancient moralists) the sage, though he would prefer not to be in this predicament, nevertheless overcomes it with his virtue; it is his body which is suffering, his spirit remains untouched (*Ep.*, 66.18ff). The wise man's security arises from an inner attitude. Poverty is to lack something, but he is content within himself; the acquisition of possessions which will be subject to the stroke of capricious fortune does not produce contentment (*De constantia sapientis*, 5.6ff). Within the soul there is an effluence of the divine spirit, within the human frame there is a god—which points to man's essential dignity and internal freedom.

Even so, Seneca was acutely aware of the weakness and misery of men, on which he laid particular stress. The soul's true life began when it had departed from the body which was its prison, a theme he handled at some length in *Ep.*, 102.23ff. And while the ideal of the Stoic sage was often put before us, this figure was far from dominating the scene. In fact, Seneca asked at one point (*De tranquillitate animi*, 7.4): 'Where will you find that man for whom we have been searching for so many centuries?' Concerning ethics, if there was no novelty of doctrine, there was notable change in the emphasis and application.

Seneca was no blindfold partisan. He felt free to criticize the official teaching of Stoicism (*De otio*, 3.1);[13] he recognized the need to add to, and improve, inherited dogma (*Ep.*, 64.7); and he advocated a liberal independence in matters of interpretation (*Ep.*, 33.7–8). In an interesting passage (*Ep.*, 84.5) he spoke of the assimilation which synthesized diverse material to form something new and different from any of the parts, a process he tended to follow himself in writing philosophy.

In Seneca, then, the ideal sage has receded, and philosophy is seen as a physician ministering not to the whole but to the sick (cf. *Ep.*, 109.17ff). Abstract theory is not what the situation demands, he says again and again, but sound practical advice. Where the early Stoics had laid down absolute moral imperatives, Seneca shows a more humane and understanding spirit. In place of the grim idea that to fall short of complete perfection by the slightest degree is morally as bad as the worst depravity ('a miss is as good as a mile'), we find that there are various classes of patients in 'progress' (*profectus*)—that is, they are making their way, slowly and painfully, towards virtue. Hope and encouragement are held out to the poor struggler. The first step is the eradication of vicious habits; evil tendencies are to be corrected, and strict control is to be kept over the corrupt inclinations of the reason. If we succeed in this, we still have to contend with the single attacks of the passions: though we have conquered irascibility, we can always fall victim to a fit of rage. The second stage in our progress can be reached if we train our impulses in such a way that the fitness of things indifferent becomes the guide to conduct. Lastly it remains to impose upon our will the quality of constant infallibility without which we are always liable to go astray, and this is to be brought about by the training of the judgment. For this whole subject see *Ep.*, 75.8ff, and compare *Epp.*, 71.30ff, 72.6ff and 109.15. Perhaps such a programme is still a shade too idealistic, but in method and outlook it has more than a little in common with the systems of moral discipline expounded by such Christian teachers as St Ignatius Loyola and St François de Sales who themselves along with their followers have shown the devout life to be fully possible.[14] And as Seneca himself remarks, 'the great thing about progress is the desire to progress' (*Ep.*, 71.36).[15]

In the quest for virtue the passions (*adfectus*), of which Zeno had identified the chief as pleasure, lust, anxiety, and fear, were always to the Stoics powerful adversaries to be beaten down and crushed. Seneca's treatment of them is orthodox (see *Epp.*, 9.1ff, 51.4ff, 85.3ff and 104.4ff). The Stoic had to attain freedom from these evils—a state of *impatientia* (which was a rendering of the Greek *apathia*) was the objective—for they were morbid and opposed to reason.

Death Seneca neatly defines as one of life's duties (*Ep.*, 77.19). It is part of the natural order. Our instincts cause us to dread it, but philosophy will help us to see it as a door leading to freedom from the inscrutable problems of life. Death is something in-different, but nevertheless it cannot easily be ignored. The soul must be hardened by long practice in the contemplation of death so as to be able to endure the sight and approach of it. Implanted in us all is a deep love of self, a desire for existence and self-preservation, and also an abhorrence of dissolution, because death seems to take away from us many goods and to remove us from the abundance to which we have become accustomed. Further, we are already familiar with the present, but are ignorant of the future into which we shall transfer ourselves, and we shrink from the unknown. And it is natural to fear the world of shades, to which death is believed to lead (*Ep.*, 82.15–16).

But death is implied by life: you will die, not because you are ill, but because you are alive; when you have recovered from a serious illness, it will not be death but ill-health that you have escaped (*Ep.*, 78.6). However, we must take a positive view. Writing to console Marcia, a Roman lady of high station, on the death of a son, Metilius, whom she greatly mourned, Seneca tells her that the young man has now escaped the power of chance; only his image—and a very imperfect one it was—has perished; he himself has become eternal and has reached a far better state. Death is not our greatest infirmity, it is in fact our greatest strength (*Ad Marciam*, 24.4ff).

Death is a release and its own reward. Suicide is perfectly

justifiable when life in accordance with reason and nature is no longer possible. Death is available as the ultimate means of our deliverance. Seneca handles this topic in *Ep.* 77. Older Stoic teachers (Panaetius, for example) had denied the possibility of personal survival, even for the wise man. Posidonius, on the other hand, had held that the sage's soul would be granted hereafter a full vision of the eternal verities, a notion that probably was inspired by Plato. Seneca (*Ad Marciam*, 25.1ff) imagines Metilius being received into the company of the sainted dead by his grandfather Cremutius Cordus, and being initiated by him into the wonders of the celestial regions—a rapturous passage that would seem to some extent indebted for its presence here to rhetorical opportunism. The Stoic tradition was divided, and Seneca is not consistent. Elsewhere he writes that death is non-existence, a state similar to that in which we were before we were born (*Epp.*, 54.4 and 77.11; also, *Troades*, 407). Again, he maintains against some at least of his school that the soul, even if we meet with a deadly accident and a watch-tower or a mountain crashes down upon us, is not dispersed under the impact but can survive (*Ep.*, 57.6). But whatever the manner of death, it is clear that Seneca does not subscribe to the theory of survival by all. Only those who by the power of reason have been raised above the common level of mere animal instinct and have lived their lives in accordance with the highest ideals deserve and are allowed to pass in spirit into the great beyond. Their souls return to their source on the divine plane (cf. *Epp.*, 41.4ff, 78.10, and 102.21ff), while those of the rest remain bound up with the material cycle on the lower plane. But survival is itself of limited duration (*Ep.*, 88.28). Ultimately the souls of the righteous will be absorbed in the cosmic process of renewal—that renewal which the Stoics held to be periodic and which involved the merging of all things and their total destruction by fire (*Ad Marciam*, 26.6–7).[16]

The contemplation of the experience of the wise man's soul after death had a particular appeal for Seneca and stirred his imagination, as we see, for example, from his eloquent words in *Ep.*, 102.28:

aliquando naturae tibi arcana retegentur, discutietur ista
caligo et lux undique clara percutiet. imaginare tecum
quantus ille sit fulgor tot sideribus inter se lumen miscentibus.

nulla serenum umbra turbabit; aequaliter splendebit omne
caeli latus; dies et nox aëris infimi vices sunt. tunc in
tenebris vixisse te dices cum totam lucem et totus aspexeris,
quam nunc per angustissimas oculorum vias obscure intueris.
et tamen admiraris illam iam procul: quid tibi videbitur
divina lux cum illam suo loco videris?

(Some day the secrets of nature will be revealed to you, that
mist up there will be dispelled, and bright light will pour in
upon you from all sides. Picture to yourself the splendour
when all the stars mingle their fires. No shadow will disturb
the clear sky; every quarter of the firmament will shine with
an unvarying brilliance; night and day are changes found
only in the lower regions of the atmosphere. Then you will
say that you have lived in darkness when you have seen the
light pure and whole as you yourself will be pure and whole
—that light which you now behold darkly through the very
narrow corridors of the eyes. And yet, though it is far away,
you already look upon it with wonder;—how will you find
the heavenly light when you have seen it in its native region?)

The strong religious feeling in Seneca is unmistakable. He
adheres to the monotheism of the school, positing God as the
first cause behind the universe. God is the creative reason, the
creative force in nature—what was technically known in Greek as
logos spermatikos or 'germinal reason' (*Ep.*, 65.12). God is the
great *artifex* or master-builder of the universe (*Ep.*, 65.19ff). The
scandalous stories of mythology he dismisses as 'the nonsense of
the poets' (*De vita beata*, 26.6), while in company with his Stoic
predecessors he holds that the various figures of the traditional
pantheon simply represent different aspects of the godhead:

quid enim aliud est natura quam deus et divina ratio toti
mundo partibusque eius inserta? quotiens voles tibi licet
aliter hunc auctorem rerum nostrarum compellare; et Iovem
illum Optimum ac Maximum rite dices et Tonantem et
Statorem, qui non, ut historici tradiderunt, ex eo quod post
votum susceptum acies Romanorum fugientium stetit, sed
quod stant beneficio eius omnia, stator stabilitorque est. . . .
hunc et Liberum patrem et Herculem ac Mercurium nostri

putant: Liberum patrem, quia omnium parens sit . . . Herculem, quia vis eius invicta sit . . . Mercurium, quia ratio penes illum est numerusque et ordo et scientia.

(For what else is nature but God and the divine reason which pervades the whole universe and all its parts? You may as often as you like address this being who created this world of ours by different names; it will be proper for you to call him Jupiter Best and Greatest, and the Thunderer and the Stayer, a title which came about not from the fact that, as historians have related, the Roman battle-line was in response to prayer stayed as the men fled, but from the fact that everything is stayed by his benefits, that he is the Stayer and Stabilizer of all . . . Our school look upon him both as Father Liber and as Hercules and as Mercury—Father Liber, because he is the father of all things . . . Hercules, because his power is invincible . . . Mercury, because reason and number and order and knowledge belong to him.) (*De beneficiis*, 4.7–8)[17]

For the Stoics the universe formed an organic whole over which presided a single and indivisible divine power.

As our souls are part of the world soul, and the world soul itself is to be identified with God, God is within us. 'A holy spirit lives within us, one who notes our good and bad deeds, and is our guardian' (*Ep.*, 41.2). 'Nothing is shut off from the sight of God. He is present as a witness in our souls, and he comes into the midst of our thoughts' (*Ep.*, 83.1). We have a natural kinship with God, and if we lead a life ordered by virtue and reason (which are identical) we shall rise to his level (cf. *Ep.*, 31.9ff). In the face of life's obstacles and difficulties obedience to God is the right path for the wise man to take: 'nihil umquam mihi incidet quod tristis excipiam, quod malo vultu; nullum tributum invitus conferam. 'omnia autem ad quae gemimus, quae expavescimus, tributa vitae sunt: horum, mi Lucili, nec speraveris immunitatem nec petieris.' ('Nothing will ever happen to me that I shall receive with sulkiness or a wry face. I shall pay all my taxes with a good grace. Now all the things which cause us to groan or feel dread are taxes levied by life—and you must not hope for immunity from them, my dear Lucilius, or seek it') (*Ep.*, 96.2).

At this point the question of destiny arises. In Stoic teaching everything was determined by an unbreakable chain of cause and effect.[18] The unity of the world depended upon the interconnection of all things (their *sympathia*). The whole of nature was an expression or embodiment of the divine law and wisdom. The universe was organized and pervaded by divine thought, which was itself imagined in material terms as an attribute of the most refined and most primary of physical substances, a subtle fiery ether. By this teaching the Stoic conviction that wisdom was all-sufficient for the well-being of mankind was provided with a foundation in what appeared to be a cosmic fact. The particle of the divine substance in each one of us—'the god within us'—united us with one another and with the totality of creation, and its pure life subsisted on the exercise of reason. All things were governed by a divine design, to discern which was the task of the implanted reason. The Stoics held to a thorough-going determinism.

Socrates had identified virtue with knowledge ('no one willingly sins'), a standpoint which the Stoics also adopted. But here two difficulties had to be faced—if virtue was knowledge, did it not then follow that vice was involuntary? If not, then ignorance must be voluntary. This alternative did less harm to morality and the Stoics chose it. But they were not yet out of the wood, for they stretched human volition to an extreme degree and came up against the determinism which was involved in their view of the physical universe.[19] How could the sinner be held responsible if his sin were strictly pre-determined? The Stoic answer was to argue that the error which lay at the heart of vice was voluntary to the extent that it could be avoided if men chose to apply reason. Effective exercise of reason would depend on the inherent strength and resolution of the soul—some Stoics, while continuing to accept the definition of virtue that equated it with knowledge, further defined it as strength and force. If the wrong action came, not from any external cause but from the man himself, then moral responsibility is saved. Morality is a matter of recognizing what the universal order demands of us and responding appropriately.

Seneca accepted this doctrine:

hanc quoque animosam Demetri fortissimi viri vocem
audisse me memini: 'hoc unum,' inquit, 'de vobis, di
immortales, queri possum, quod non ante mihi notam

voluntatem vestram fecistis; prior enim ad ista venissem ad
quae nunc vocatus adsum. vultis liberos sumere? vobis illos
sustuli. vultis aliquam partem corporis? sumite; non magnam
rem promitto, cito totum relinquam. vultis spiritum?
quidni? nullam moram faciam quo minus recipiatis quod
dedistis. a volente feretis quicquid petieritis. quid ergo est?
maluissem offerre quam tradere. quid opus fuit auferre?
accipere potuistis; sed ne nunc quidem auferetis, quia
nihil eripitur nisi retinenti.'

(I remember having heard that most gallant man, Demetrius,
make this spirited utterance: 'Immortal gods,' he said, 'I can
make this one complaint against you, that you did not make
your will known to me sooner, because I should have
reached earlier that state in which, after having been
summoned, I now am. Do you wish to take my children? It
was for you that I fathered them. Do you wish to take some
part of my body? Take it—it is no great thing that I am
offering you, and I shall be leaving the whole thing behind
soon. Do you wish to take my life? Why not? I shall not
hinder you from taking back what you gave. You shall have
whatever you ask of me, and it will be with my free consent.
What is my trouble, then? I should have preferred to offer
rather than to hand over. What need was there to take by
force? You could have received it as a gift; but even now
you will not take it away by force, because nothing can be
torn from a man's possession unless he holds on to it.') (*De
providentia*, 5.5–6)

Seneca goes on to say that he is under no compulsion, suffers
nothing against his will, and is not God's slave but his follower,
and the more so, in fact, since he knows that everything is under
the control of a law which is fixed and enacted for all time. 'Fata
nos ducunt et quantum cuique temporis restat prima nascentium
hora disposuit. Causa pendet ex causa, privata ac publica longus
ordo rerum trahit. Ideo fortiter omne patiendum est quia non, ut
putamus, incidunt cuncta sed veniunt. Olim constitutum est quid
gaudeas, quid fleas . . .' ('Fate guides us, and what length of time
remains for each of us was settled at the first hour of birth. Cause
is connected with cause [cf. *Ep.*, 77.12: 'the chain of causes'],
and all public and private issues a long sequence of events

directs. Everything should therefore be endured with fortitude since all things do not, as we suppose, simply happen but come about. Long ago it was decided what would make you rejoice, what would make you weep . . .') (*De providentia*, 5.7). We may compare his fine words (*De vita beata*, 15.5): 'omnemque temporum difficultatem sciet (virtus) legem esse naturae et ut bonus miles feret volnera, numerabit cicatrices, et transverberatus telis moriens amabit eum pro quo cadet imperatorem; habebit illud in animo vetus praeceptum: deum sequere!' ('Virtue will know that every trouble that time brings comes by a law of nature, and like a good soldier she will bear the wounds, she will count her scars, and pierced with darts she will, as she dies, love him for whom she falls—her captain; she will keep in mind that old command, "Follow God!"') In *Ep.*, 96 Seneca treats the same theme, as he does also in *Ep.*, 107 which he concludes with a rendering of some lines by Cleanthes[20] conveying the Stoic doctrine succinctly. The last line appears to be Seneca's own:

> Lead, o Father and Master of the lofty heavens,
> Whitherso'er it pleases thee; I shall obey
> At once. I stand prepared and eager. Though I would
> Refuse, I shall with groaning go and suffer in
> My sin that which I might have done in virtuousness.
> Fate leads the willing man, the unwilling drags along.

> (duc, o parens celsique dominator poli,
> quocumque placuit: nulla parendi mora est;
> adsum impiger. fac nolle, comitabor gemens
> malusque patiar facere quod licuit bono.
> ducunt volentem fata, nolentem trahunt.)   *Ep.* 107.11

Like a dog tied to a cart, we can either run with it willingly, or resist and be pulled along.

The stress which the Stoics in their psychology laid on the essential unity of the rational self that is the source of voluntary action prevented them from accepting Plato's analysis of the soul into a controlling element and elements requiring control. Seneca, however, seems to have accepted a rational and an irrational part of the soul (cf. *Ep.*, 92.1 and 8ff).[21] Human behaviour does display remarkable contrasts, and no doubt this doctrine was put forward to take account of the facts of experience, but even so for Seneca the ultimate ideal remained—a trained judgment which imparts to the will an undeviating accuracy in the avoidance of all error.

Voluntary withdrawal from life was permissible not only as providing a refuge in suffering but also as a final assertion of man's moral freedom. A general feeling of despair and insecurity was bred in many amongst the privileged classes at Rome during the first century A.D. as they viewed the results of moral corruption and arbitrary rule. The comfort that Stoicism had to offer was eagerly sought by many. It taught them, driven in upon themselves by political conditions, to build up spiritual power through severe self-examination, and it taught them resignation in face of the chances and changes of life.

The vicissitudes of fortune frequently moved Seneca to proffer earnest counsel. We are to rise superior to it, and we can really do so:

> errant enim, Lucili, qui aut boni aliquid nobis aut mali iudicant tribuere fortunam: materiam dat bonorum ac malorum et initia rerum apud nos in malum bonumve exiturarum. valentior enim omni fortuna animus est et in utramque partem ipse res suas ducit beataeque ac miserae vitae sibi causa est.

> (For those people are mistaken, Lucilius, who consider that anything good, or evil, is bestowed upon us by fortune; she gives us simply the raw material of goods and ills, the primary sources of things, which, in our hands, will turn out for good or ill. For the soul is stronger than any kind of fortune, and by its own agency it directs its affairs either way, and it produces for itself a life that is happy or wretched.)
> (*Ep.*, 98.2)

The treachery of fortune is touched on in *Ep.*, 8.3f (her 'gifts' are snares), and the whole of *Ep.*, 13 is intended to show how fear of fortune is baseless. The same theme occurs elsewhere (*e.g. Epp.*, 16.4; 18.6f; 72.7f; 98 *passim*).

It was wise to depart when because of external circumstances life in accordance with nature was no longer a possibility. The point of decision was a matter open to varying interpretation amongst Stoics; some believed that a noble purpose justified suicide; others were content with something less exalted. However, the general teaching of the Stoics on the subject was quite strict, according to what Diogenes Laertius tells us (7.130): the sage would withdraw from life for the sake of country and friends and if he fell victim to pain too severe to bear or mutilation or incurable disease. Seneca's position did not differ much from this. In *Ep.*, 120.14, he likens the body to a guest-house which we must leave immediately it becomes clear that we are a burden to our host. In *Ep.*, 58.33ff, he writes thus:

> Plurimum enim refert, vitam aliquis extendat an mortem. At si inutile ministeriis corpus est, quidni oporteat educere animum laborantem? et fortasse paulo ante quam debet faciendum est, ne cum fieri debebit facere non possis; et cum maius periculum sit male vivendi quam cito moriendi, stultus est qui non exigua temporis mercede magnae rei aleam redimit.

> (It makes a very great difference whether a man is lengthening his life or his death. But if the body is unable to render service why should we not release the struggling soul? And perhaps one ought to do this a little before the debt is due so that, when it does fall due, one is not unable to carry out the deed. Since the danger of living in misery is greater than that of dying soon, the man is foolish who refuses to win a hazard of substantial gain by staking a small amount of time.)

In *Ep.*, 70.5f we find these words:

> sapiens vivit quantum debet, non quantum potest. . . . cogitat semper qualis vita, non quanta sit. si multa occurrunt molesta et tranquillitatem turbantia, emittit se; nec hoc tantum in necessitate ultima facit, sed cum primum illi coepit suspecta esse fortuna. . . .

> (The wise man lives as long as he ought, not as long as he can. . . . He always considers the quality of his life and not its quantity. If many obstacles trouble him and disturb his peace of mind he sets himself free. And this course is open to him not only when the crisis is in its final stage but

as soon as he begins to suspect fortune of treachery. He looks about carefully to decide whether his life had not best end there. . . . It is a question not of dying sooner or later, but of dying well or ill. Now to die well is to escape from the danger of living ill.)

Seneca's own eventual suicide in A.D. 65 anticipating an act of violence on the part of the emperor Nero was fully in accord with the ideas expressed here.[22] His play, the *Phoenissae*, contains (63-215) a dialogue between Oedipus and Antigone on this same theme in which there are some correspondences with passages in the *Epistulae Morales*—we may compare, for example, 1.79, 'tantis in malis vinci mori est', ('amidst such sorrows to be defeated is to die'), with *Ep.*, 58.36, 'sic mori vinci est', ('to die under such circumstances is to be defeated') (both contexts refer to the sufficiency of grounds for suicide), and l. 146ff, with *Ep.*, 70.14 (how easy suicide is and how many ways there are to effect it). Lines 190ff and *Ep.*, 78.2 point out that sometimes courage is necessary *not* to commit suicide.

'At whatever point you leave off living, provided that you leave off nobly, your life is a completed whole' (*Ep.*, 77.4). This thought is a favourite one with Seneca and seems to sum up well his views on death and suicide, on which he constantly meditated. Under a cruel and capricious autocrat life for people of wealth and status was full of danger and uncertainty. Many found in Stoicism an answer to some at least of the main difficulties of existence, and many, as readers of Tacitus' *Annals* know, sought the Stoic way out when these difficulties could no longer be borne in a manner consonant with what the school had shown them to be fitting.

The Stoic pantheistic doctrine of the universe involved strong emphasis on the idea of divine providence—so much so that Semitic influence has been suspected.[23] The idea is present throughout the Old Testament and is carried over into the New: God is looking ahead and guiding events in nature and history. The Bible sees this happening from the creation onwards, through the life of Israel, through the work of Christ, through the history of the Church and in the affairs of mankind generally. Zeno himself, the founder of the Stoic school, was perhaps of Semitic race, but it is safest to avoid speculation and simply point to the likeness in teaching. Seneca subscribed to the school's position. The work *De providentia* at large is concerned to show that adversities are the wise man's training ground provided by God's beneficence, and it closes with a passage on suicide as a reasonable course when trials become too burdensome. He begins the treatise with a statement on the divine foresight which is the planning and directing force behind all things in the world (2–4).

On prayer Seneca commends a saying which he found in a Greek philosopher: 'tunc scito esse te omnibus cupiditatibus solutum, cum eo perveneris ut nihil deum roges nisi quod rogare possis palam.' ('Know that you have been set free from all desires when you have reached the point where you pray to God for nothing except that for which you can pray openly') (*Ep.*, 10.5). Elsewhere he sounds the same note of warning (*Ep.*, 60 and *Ep.*, 117.23f): too many people pray for what is really harmful (a common subject for moralists—compare Juvenal's great tenth satire, creatively rendered by Samuel Johnson under the title *The Vanity of Human Wishes*). The cardinal virtues of prudence, temperance, justice and bravery are the qualities for which we should properly pray, says Seneca in conformity with the teaching of his Stoic predecessors. In *Ep.*, 85 he gives extensive treatment to these basic qualities, referring to the views of other schools as well, while shorter discussions of them are found in *Ep.*, 67.3ff, *Ep.*, 88.29ff and *Ep.* 95.55ff.

And this takes us to the question of value. According to Stoic dogma, to be virtuous (that is, to live in harmony with reason) was the only good, and not to be virtuous the only evil. Everything not related to these standards was neither good nor evil and was therefore negligible or indifferent. Indifferent things (*adiaphora* in Greek; *indifferentia, media* in Latin) are treated by Seneca at several points—*Ep.*, 66.36ff, *Ep.*, 82.10ff and *Ep.*, 109.12f. However, orthodox Stoicism was prepared to admit that for the wise man there were certain things to be *preferred* (*proēgmena* in Greek; *praeposita, praecipua, promota, potiora, producta* in Latin—Seneca discusses *producta* in *Ep.*, 74.17ff) which included, for example, health and self-preservation; and other things again to be *avoided* (*apoproēgmena* in Greek; *remota, reiecta* in Latin) amongst which were pain, illness, death. Virtuous conduct was the criterion for preference and avoidance. But the presence or absence of *producta* and *remota* could not have any effect upon the wise man's happiness. Reason for him was the only real good, which made him independent of the inconstancy of fortune. Pleasure for him was not a good, hence his temperance; pain and death were not evils, hence his bravery; and he was immune to the influence of prejudice or favour, hence his justice. Yet Seneca's object, as has already been remarked, was not to press the original absolute claims and demands of the school but to deal in a humane and direct way with people's problems and attempt to speak encouragingly to their condition.

In two very interesting letters (94 and 95) Seneca offers a useful discussion of the leading concepts in Stoic moral theory. In *Ep.*, 94 he considers the question whether doctrines without precepts are sufficient for the philosopher and student; in *Ep.*, 95 whether precepts without doctrines are enough. In view of the many duties and choices which confront us amidst the complexities of life, Seneca comes to the conclusion that they are both necessary and are complementary to one another. He shows clear command of the ideas and the technical vocabulary which expresses them. The external presentation of knowledge (*epistēmē* in Greek; *scientia* in Latin) and of what the Stoics called innate ideas (*prolēpseis*; *notiones communes*) is in the form of incontrovertible statements (*axiōmata*; *pronuntiata*) and of dogmas and principles (*dogmata*; *decreta, placita, scita*). Determined by definitions (*horoi*; *definitiones*), they are tested by their moral value (*axia*; *honestum*), by the standard or canon of judgment (*critērion*; *norma iudicii, lex, regula*), and by the universal law of reason (*orthos logos*; *recta ratio*). In this way the tenets of philosophy are contrasted with opinion (*doxa*; *opinio*) and a comprehension (*catalēpsis*; *cognitio*) which fails to reach completeness and perfection. When a person fully understands and thoroughly puts into effect such doctrines the conduct that results is described as 'absolute duty' (*catorthōma, teleion cathēcon*; *perfectum officium*). Acts in this class are completely appropriate.

In the second of the two letters Seneca turns to the preceptorial part (*pars praeceptiva*) of philosophy which is concerned with intermediate duty (*cathēcon*; *medium, commune officium*).[24] An act in the intermediate category is incompletely appropriate, while the third category of act consists of what is inappropriate. Virtue cannot be exercised except in the midst of human society, which in turn means the assumption of certain responsibilities—intermediate duties (such as earning a living, supporting one's family, taking part in public life). This whole preceptorial department of philosophy is thus bound up with the real problems of daily life and the *indifferentia* or things indifferent, and Seneca proceeds to an analysis, diffuse and quite lengthy, of the technical divisions and related terms involved, yet another indication of his wide knowledge of the substratum of his school's tenets.

The Stoics seem to have varied in their view of good repute (*eudoxia* in Greek; *gloria, claritas* in Latin). At first, when the influence of Cynicism was greater, they professed both an external and an internal indifference to it; ultimately they followed common sense and included it among the things to be preferred—cf. Seneca, *Ep.*, 102.3ff. In *Ep.*, 94.64ff he writes about the misguided desire for it which has bad consequences, but in *Ep.*, 79.13ff he calls fame the shadow of virtue since it brings to attention the good examples set by the wise.

Stoic teaching recognized 'first objects according to nature' (*prōta kata physin* in Greek; *prima naturae* in Latin) which referred to those things primarily and naturally sought by the animal organism right from the very beginning of its existence as being conducive to its preservation. Amongst these first objects they included freedom from bodily pain, but they refused to find a place for pleasure here, holding it to be not the result of uncorrupted natural impulse but an accompaniment or 'aftergrowth'. By a later modification of their teaching cheerfulness was taken to be the ultimate aim to which the practice of virtue was simply a means. Restraint had to be exercised—'real joy is a serious matter', says Seneca (*Ep.*, 23.4). He advises the avoidance of pleasure in *Ep.*, 104.34, and in *Ep.*, 124.2ff remarks that those who follow pleasure make the grave mistake of limiting it to the senses. The pleasure that comes from plain living is extolled in *Ep.*, 21.10–11, while in *Ep.*, 122.2ff the pleasure some take in table luxury and late hours is castigated. Worldly pleasure is vain and delusory and must be dearly paid for (*Epp.*, 27.2f, and 39.5f); the allurements of pleasure are provocations to vice (*Ep.*, 51.4ff). Drunkenness he condemns on more than one occasion, most extensively in *Ep.*, 83 which is a sustained sermon against this offence that violates the cardinal principle of self-control.

Concerning wealth (officially categorized amongst the things indifferent) there are inconsistencies between his preaching and his practice: 'Seneca, *in his books* a philosopher' (John Milton's epigrammatic verdict). He expresses scorn of wealth (*Ep.*, 108.11ff), stigmatizes it as a handicap in the pursuit of philosophy (*Ep.*, 17 *passim*), points to it as a source of corruption (*Ep.*, 87.22ff), urges that it be avoided (*Ep.*, 104.34), reflects on its emptiness (*Ep.*, 110.14ff), and rails against it as a curse (*Ep.*, 115.9ff). And yet, despite all these protests, he was himself a very rich man, the owner (sure sign of exceeding affluence) of five hundred citrus wood tables.[25] In the *De vita beata* he honestly acknowledges the case against him and ably defends himself with the engaging humility that characterizes all his utterances on this topic (17.3ff):

> non sum sapiens ... nec ero. exige itaque a me, non ut optimis par sim, sed ut malis melior. hoc mihi satis est, cotidie aliquid ex vitiis meis demere et errores meos obiurgare. non perveni ad sanitatem, ne perveniam quidem ... hoc ... Platoni obiectum est, obiectum Epicuro, obiectum Zenoni; omnes enim isti dicebant non quemadmodum ipsi viverent, sed quemadmodum esset ipsis vivendum.

> (I am no sage ... and never shall be. And so don't demand that I should be equal to the best, but that I should be better than the bad. It is enough for me if every day I discard some of my vices and blame my mistakes. I have not yet attained perfect health, nor in fact shall I attain it . . . . The same charge has been levelled against Plato, Epicurus and Zeno; they did not profess to say how they lived, but only how they ought to live.)

Later in the same work he points out that through wealth the philosopher is enabled to put his theories into practice and to exercise the qualities he has developed. If we refuse wealth admission to our homes we thereby reveal that we are ignorant of the art of using it properly (23.3). Elsewhere (*De constantia sapientis*, 14.2) he argues that the value of money for doing good must not be under-rated, even though its possession may lay us open to particular temptations. In fact, he places riches amongst the *potiora* or things to be preferred (*De vita beata*, 22.4), thus diverging from the tradition of his school. No doubt today socialist millionaires would justify their position along the same lines as Seneca.

The powerful hunger for righteousness and purity of heart that marked Stoicism as a whole is evident in Seneca. On true morality he writes thus (*De beneficiis*, 1.6.1–2): 'Itaque non quid fiat aut quid detur refert, sed qua mente, quia beneficium non in eo quod fit aut datur consistit, sed in ipso dantis aut facientis animo.' ('What counts is not what is done or given, but the attitude behind the action, since a benefit consists not in what is done or given, but in the intention of the giver or doer.') Following Stoic doctrine, he states that sin can be removed through knowledge (cf. *Epp.*, 28.9ff, 29.4ff, 42.1ff, 50.4ff, for example). He also recognizes the power of conscience (cf. *Epp.*, 43.5; 97.12ff), and stresses the possibility of amendment of life in conformity with the concept of moral progress (cf. *Epp.*, 25 and 112).

Virtue was a matter of discerning the real values, of appropriating them, and of making the right choices accordingly. Seneca's earnest devotion to this ideal was genuine and is well exemplified by the vision of virtue which he enthusiastically presents in *Ep.*, 115.3ff. Virtue is identical with truth (*Ep.*, 71.16) and can kindle and inspire the imagination (*Ep.*, 64.6ff) and raise us above the limitations of our material environment (*Ep.* 66.2ff—a letter which interestingly considers various aspects of virtue from the Stoic standpoint).

With the Stoic philosopher's insistence on the claims of individual virtue went an equal insistence on membership of a cosmopolitan society, and this notion of a 'city of Zeus' remained throughout a distinctive Stoic dogma.[26] The proposition that man was born not for himself but for mankind was the most important part of their contribution to practical morality. 'Nullum inveniri exilium intra mundum potest; nihil enim quod intra mundum est alienum homini est.' ('Inside the world no place of exile can be found, for nothing that is inside the world is foreign to mankind') (Seneca, *Ad Helviam*, 8.5; cf. *De otio*, 4.1). We should live in the conviction that the whole of this world is our native land (*Ep.*, 28.4). No distinction was to be made between Greek and barbarian, Roman and stranger, male and female, bond and free. All were members of one body for all partook of reason, and all were equally men.

But this belief did not give rise to any movement for the abolition of slavery, for the Stoics attached little importance to external circumstances. Seneca, however, to his everlasting credit tried to reduce its evils in practice, pleading for humanity in masters' treatment of their slaves.[27] In *Ep.* 47 he gives his views which recur in *De clementia*, 1.18, *De ira*, 3.35, and *De beneficiis*, 3.18ff: 'Vis tu cogitare istum quem servum tuum vocas ex isdem seminibus ortum eodum frui caelo, aeque spirare, aeque vivere, aeque mori! . . . sic cum inferiore vivas quemadmodum tecum superiorem velis vivere.' ('Please remember that the man you call your slave sprang from the same beginnings, is smiled upon by the same sky, and breathes, lives and dies just as you do yourself. . . . Treat your inferiors as you would be treated by your betters') (*Ep.* 47.10–11). Seneca's humanitarianism stood in strong contrast to the haughty, cruel and insulting treatment that was often, as he remarks, meted out to slaves.

Associated with this liberalism in Seneca was an enlightened attitude to the education of women. He repudiated the suggestion that they were naturally less gifted than men (*Ad Marciam*, 16.1), and he regretted that his father's old-fashioned outlook prevented his mother from acquiring a proper grounding in philosophical studies (*Ad Helviam*, 17.4).

Full participation in political life was enjoined by Stoic doctrine, in contradistinction to the quietism of the Epicureans. Both Zeno and Chrysippus wrote works on their ideal political community, and Chrysippus believed that statesmanship was the region in which the Stoic wise man could best exercise his virtue. Seneca's commitment to politics was deep—he was a politician who happened also to be a philosopher, as was observed at the outset, and not a philosopher who happened to be a politician. He tried to exert a moderating influence; the treatise *De clementia* was addressed to the young Nero at the start of his reign in A.D. 54 when Seneca passed from being his tutor to being a minister. He did not always succeed in living up to his creed; during his years of banishment in Corsica (A.D. 41–9) he showed an un-Stoic dejection, grovelling shamefully to the emperor Claudius' powerful freedman and secretary, Polybius (see *Ad Polybium passim*), and later in the *Apocolocyntosis*, a witty but cruel skit on the dead Claudius, we find both meanness of spirit and uncharitableness of judgment concerning a man who was by no means a contemptible ninny. Five years later (A.D. 59) he connived at the murder of Agrippina, carried out at the orders of her son, Nero, who had succeeded Claudius. But condemnation is easy; Seneca's aspirations were of the highest and most honourable; the times were difficult and his position was one that presented special temptations and trials. A man's good actions so often escape notice. It is hard to believe that Seneca the Stoic had no leavening effect at all upon his age.

Yet the theme of retirement as opposed to participation in affairs appears from time to time in his writings, most notably in the fragmentary work *De otio*. Against the strict Stoic view, summed up in Zeno's dictate that the wise man will engage in politics unless something prevents him, Seneca upholds the moral value of abstention. At every age, he argues, it is allowable to give up action in favour of a contemplative existence, and those who have grown old in active duty have an especial right to follow this course. When corruption is universal in the polity, deliberate withdrawal is permitted under both the Stoic and the Epicurean codes. There are two commonwealths to which we belong—'the one a vast and truly common state . . . in which we measure the limits of our citizenship by the path of the sun; the other, the one to which the accident of birth has assigned us' (*De otio*, 4.1). The wise man may better serve the greater commonwealth by retreating in order to speculate on the laws of morality and of nature. Nature has designed that we study her vast and wonderful works; our research must be directed so as to pass 'from revealed to hidden things and discover something more ancient than the world itself . . . Our thought bursts through the ramparts of the sky and is not content to know what is shown' (ibid., 5.5–6). It is likely that the *De otio*, with its defence of leisure from affairs, belongs to the last period of Seneca's life which begins with his voluntary withdrawal from the court in A.D. 62, the year in which its addressee, Annaeus Serenus, probably died. The impulse towards scientific enquiry which we encounter in it connects it with the *Naturales Quaestiones* which also dates from the author's last years. The circumstances of his own life helped to form Seneca's attitude to the question of retreat; it is mentioned several times in the letters (e.g. 19.11; 21.1ff; 22 *passim*), and *Ep.* 73 is particularly of note for the autobiographical hints it gives and for its indication of Seneca's own attempts to cut loose from the life of the court and gain the leisure and detachment of the sage.

Simplicity and frugality of living were always a central part of the Stoic ethic, and Seneca commends these frequently. Perhaps his most interesting treatment of the question is in *Ep.*, 108 *passim*. At section 17ff of this letter he reveals that in his youth he had leanings towards the asceticism of the Pythagoreans (who abstained from flesh). In the preceding section he remarks that throughout his life he has avoided perfumes (a regular ingredient of the Roman toilet for both men and women), wine and the excessive use of the bath to which so many Romans were addicted. A Stoic had to be self-sufficient. The wise man would keep clear of anything that could threaten and impair his self-sufficiency.

More than once Seneca remarks that he has it in mind to produce a systematic work on moral philosophy (*De providentia*, 1.1; *Epp.*, 106.2; 108.1; 109.17), but apparently this never came to anything. The letters with their sound, practical advice attractively presented form a useful handbook. Various types of composition recognized in ancient epistolography occur. We have consolation for the bereaved (*Epp.*, 63 and 99), and the theme of friendship (*Epp.*, 3; 9; 19.10f; 35; 48.2ff; 55.9ff, for example) which was standard amongst the moralists. Seneca (*Ep.*, 94.40) affirms that we need the society of good men if we are going to improve—a thought he frequently expresses (cf. *Epp.*, 25.6, and 52.8, for example). Old age with its various infirmities and problems receives sympathetic handling (*Epp.*, 12; 26.1ff, for example), while a number of old men (e.g. Aufidius Bassus in *Ep.*, 30.1ff, Claranus in *Ep.*, 66.1ff and Seneca himself in *Ep.*, 67.1ff) are commended in characteristically Roman laudations for their heroic struggle against ill-health.

Seneca's generous spirit and unprejudiced breadth of vision are seen nowhere more clearly than in his estimate of Epicurus and his teaching. In the letters he frequently refers to, or quotes from, this leader of a rival school—cf. 18.9; 12.10; 90.35, for example. The best ideas are common property, he says after citing a remark of Epicurus (*Ep.*, 12.11); he was ready to use good material whatever its source. On the character and creed of Epicurus he has this to say in *De vita beata*, 13.1.2:

in ea quidem ipse sententia sum—invitis hoc nostris popularibus dicam—sancta Epicurum et recta praecipere et si propius accesseris tristia; voluptas enim illa ad parvum et exile revocatur et, quam nos virtuti legem dicimus, eam ille dicit

voluptati: iubet illam parere naturae. . . . ille quisquis desidio-
sum otium et gulae ac libidinis vices felicitatem vocat, bonum
malae rei quaerit auctorem et, cum illo venit blando nomine
inductus, sequitur voluptatem non quam audit sed quam
attulit.

(Personally I believe—and I shall say it though the members
of our school may protest—that the doctrines of Epicurus are
upright and holy and, if you consider them closely, austere.
Pleasure according to his well-known tenet is reduced to a
minimum, a mere shadow, and he lays down the same rule for
it as we Stoics do for virtue, requiring that it obey nature. . . .
Whoever applies the word 'happiness' to slothful idleness and
alternate indulgence in gluttony and lust casts about for a good
sponsor to whom to appeal in the defence of an evil practice,
and when, attracted to this school by a tempting word, he
has joined it, the pleasure that he then pursues is not the
one he is taught but the one he has brought.)

In *Ep.*, 58.6–24 and 30–1 Seneca expounds the Platonic idea of
being, and in *Ep.*, 65 he deals with causes, giving first the Stoic
teaching (2–3), next Aristotle's (4–6), and next Plato's (7–10). He
then criticizes that of Aristotle and Plato (11–14). His sources
for this kind of knowledge are uncertain; lecture notes, anthologies and text-books, as well as first-hand inspection of some at
least of the more important among the original works are all
possible. The fairly large number of references by name to
Posidonius in Seneca's writings suggests that he had in fact read
him. As we have already seen, his command of Stoic technical
philosophy, however it came to him, was not negligible. In the
letter to which we have just referred (58.15ff) there is a discussion
of the Stoic categories.[28] In *Ep.*, 106 *passim* Seneca presents the
Stoic view of virtue and the emotions as corporeal, and in *Ep.*,
113 continues the subject, discoursing on the vitality of the soul
and its attributes.

The function of the nine tragedies in Seneca's scheme of
philosophical exposition, briefly referred to at the beginning, has
been studied in the fundamental work of O. Regenbogen[29] who
examines the treatment in them in accordance with Stoic principles of suffering and death. Under these principles strong

emotions of any kind are condemned, and in these pieces the baneful results of grief, anger, jealousy, ambition, pride, etc., are depicted. Really dramatic scenes are rare, but one in *Troades* (525–814) between Andromache and Ulysses is particularly notable and is singled out by Regenbogen for attention. Ulysses has come to fetch Hector's son Astyanax for execution, but the mother, Andromache, has hidden the boy in his father's tomb. Occupying nearly a third of the whole piece and having no counterpart in Euripides' play of the same name, the scene shows in its presentation of Ulysses' shrewd cunning and the grief of the heart-broken Andromache a depth of psychological insight not found in Greek drama, as Regenbogen remarks. In the passage of *Agamemnon* (108–225) in which Clytaemnestra talks with the Nurse there is a characteristically Senecan turmoil of conflicting emotions, a state to be avoided at all costs by the Stoic—cf. *De vita beata*, 8.6: 'And so you may boldly declare that harmony of the soul is the highest good; where concord and unity are, there must the virtues be. The vices are accompanied by discord.'

In the few pages of excellent analysis that he gives to the plays, Pohlenz[30] warns us not to separate Seneca the philosopher and Seneca the tragedian. The dramas (never intended for the stage) show us man struggling against whimsical fortune and constantly falling victim to his own blind infatuation. In *Troades* the demands of the political situation bring about the death of Astyanax (for only through it can Greece be safe from any future Trojan war); in *Phoenissae* Iocasta, a figure of grief and shame, is in the grip of a cruel dilemma posed by natural affection as her two sons Eteocles and Polynices prepare to wage war on one another for the kingship of Thebes; and in *Thyestes* the Aeschylean notion of great power leading to the sinful pride that brings ruin in its train is worked out. It was the destructive passions of men which principally interested Seneca, in which respect he resembled Euripides. While Euripides viewed the whole person from whom the passions emanated, Seneca, says Pohlenz, gave the passions an existence of their own and through individual examples illustrated their course. As a student of psychology Seneca, Pohlenz finds, tended to leave philosophical theory behind. The combat between intellect and passion is there, but when he treats revenge or a mother's love his characters are not just impersonations of emotions set out to be paradigmatic of

Stoic theory. Yet Pohlenz would agree with Regenbogen that between the prose writings and the tragedies there is a correspondence in general outlook and in certain themes.

'The mere name of philosophy is an object of scorn' (*Ep.*, 5.2); 'the name of philosophy . . . worshipful and sacred' (*Ep.*, 14.11). Both the ostentatious squalor of some would-be philosophers and dialectical subtleties were equally repellant to Romans, as Seneca knew; down-to-earth advice about living was what people required and he set about supplying it. The neglect of irrational forces in human nature was a leading feature of post-Aristotelian thought, and the Stoa, in its first stage, was over-intellectualized. A leader in its third stage, Seneca diffused a humanitarian spirit. On the whole the first century A.D. at Rome displayed a greater degree of humanity in personal dealings, which arose no doubt from the spread of Stoicism with its distinctive social philosophy, and some of the credit for spreading it must go to Seneca. There was much in Stoicism to appeal immediately to the Roman character. Alone among the ancient systems of thought it explicitly recognized and made psychological allowance for the motive of duty, a motive for which the Romans already had a deep natural respect. As popularizer, Seneca, though himself conversant with the technical, more complicated areas of his school's doctrines, took care to emphasize those parts of his saving message which would find readiest response in the hearts and minds of his fellows as having widest application to their situation.

And he did this in a style which, being pithy and sententious, was calculated to catch the ears of contemporaries.[31] We may fitly close with a few examples chosen from multitudes of his epigrams:

nemo se iudicet quicquam debere qui tempus accepit, cum interim hoc unum est quod ne gratus quidem potest reddere.

(No one who has taken up your time would reckon that he owes you anything, and yet this is the one loan which even a grateful borrower cannot repay.) (*Ep.*, 1.3)

longum iter est per praecepta, breve et efficax per exempla.

(The learner's path is made long by rules, short and successful by examples.) (*Ep.*, 6.5)

quisquis exit in lucem iussus est lacte et panno esse contentus:
ab his initiis nos regna non capiunt.

(At birth we have to be satisfied with a little milk and a rag;
so we begin, but soon whole kingdoms are not big enough
for us.) (*Ep.*, 20.13)

nemo enim patriam quia magna est amat, sed quia sua.

(Men love their native land, not because it is great but
because it is their own.) (*Ep.*, 66.26)

quomodo fabula, sic vita: non quam diu, sed quam bene acta
sit refert.

(Life is like a play; it is not the length that matters but the
quality of the acting.) (*Ep.*, 77.20)

otium sine litteris mors est et hominis vivi sepultura.

(Retirement without literature is a living burial.) (*Ep.*, 82.3)

hoc agamus ut quemadmodum pretiosa rerum sic vita
nostra non multum pateat sed multum pendeat.

(Life should resemble precious metals and weigh much in
little bulk.) (*Ep.*, 93.4)

quaedam absciduntur facilius animo quam temperantur.

(It is easier to abstain than be temperate.) (*Ep.*, 108.16)

tam omnibus ignoscere crudelitas quam nulli.

(It is as much an act of cruelty to pardon all as to pardon
none.) (*De clementia*, 1.2.2)

non minus principi turpia sunt multa supplicia quam medico
multa funera.

(A host of executions discredits a king, just as a host of
funerals discredits a doctor.) (*De clementia*, 1.24.1)

omnis ex infirmitate feritas est.

(All ferocity arises from a sense of weakness.) (*De vita beata*, 3.4)

vivere tota vita discendum est et . . . tota vita discendum est mori.

(It takes the whole of life to learn how to live—and the whole of life to learn how to die.) (*De brevitate vitae*, 7.3)

puto multos potuisse ad sapientiam pervenire nisi putassent se pervenisse.

(I imagine that many men would have arrived at wisdom if they had not imagined that they had already arrived.) (*De tranquillitate animi*, 1.16)

Notes

1 On Seneca's style, its spirit and purpose, see H. MacL.Currie, (1966).
2 See Pierre Grimal's excellent edition, Paris, 1953.
3 See O. Regenbogen, 'Schmerz und Tod in den Tragödien Senecas', *Vortr. Bibl. Warburg* 1927–8, Leipzig-Berlin, 1930, 167–218, a very valuable study.
4 On the *Naturales Quaestiones* see G. Stahl's very useful article, *Hermes* 92, (1964), 425ff.
5 Empedocles, c 493–c 433 B.C., philosopher, poet, scientist, orator, statesman, mystic, thaumaturgist and claimant to divine honours—one of the greatest figures of his time. For a good account, see Werner Jaeger, *The Theology of the Early Greek Philosophers* (Oxford paperback, 1967), ch. 8 *passim* with the literature there cited.
6 On Posidonius, A. D. Nock's paper in *JRS* 49 (1949), 1ff has much of value to say in brief compass.
7 R. D. Hicks (1911), 23.
8 Chrysippus, second founder of the school ('Without Chrysippus there would have been no Stoa', *Diogenes Laertius*, 7.183), a man of very acute intellect and great literary industry (705 rolls are attributed to him, *Diog. Laertius*, 7. 180), but no stylist. Logic, law and divination were among the many subjects he handled. His fragments occupy the 348 pages of von Arnim's second volume and nearly 200 of his third. See Gould, (1970), for an up-to-date assessment of him and his thought. His importance for the school lies in the logical foundation which he laid for it.

9 Briefly, indifferent things are those which have no direct connection with either happiness or unhappiness.

10 Punishment in this life has a reformatory function (Seneca, *De clementia*, 2.22.1), and hereafter (*Ad Marciam*, 25.1).

11 Seneca is an important witness concerning Posidonius. A. D. Leeman's article, 'Seneca and Poseidonios: a philosophical commentary on Seneca, *Ep.*, 102. 3–19', *Mnemosyne* 5 (1952), 57–79 is instructive.

12 Heraclitus of Ephesus (flourished c 500 B.C.) thought of the universe as a conflict of opposites under the control of eternal Justice—a conflict in which he found both the apparent relativity of nature and her inner unity. His influence upon Stoic physics and Stoic thought in general was profound. For him and early Greek philosophy at large see the *Cambridge Ancient History*, vol. 4, 'Mystery-religions and Presocratic Philosophy' by F. M. Cornford; J. Burnet, *Early Greek Philosophy* (4th ed., 1930); W. Jaeger, *The Theology of the Early Greek Philosophers* (Oxford paperback, 1967), especially ch. 8 for Heraclitus. *The Presocratic Philosophers* by G. S. Kirk and J. E. Raven (Cambridge, 1957) is for the more advanced student; on Heraclitus see ch. 6.

13 *De otio*, 3.1: 'I shall show that the Stoics also accept this teaching [i.e. that the contemplative life in seclusion, even from one's earliest years, and retirement after one has served the state well are equally permissible] not because I have made it my rule to advance nothing contrary to the doctrine of Zeno or Chrysippus, but because the matter itself allows me to adopt their opinion; for if a man always follows the opinion of one person his place is not in the senate but in a faction.'

14 See *Spiritual Exercises* by Ignatius Loyola (latest English trans. by L. J. Puhl, 1968), and J. Brodrick, *St Ignatius Loyola: the Pilgrim Years* (Burns & Oates, 1956). The *Introduction to the Devout Life* (Christian Classics, 1962) and *The Love of God* by St François de Sales (Christian Literature Crusade, 1965) are both recent translations into English; see too A. J. M. Hamon, *Life of St Francis de Sales* (2 vols, Burns & Oates, 1925–9). Christian writers held Seneca in great respect; his edifying works convinced them that if he was not actually a Christian he was certainly not far from being one (this, despite the fact that he commends suicide)—cf. *saepe noster* (Tertullian, *De anima*, 20), and *potuit esse uerus dei cultor si quis illi monstrasset* (Lactantius, *Diu. Inst.*, 6.24.14). There is a genuine resemblance between popular Stoic ethics and those of Christianity. A forged correspondence between Seneca and St Paul survives which St Jerome knew (*De viris illust.*, 12) but not apparently anyone earlier. See J. N. Sevenster, *Paul and Seneca* (Leyden, 1961). See too W. K. C. Guthrie, *History of Greek Philosophy*, vol. 1 (Cambridge, 1962), ch. 7.

15 This is a favourite thought with Seneca—cf., for instance, *Ep.*, 34.3: *pars magna bonitatis est velle fieri bonum* (which parallels *Phaedra*, 249: *pars sanitatis velle sanari fuit*), and *Ep.*, 80.4: *quid tibi opus est ut sis bonus? velle.* This thought is related to the philosophical question of willing and knowing (for which see *Epp.*, 20.5; 37.5; 81.13; 115.5). Pohlenz argued that Seneca, unlike his Stoic predecessors, put a special emphasis on the will, but Rist (1969), ch. 12 ('Knowing and Willing'), concludes that

Seneca did not make any significant variation on the doctrine of the Old Stoa concerning this issue.

16 ἐκπύρωσις (complete destruction by fire) and ἀποκατάστασις τοῦ παντός (renewal of the whole) are the technical terms.

17 The Stoics rationalized and allegorized the old myths (in which a lead had already been given by Democritus, Empedocles, some of the Sophists and the Cynics). Zeno sought out or invented 'natural principles' (φυσικοὶ λόγοι) and moral ideas in the traditional legends and in the poetry of Homer and Hesiod. Etymology was widely applied with the wildest results; mythological explanations were often based on the most outlandish etymological conjectures. Hercules and Odysseus were the Stoics' favourite heroes and practically every incident in their adventures was used to yield some moral meaning. On ancient allegory see J. Tate, *CR*, 41 (1927), 214ff, *CQ* 23 (1929), 41ff; 142ff; 24 (1930), 1ff; 28 (1934), 105 ff.

18 Seneca defines fate as the necessity of things (*Nat. Quaest.*, 2.36).

19 For this whole subject see the full discussion by Rist (1969), ch. 7 ('Fate and Necessity'), and A. A. Long, 'Freedom and determinism in the Stoic theory of human action' in Long (1970), 173–99.

20 Cleanthes, *fr.* 527, von Arnim. Cleanthes, Zeno's pupil and successor, used his poetic ability to advance the Stoic cause. His hymn to Zeus in thirty-eight hexameters (translated with brief introduction and notes by E. H. Blakeney, S.P.C.K., 1921) is full of genuine religious feeling. On the use of poetry to present moral truth cf. *Ep.*, 33.6 and *Ep.*, 94.27. At *Ep.*, 108.10 Seneca quotes a saying of Cleanthes (*fr.* 487, von Arnim): 'As our breath produces a louder sound when it passes through the long and narrow opening of the trumpet . . . even so the constricting rules of poetry clarify our meaning.'

21 On this Posidonian psychological dualism see Rist (1969), ch. 11 ('The Imprint of Posidonius').

22 For Seneca on suicide cf. also *Epp.*, 24 (especially section 25 to the end) and 30.15. Rist (1969) devotes his thirteenth chapter to a discussion of the Stoic attitude to this subject. He rightly finds Seneca's wise man to be fundamentally in love with death, but when he says that Seneca's emphasis on suicide is an emphasis on 'a negative concept of freedom which is almost totally absent among the early Stoics' (248–9) he is surely overlooking the fact that the people whom Seneca was trying to help were living in a different world from that which Zeno and Chrysippus knew.

23 Zeno, the founder of the school (335–263 B.C.), born at Citium in Cyprus, was perhaps of Phoenician (and so Semitic) stock. Bevan (1913), makes much of this possibility.

24 I. G. Kidd's important paper, 'Stoic Intermediates and the End for Man', *CQ*, n.s. 5 (1955), 181–94 (reprinted in Long (1970), 150–72) should be consulted.

25 For Seneca's great wealth see Tacitus, *Annals*, 15.64.6; Juvenal, 10.16 (*Senecae praedivitis*), and Dio Cassius, 61.10.2.

26 See Baldry (1965), *passim*.

27 From Cleanthes to Seneca the theme of benevolence and charity con-

stantly figures in Stoic teaching. The spirit of philanthropy and compassion is particularly noticeable in Seneca—cf., for example, *Ep.*, 95.33 and 52.

28 Rist (1969), ch. 9, considers the Stoic categories and their uses.

29 See n. 3 above. Regenbogen's approach to the tragedies has been productive of a whole school of criticism—see Michael Coffey in *Lustrum* 2 (1957), 113ff for bibliography covering work on the tragedies from 1922 to 1955. Cf. also C. Garton, 'The background to character portrayal in Seneca', *CPhil.* 54 (1959), 1ff.

30 Pohlenz (1964), 324–7.

31 Cf. Tacitus' assessment of Seneca's status as a writer (*Ann.*, 13.3): *ingenium amoenum et temporis eius auribus accommodatum.*

BIBLIOGRAPHICAL NOTE

Seneca wrote much, and his surviving works (which provide few indications to assist us in dating them) are of considerable bulk. First, there are ten *Dialogi* (Seneca's own title, though it is the conversational atmosphere rather than the form of dialogue which we meet in them), three of which are *consolationes* or consolatory pieces—*Ad Marciam* (Marcia had lost a son), *Ad Polybium* (Polybius, the emperor Claudius' influential freedman, had lost a brother), and *Ad Helviam* (written from his Corsican exile to his mother Helvia to soothe her grief over the mishap that had overtaken him). The *De providentia* demonstrates that any suffering the virtuous undergo is part of Providence's scheme for training them, the *De constantia sapientis* that the Stoic wise man has no fear of suffering. The *De ira* discusses the nature of anger, its futility and cure, the *De vita beata* the Stoic teaching on happiness, the *De otio* (a fragment) the implications for the Stoic of retirement from public life, the *De tranquillitate animi* the anxieties and troubles of the unwise who have not taken to philosophy, the *De brevitate vitae* the sufficiency of life, however short, provided that no time be wasted. Next, there are three prose treatises: the *De clementia*, on mercy as a necessary quality in the autocrat, addressed to the young Nero and because of the reference to his age at 1.9.1, to be dated to the year A.D. 55 or 56; the *De beneficiis*, a long and rambling work on benefits; and the *Naturales Quaestiones* in seven books which treats in a popular manner various aspects of meteorology and astronomy, a work with little scientific merit. The *Epistulae Morales*, a collection of 124 letters addressed to his friend Lucilius on moral themes, belong to the period A.D. 63–64. The *Apocolocyntosis*, a Menippean satire in a mixture of prose and verse, is a bitter though not unamusing skit on the dead and officially deified emperor Claudius.

Nine tragedies have come down to us: the *Hercules Furens*, *Thyestes*, *Phoenissae*, *Phaedra*, *Oedipus*, *Troades*, *Medea*, *Agamemnon*, *Hercules Oetaeus*. The *Octavia*, the only *praetexta* or serious drama on a Roman historical subject which has survived, contains allusions to Nero's end and would seem thus to be the product of a later hand.

At least eighteen prose works have not survived, among them *De superstitione*, an attack on the popular conception of the gods, and *De matrimonio*, which seems to have been an interesting discussion on marriage. A collection of 77 verse epigrams has been preserved, but they are not all from Seneca's pen.

Select Bibliography

SENECA, Loeb Classical Library.

CICERO, *De officiis*, *De finibus* III and IV, *De natura deorum* II (all in Loeb Classical Library).

ABEL, K. *Bauformen in Senecas Dialogen*, Heidelberg, 1967.

ANDREWS, A. C. 'Did Seneca practise the Ethics of his Epistles?' *CJ* XXV (1930), 611ff.

VON ARNIM, H. *Stoicorum veterum fragmenta* (4 vols), Stuttgart, 1902–24.

ARNOLD, E. V. *Roman Stoicism*, Cambridge, 1911.

BAILLY, A. *La Vie et les pensées de Sénèque*, Paris, 1929.

BALDRY, H. C. *The Unity of Mankind in Greek Thought*, Cambridge, 1965.

BEVAN, E. *Stoics and Sceptics*, Oxford, 1913.

CANCIK, HILDEGARD, *Untersuchungen zu Senecas epistulae morales*, Hildesheim, 1967.

CURRIE, H. MACL. 'The Younger Seneca's style', *Bulletin of the Institute of Classical Studies*, London, 13 (1966), 76ff.

EDELSTEIN, L. *The Meaning of Stoicism*, Oxford, 1966.

GOULD, J. B. *The Philosophy of Chrysippus*, Leyden, 1970.

GRIMAL, PIERRE. *Sénèque: sa vie, son oeuvre*, Paris, 1948.

GUILLEMIN, A.M. 'Sénèque, directeur d'âmes', *Rev. Ét. Lat.* 30 (1953), 202ff.

HICKS, R. D. *Stoic and Epicurean*, Longmans, 1911.

HOLLAND, F. *Seneca*, Longmans, 1920.

LONG, A. A. (ed.). *Problems in Stoicism*, Athlone Press, 1970.

MARCHESI, C. *Seneca*, Messina, 1920.

MARTHA, C. *Les Moralistes sous l'empire romain*, Paris, 1865.

MATES, B. *Stoic Logic*, University of California Press, 1953.

MORE, P. E. *Hellenistic Philosophies*, Milford, 1923.

MOTTO, A. L. *Seneca Sourcebook: a Guide to the Thought of Seneca in the extant Prose Writings*, New York, 1970 (a notable work which came too late for me to make any use of it in the writing of this chapter).

POHLENZ, M. *Die Stoa*, Göttingen, 3rd. edn, 1964.
RIST, J. M. *Stoic Philosophy*, Cambridge, 1969.
SAMBURSKY, S. *Physics of the Stoics*, Routledge & Kegan Paul, 1959.
WATSON, G. *The Stoic Theory of Knowledge*, Belfast, 1966.
WALTZ, R. *La Vie politique de Sénèque*, Paris, 1909.
WENLEY, R. M. *Stoicism and its Influence*, Harrap, 1924.

III

Lucan's Political Views and the Caesars

O. A. W. Dilke

Lucan wrote his historical epic under the last of the true Caesars; his subject was the civil war won by the first of the dynasty. To what extent was his view of Julius Caesar coloured by his view of Nero? How did these views change, if they did, within the framework of his poem? In trying to elucidate these questions, it will be convenient to start with the poet's view of Caesar, next to consider his attitude towards Augustus and the imperial house in general, and finally to assess his relationship with Nero.

Julius Caesar[1]

It is sometimes assumed or implied that Lucan's attitude towards Julius Caesar and the imperial house down to Nero remained virtually unchanged throughout the ten books of his poem that he lived to complete. According to this view, Lucan was biased against Caesar from the outset, and anything ostensibly flattering he may say about Nero in the exordium must be regarded as ironical. If we were dealing with a middle-aged poet of conservative outlook, such a view might commend itself. But we are not: we are dealing with a young man, '*ardens et concitatus*', who was perhaps only about nineteen when he began the poem and only twenty-five when he died.

His family and educational background,[2] strongly influenced by his uncle, the younger Seneca, and his tutor, Cornutus, impregnated him with the intellectual antagonism of the Stoic opposition to all forms of tyranny. The word *tyrannus* came to mean not merely an unconstitutional ruler, but a despot who suppressed *libertas*,[3] especially freedom of action and freedom of speech. This attitude had its origins, as far as the leading characters in the civil war were concerned, in the late Republic.

The cult of Cato of Utica had developed very rapidly.[4] The question debated in Cicero's *Cato*, Hirtius' refutation, Caesar's *Anti-Cato* and Brutus' *Cato*, works all dating from 46–45 B.C. and none of whose writers was a Stoic, was whether Cato was '*omnium gentium uirtute princeps*' (Cic., *Phil.*, XIII.20). By the end of 45 his supporters had virtually turned him into a saint; and this produced, for many, the image of Caesar as a tyrant. At a later stage we find even Velleius, loyal to the principate, writing of Cato as '*homo uirtuti simillimus et per omnia ingenio dis quam hominibus propior*' (II.35.2) ('a man most resembling *uirtus* and in all respects intellectually closer to gods than to men').

The cult of Brutus was less tolerated under the early empire than that of Cato. Brutus had been not only one of the two chief tyrannicides[5] but the leader of the forces which fought Octavian as well as Antony. His descent from L. Junius Brutus, expeller of the Tarquins, and his adoption of *libertas* as his motto also endeared him to Republican sentiment. Pollio, whose work on the civil wars may well have been among Lucan's sources, was one of the earliest to glorify him and Cassius. The literary revolt continued throughout the first century A.D. In A.D. 25 A. Cremutius Cordus was tried, among other charges, for praising Brutus, calling Cassius 'the last of the Romans', and being disrespectful to Julius Caesar and Augustus. He committed suicide, and his *Annals* were publicly burnt. The birthdays of Brutus and Cassius continued to be celebrated by their supporters, just as Lucan's birthday was celebrated by Statius (*Silv.*, II.7). Juvenal (v.36). records their celebration by Thrasea and his son-in-law Helvidius Priscus in Nero's reign Lucan's admiration of Brutus is such that he falsifies history by making him try to kill Caesar on the battlefield (VII.586–96).

If Brutus was the lover of *libertas* and hater of tyranny, Cassius was the personal enemy of Julius Caesar, although he had earlier benefited by Caesar's policy of *clementia*. It was another member of the same *gens*, C. Cassius Chaerea, who assassinated the Emperor Gaius; he was given by the consuls the password *libertas*, but was executed by the praetorian guard. The antipathy of the two families comes out clearly in an episode which occurred three years after Lucan's death. Tacitus (*Ann.*, XVI.7–9) tells us that

C. Cassius Longinus, the celebrated jurist, was then accused of revering among the waxen images of his ancestors one of the tyrannicides, with the inscription *duci partium*, 'to the leader of the cause'; this was coupled with an accusation of plotting a conspiracy, and he was exiled.

Seneca and Lucan took over this strong Republican tradition, which idealized not only the Stoic Cato but (an illustration of the eclectic nature of philosophy under the early empire) the Academic Brutus and the Epicurean Cassius as embodiments of Roman virtues. Cato was to them a superhuman figure who approached the Stoic ideal of the perfect man.[6] One might imagine from this approach that their impression of Julius Caesar, Cato's bitter enemy, would have been fiercely hostile throughout. But in fact Seneca paints what has been called a 'negative' portrait of Caesar, stressing his clemency as well as his struggle for personal power.[7] One only wonders whether the former would have been regarded as the type of *clementia* treated by some philosophers as objectionable (Sen., *De Clem.*, praef. II.1).

Lucan, when he began writing his poem, was young and much influenced in style and content by Seneca, in content also by Livy,[8] who was so partial as to be dubbed 'Pompeian' by Augustus. As a result of the Senecan influence, his initial portrait of the dictator is ambivalent, and it is only as the poem develops that unmitigated hostility sets in.

'Au point de vue politique', writes Jacqueline Brisset, 'Lucain ne garde même pas l'apparence de l'impartialité.'[9] She amplifies this by a claim that Lucan asserts from the outset that Caesar's aggression was premeditated.[10] What the poet writes (1.183–5) is:

> iam gelidas Caesar cursu superauerat Alpes
> ingentesque animo motus bellumque futurum
> ceperat. ut uentum est parui Rubiconis ad undas . . .

> (Caesar had dashed across the frozen Alps
> And in his mind had plotted vast revolts
> And war to come. As soon as he arrived
> At Rubicon's small river, . . .)

This entirely omits Caesar's stay in Ravenna, during which he sent a compromise offer to the Senate and awaited their reply. But this omission is not made out of bias against Caesar. It is part of

Lucan's customary technique of telescoping events in such a way as to secure the greatest possible dramatic effect.[11] For example, when Pompey fled from Larissa after the battle of Pharsalia, he called first at Amphipolis, then at Lesbos, where Cornelia had taken refuge. Rubicon, like Lesbos, offered scope for rhetorical poetry; Ravenna, like Amphipolis, did not.

An examination of Book 1 will suggest that Lucan started by being impartial as far as his Stoic background, Republican tradition of historiography, and perhaps immature beliefs permitted him. Julius Caesar is not mentioned in the first hundred lines: in 1.41 *Caesar* is clearly to be taken as vocative, referring to Nero. The *furor* denounced in 1.8 is not Caesar's fury, but the sheer madness of embarking on any civil war; it is this that to Lucan's mind in the early stages of the poem constitutes the really heinous crime. In the section dealing with the causes of the civil war[12] the poet blames the First Triumvirate's lust for power (1.84f), but does not attach responsibility for the civil war to one side more than the other. He even writes (1.126f):

> quis [i.e. uter] iustius induit arma
> scire nefas.

> (Which of the two
> Had better right to start hostilities
> We may not know.)

The characters of Pompey and Caesar are likewise nicely weighed up with impartiality. Lucan even balances the number of lines (1.129–57):

Half-line summary } $= 14\frac{1}{2}$ lines
Pompey's character }

Caesar's character $= 14\frac{1}{2}$ lines

Almost exactly half of each, $7\frac{1}{2}$ and 7 lines respectively, is occupied by a simile from nature, Pompey being likened to an oak and Caesar to lightning,[13] so as to contrast immobile with mobile strength. The immobility of the oak is brought out by the metre: each line of the oak simile (136–43) ends with a disyllable, with or without preceding preposition, and three lines, 140–2, have spondees in each of the first three or four feet,[14] an effect found in only the last line of the lightning simile. There are also verbal reminders. Pompey *stat magni nominis umbra* (135); the section on Caesar also refers to *nomen*.[15] Pompey's joy (*gaudere*, 133) and Caesar's (*gaudens*, 150, echoed in II.439f)[16] both reveal defects of character, on the one hand vanity, on the other a destructive tendency. Each has some merits as well as demerits:[17] adjectives like *acer* and *indomitus* (146) are eulogistic, the latter meaning 'invincible' rather than 'headstrong' (Duff).

A further glimpse of Lucan's view of Caesar in the first book is afforded by 479ff. Rumours circulating in Rome of the invader's monstrous behaviour are deflated by the poet's comment (484–6):

> sic quisque pauendo
> dat uires famae, nulloque auctore malorum
> quae finxere timent.

> (Thus each by panicking
> Gave strength to rumour, and as none confirmed
> Disasters, only feared their own inventions.)

In line 522, *timent* reappears at the end of the sentence: *Pompeio fugiente timent* (they feared as Pompey fled); a comparison of the two shows that, whereas Caesar turns out to be less monstrous than was rumoured, Pompey's reputation suffers an unprecedented blow.

The first half of the second book does not vary the emphasis. In II.68ff Lucan makes an anonymous elder recount the horrors of the civil war between Marius and Sulla. The fact that the minds of listeners or readers are turned towards those earlier atrocities tends, if anything, to mitigate any excesses committed by Caesar's invading force. Brutus acknowledges no leader but Cato. Cato, though he decides to follow Pompey, recognizes that he too, if he wins, will want to rule the world (II.320–2). Again we have the Senecan approach (cf. n.7), an unwillingness to extol Pompey too much; though one can see the origins of it in Cicero's letters, especially in *dominatio quaesita ab utroque est* (overlordship has been aimed at by both leaders) and what follows (*Ad Att.*, VIII.11.2).

The change of heart begins to be visible in the second half of Book II, written perhaps at a period when the relations between Nero and Lucan were beginning to deteriorate. Whereas at the beginning of Book I *furor* is associated with civil war, in II.439f it is transferred to Caesar:

> Caesar in arma furens nullas nisi sanguine fuso
> gaudet habere uias.
>
> (Caesar, who madly rushes into war,
> Exults that only bloodshed opens routes.)

He delighted, so Lucan would have us believe, at finding battle succeeding battle, and preferred ravaging the land to occupying it without a blow. Admittedly the tone is only an elaboration of 1.150, referred to above; but the streak of cruelty and vandalism is harped on far more and localized in Italy itself. More conclusive evidence of prejudice is to be found in the treatment of the siege of Corfinium (II.478ff). The defence of this town by L. Domitius Ahenobarbus was in fact pointless[18] and contrary to Pompey's orders. Yet in Lucan it is glorified and Domitius made a hero, branding Caesar for his madness (544). After this it is refreshing to find Lucan summarizing thus the energetic commander (657):

> nil actum credens cum quid superesset agendum.
>
> (Thought incomplete deeds were like none at all . . .)

The Stoic admires quick action and finds Pompey's inactivity at this stage repugnant.

From the beginning of Book III idealization of Pompey and ranting hatred of Caesar become more prominent. Pompey is frequently called by his *cognomen* Magnus;[19] now he is greater still (III.37):

> maior in arma ruit certa cum mente malorum.
>
> (Rushed into battle greater than before,
> His mind now set on woe.)

Realization of impending disaster makes him resolved; this is the mark of a Stoic sage.[20]

The hatred of Caesar comes out in III.80–83:

> non illum laetis uadentem coetibus urbes
> sed tacitae uidere metu, nec constitit usquam
> obuia turba duci. gaudet tamen esse timori
> tam magno populis et se non mallet amari.

(No cities full of joyful throngs looked out
Upon his march: they looked with silent fear,
And no crowd ever stayed to meet the general.
Yet he was glad that he in Italy
Was feared, and would not have preferred men's love.)

From here right to the end of what Lucan lived to write (with
exceptions such as v.270–1), Caesar is associated with all the vices
typical of those denounced in Roman invective against tyranny:
anger, cruelty, ambition, pride, and others. A desire for kingship
is frequently imputed to him, especially in v.207, 666–8; vii.240,
386, 593–6. At times he is depicted as a veritable monster of
depravity. In vii.551 Lucan writes of the heart of the battle-line
at Pharsalia:

> hic furor, hic rabies, hic sunt tua crimina, Caesar.

> (Here Caesar's madness is, his rage, his crimes.)

In vii.699f Caesar is made to give orders for a feast to be held on
the spot from which he can best see the corpses weltering in
blood and recognize their faces. He has become a truly fiendish
character, comparable with Satan in *Paradise Lost*.[21]

In one passage (*De Ben.*, ii.20.2) we find Seneca actually disapproving of the assassination of Caesar. This attitude is not
echoed in Lucan. But it is only from Book v that we see him
looking forward (from his dramatic date) with glee to the Ides of
March, when just as L. Junius Brutus expelled the despot Tarquin,
so his descendant shall strike down the new despot: v.206f;
vii.449–51, 781–3; x.338–42, 526–9.

Increasing vilification of Caesar results from Book vii onwards
(except viii. 276ff) in more idealization of Pompey.[22] Here
Lucan perhaps followed propagandist tracts, now lost, of the
civil war period[23] or rhetorical *suasoriae*. It is to deflect blame from
Pompey for the start of the battle of Pharsalia that Cicero is unhistorically introduced as being present (vii.62ff).[24] In reality
Cicero remained at Dyrrhachium; but in Lucan's poem he is made
spokesman for the Pompeian hot-heads who are demanding an
immediate fight. Pompey, when he flees from the battle
(vii.669ff), is portrayed as in no way lacking courage, but either
feeling that the whole world will die for him or wanting to conceal
his death from Caesar! He leaves the battle-field free from care,

with the burden of fate laid down (687), and can even pity the conqueror, his relative by marriage (701).[25] When on his arrival in Egypt he is stabbed by a Roman soldier in the pay of the young Ptolemy's regents, he exclaims (VIII.629-31):

> spargant lacerentque licebit,
> sum tamen, o superi, felix, nullique potestas
> hoc auferre deo.

> (Although my limbs are rent and scattered, yet
> The gods can see that I am fortunate;
> This no god has the power to take away.)

The idealization reaches its peak after the assassination. Stoic doctrine[26] held that the souls of the righteous rose to the orbit of the moon, so Book IX begins with Pompey's soul rising to this intervening space between earth's atmosphere and the upper air, gazing peacefully at earth and the heavenly bodies, and finally settling in the hearts of Brutus and Cato. This is a very different Pompey from the 'shadow of a mighty name' that we encountered in Book I, as much exalted as Caesar is degraded.

Augustus and his Immediate Successors

Whereas in assessing Julius Caesar modern scholars have reacted against Mommsen's over-idealized portrait, Augustus tends to be praised for all but his acquiescence in the proscriptions. Virgil, Lucan's foremost predecessor in Latin epic, had glorified the Augustan regime, and Ovid in the conclusion to his *Metamorphoses* had also paid it homage. So it may come as a surprise to modern readers to find the few allusions to him in Lucan hostile. In 1.639ff P. Nigidius Figulus, the neo-Pythagorean astrologer, is made to prophesy the future of Rome as it is affected by the outbreak of civil war.[27] The cessation of such a struggle is described in the words *cum domino pax ista uenit* (that peace comes with a *dominus*) (670), where *dominus* is an arbitrary despot. Although historically Nigidius Figulus was anti-Caesarian, Getty was wrong in referring this to Julius Caesar.[28] Lucan has just said (668) that the civil war will go on for years, and if he is thinking of one man in particular it is Octavian. Bardon[29] argues that this part of the poem was written before Nero had shown Lucan special favour by recalling him from Greece and enrolling him in his clique of young poets, but the chronology is difficult to determine. Augustus is also alluded to in a mention of the temple erected to Diuus Iulius, in Lucan's eyes a cruel tyrant (VIII.835).

The political power of the emperors is coupled with other features repugnant to the Stoic opposition: in III.168 Lucan complains that after the seizure of the treasury Rome became for the first time poorer than a Caesar, a complaint particularly appropriate to the principate of Augustus. The whole mystique, built up by Julius Caesar and his heir, of the descent of the *gens Iulia* from Aeneas is dismissed as a fairy story (*fabula*, III.212). But these are mild references compared with IV.821ff:

> ius licet in iugulos nostros sibi fecerit ensis
> Sulla potens Mariusque ferox et Cinna cruentus
> Caesareaeque domus series . . .

> (Though powerful Sulla, Marius the fierce,
> Bloodthirsty Cinna and the dynasty
> Of Caesars have created their own right
> To murder us . . .)

Whereas the acquisition of power by Augustus was treated guardedly by Seneca,[30] to Lucan the whole dynasty of Caesars was, at least from this point in the poem onwards, one of bloodthirsty tyrants like Sulla, Marius and Cinna (although *potens* is not derogatory like the epithets he uses of the other two): they had bribed their way to power and could execute anyone at will.

There is an implied objection, in these lines, to the hereditary principle. Stoics argued that, in a state where monarchy was desirable or inevitable, the succession should be by adoption, not by direct descent or kinship with the imperial family. Helvidius was later to appeal to Vespasian to introduce adoptive succession but the emperor replied, 'My son succeeds me or no one.' None of Augustus' four successors who were related to him or Livia, apart from Nero in his formative years, appealed in the least to Stoic views of the monarchy; and the question of adoptive succession must have loomed large at a time when there was no heir apparent.

In V.385–99 comes a regular list of complaints about political curtailments by the tyrannical principate (*dominis*) so long flattered by lies from Roman lips: the seizure of the consulship, which ever since Caesar's domination has been an empty name; the rigging of popular elections; the abolition of the right to obstruct political business by resort to augury: Lucan, however sceptical of the state religion, nevertheless, as an upholder of republican institutions, deplores the loss of magistrates' privileges, even of Bibulus' kind; the frequent appointment of *consules designati*, which cheapened the venerable office of consul. From Book VI onwards we also find invective against the deification of emperors (VI.807-9; VIII.835; especially VII.455-9). To Lucan the only Roman who, if freedom came back, deserved to be deified, the true *pater patriae* rather than any emperor who usurped that title, was Cato of Utica (IX.601-4).

Finally he feels that the next generation after the battle of Pharsalia and all succeeding generations have had a raw deal: what have they done to deserve to be born into a *regnum* (VII.638ff)? The emperors are nothing short of *reges*, the word hated by Romans of Roman overlordship ever since the expulsion of the Tarquins. The constant struggle is between freedom and a Caesar (VII.695f); but freedom seems to have been banished for ever beyond the Tigris and the Rhine (VII.432f).[31] What if the two statements are inconsistent? At one moment the opposition must have felt that the cause was lost, at another that the struggle was on as keenly as ever. The invective against Alexander the Great in Books IX and X[32] admittedly has traditional features: the theme was associated with certain schools of philosophy and bears the stamp of the *suasoria*[33]—in fact numerous features of Lucan's poem are strongly reminiscent of the rhetorical training which played so large a part in Roman education. But to many listeners or readers the denigration of Alexander would have wider implications. Brisset thinks they would have treated it as an allusion to Caligula or Nero; Morford says 'the real object of the denunciation is Caesar.'[34] One cannot help wondering, however, whether the real target was Alexander's descendant Cleopatra, with the possibility of Rome in servitude to her and her offspring (less terrible to Lucan than to Virgil and Horace only through the passage of time).[35] A principate was bad enough; one by a woman would have been far worse; one by a foreign woman worst of all:

> Leucadioque fuit dubius sub gurgite casus,
> an mundum ne nostra quidem matrona teneret. (X.66f)

(In Actium's waters
It was a doubtful issue if a woman
Not even Roman would subdue the world.)

Augustus at least spared Rome that.

Nero

By the time Nero succeeded to the principate, some hundred
years after the civil war, only an insignificant minority can have
desired an actual return to a republic. Opposition to the principate
was therefore slight so long as Nero was young, particularly in the
first five years of his rule. As it grew, it emerged as an opposition
headed by senators, philosophers and literary men, in many cases
men who were a combination of these. The man in the street
tended to be either apathetic or a supporter of the principate.

We can discern several political approaches by Stoics under
Nero. One is a policy of involvement, and of this Seneca in the
early part of the principate was the chief advocate. In A.D. 49 he
had been appointed tutor to Nero; five years later, on the young
prince's accession, he became a powerful minister, sharing with
Burrus the control of political affairs. In this capacity he became a
multi-millionaire, and he was thought to have been implicated in
the murder of Nero's mother Agrippina. His downfall came after
the death of Burrus and the rise of Tigellinus, but he was allowed
to remain in retirement until the Pisonian conspiracy, after the
failure of which he and Lucan were among those who committed
suicide. Less involved than Seneca, Rubellius Plautus, great-
grandson of Tiberius, went into voluntary exile in Asia Minor at
Nero's suggestion; but even this did not save him when Seneca
lost power and Tigellinus came to the fore.

Thrasea Paetus, like Livy a native of Padua, was the leader of
the Stoic opposition under Nero and a biographer of Cato. His
wife, Arria, was daughter of the Arria who handed to her husband,
Caecina Paetus, who had been condemned for conspiracy under
Claudius, the dagger with which she had stabbed herself, saying
Paete, non dolet (It doesn't hurt, Paetus). When the senate voted
honours to Nero after he had ordered the death of Agrippina,
Thrasea walked out of the senate-house. He was successful in
persuading the senate to banish rather than execute the praetor
Antistius, who had written lampoons on Nero. For these and

other offences he was forbidden to approach the emperor to congratulate him on the birth of a daughter. Despite a virtual retirement for three years, he fell victim after the Pisonian conspiracy to what Tacitus (*Ann.*, XVI.21) describes as Nero's determination to murder Virtue herself. It is difficult to see whether more of Thrasea's antagonism was directed against Nero or against the principate; but a possible clue is to be found in the uncompromising attitude of Helvidius Priscus, his son-in-law and disciple, to Vespasian. In contrast to the unscrupulous and eccentric Nero, Vespasian, even if he lacked Nero's artistic talent, was a considerate man. Yet if we are to believe Epictetus, Helvidius frequently indulged in insolent argument in public with the emperor, for which he was first banished and then executed. Among other things, he insisted on addressing him as *Vespasiane* and not by his imperial titles. If, then, we compare Helvidius' attitude, we shall consider it likely that Thrasea too was chiefly inspired with hatred of the principate itself. Lucan had much in common with both of them, with a mixture of Thrasea's grandeur and Helvidius' pettiness.

All were clearly inspired with that hatred of tyranny with which many Roman youths who studied in Athens became imbued. Lucan, like many other young Romans, had his education rounded off in Athens. To obtain an insight into the justification of violence to counter despotism, we need to look at the spurious letters of Chion of Heraclea.[36] Clearchus, tyrant of Heraclea Pontica, was in 353–2 B.C. assassinated by Chion, a disciple of Plato, and other young men. Probably in the first century A.D., seventeen letters ascribed to Chion were circulated; they praise philosophy as giving the strength to resist force from outside, and speak of the lot of all who suffer tyranny as slavery. We may compare Lucan VII.641, of Pharsalia, *uincitur his gladiis omnis quae seruiet aetas* (these swords have conquered every age of slaves); VII.382, a *sententia* at the end of Pompey's harangue to his troops before the battle, . . . *ne discam seruire senex* (not to learn as an old man to be a slave); and other passages.

Stoic poets did not necessarily cross swords with the Establishment, but caution was needed to avoid offence. The satirist Persius, like Lucan a pupil of the Stoic philosopher Cornutus (said to have been banished for hinting that four hundred books would be unduly long for a projected historical epic by Nero), was serious where Lucan tended to be flippant or irreverent; but whether he attacked the principate openly we do not know, since Cornutus, acting as his literary executor, expunged any passages that could possibly give offence. It is unlikely that Persius' lines *torua Mimalloneis inplerunt cornua bombis* . . . (they filled grim horns with Mimallonean booms) (1.99–102), were quoted from Nero's poetry. Ancient sources say that he died of a stomach disease, and a modern theory that he was poisoned is highly conjectural.[37]

It remains, under the heading of opposition to Nero, to consider C. Calpurnius Piso, leader of the unsuccessful conspiracy. He was a member of one of the most distinguished Roman families and had a generous character and a grand manner. But it looks as if he had had a personal grudge against the house of Caesar ever since Gaius robbed him of his bride, Livia Orestilla, and banished him. He reminds one of the senate, in Lucan VII.696f, which by fighting on after the rout of Pompey showed that it had been fighting for itself (*sibi* emphatic).

No one denies that Lucan's attitude to Nero changed: the only question is at what stage. When Lucan was young, Nero was being hailed as the young prince who, as lover of the arts and guided by philosophers, would bring back the Golden Age. This is the tone of Calpurnius Siculus and of the Einsiedeln eclogues. It is not surprising that Lucan too joined in this acclaim, though evidently later, receiving preferment and competing in the Neronian festival of A.D. 60 with a poem in praise of the emperor. Two or three years later three books of the *De Bello Civili*[38] were published, but a quarrel broke out between Lucan and Nero. According to one story, which seems not improbable, Nero, himself a poet, deliberately walked out of a *recitatio* of Lucan's. Ever since the Augustan age budding poets had depended to a large extent on these poetry readings, with their opportunities for showing off brilliance, to launch them on their careers; and a studied insult of this sort would rankle like nothing else. The quarrel resulted in a ban on further publication. In A.D. 65 Lucan, still only in his mid-twenties, joined the Pisonian conspiracy against Nero, and on its detection committed suicide.

In the opening of his poem, after stating his theme,[39] he laments the destructiveness of civil war and its terrible after-effects. But, he consoles himself, there is at least one advantage (1.33–7):

quod si non aliam uenturo fata Neroni
inuenere uiam magnoque aeterna parantur
regna deis caelumque suo seruire Tonanti
non nisi saeuorum potuit post bella gigantum,
iam nihil, o superi, querimur.

(But if the Fates could find no other way
For Nero's coming, if the gods above
Pay a high price for their eternal rule,
If Jupiter could only be obeyed
After a war against the savage Giants,
Then I have no complaint against the gods.)

This theme is elaborated, and then the poet turns to a eulogy of the young emperor, occupying $14\frac{1}{2}$ lines[40] (1.45–59). When Nero's life on earth is over, not only will he be deified but every god will make way for him; he will be able to choose his abode, but unless he remains in the centre of the heavens the axis of the world will feel his weight; let his area be cloudless. The exordium winds up with a vision of world peace and brotherhood to come at that time, and a dedication to the emperor, who to Lucan is already a deity (*numen*) (60–6).

This idea that the poet could in a short space of time, while composing the *De Bello Civili*, have fundamentally changed his view of Nero seems unacceptable to many modern writers.[41] They regard the procemium as sarcastic and intentionally ambiguous, sometimes even as a skit on certain physical defects of the emperor.

As with some other features which in extant epic poetry are confined to Lucan, we must turn to his uncle Seneca to obtain the closest parallel. In the first year of Claudius' principate, A.D. 41, the younger Seneca was relegated to Corsica on a charge of adultery with Julia Livilla, sister of the emperor Gaius and niece of Claudius. He was eventually restored in A.D. 49. From Corsica he wrote his *Consolatio ad Polybium* dedicated to Claudius' influential secretary, hoping that through flattery both of him and of Claudius his request for recall would be granted. The adulation of Claudius (12–13) starts with the wish that the gods and goddesses may long lend him to the earth; this stock theme is exactly paralleled in Horace, while in Lucan there is merely a wish for long life.[42] Later Claudius is called a constellation or sun (*sidus*);

may he even shine on the darkened and depressed world. Similarly the dedication to the English Bible refers to 'some thick and palpable clouds of darkness' expected on the death of 'that bright Occidental Star, Queen Elizabeth' which have been dispelled by 'the appearance of your Majesty, as of the Sun in his strength'. Seneca prays that the emperor may pacify Germany, open up Britain and celebrate new triumphs.

Style and content of Lucan's procemium are to some extent based on Virgil, *Georgics* I. Both poets verge on the grotesque in their suggestions of future activities and alternative realms. But Lucan has also in mind either his uncle's flattery of Claudius or a rhetorical pattern on which both are drawing. Germany and Britain are replaced by China, Armenia and the source of the Nile, areas which, with some exaggeration, represent actual schemes in Nero's principate.[43] *Mutato sole* (though its sun is changed) (49) echoes Seneca's *sidus*; the triumphs of Claudius are earthly, whereas Nero is envisaged mounting Phoebus' chariot; instead of Fortune guarding the emperor, the Fates pave the way for him (33f).

We may conclude that Lucan, like Seneca, was acting the courtier. No doubt he realized the emptiness of the traditional eulogy, which owed its inspiration to the court-poets of Alexandria,[44] but he hoped by it to secure Nero, himself a poet and champion of the arts, as patron of his poem. Even if the first flush of enthusiasm for the young prince had passed, adulation was still rife: Greece had recently hailed him as Zeus.[45] The parallel between Jupiter's fight for supremacy and the succession of Nero is couched in the language of panegyric (1.35f); editors compare Pliny's *Panegyricus*.

The idea that there is latent satire in the opening lines is not new: it is found in the Bern scholia and in Arnulf.[46] There it is associated with skits on physical defects of Nero, actual or supposed, whereas modern writers for the most part play down such puerile humour.[47] The fact is that the ancients were very conscious of the specific field of each genre, and the opening of an epic was no place for a skit of any kind. If we disregard some of the over-elaborate formalism of the eulogy, the lines undoubtedly have a certain dignity, and the yearning for universal peace seems genuine enough (1.60–2). Lucan had a high regard for the calling of bard, as we can see from the famous passage IX.980–5:

o sacer et magnus uatum labor! omnia fato
eripis et populis donas mortalibus aeuum.
inuidia sacrae, Caesar, ne tangere famae;
nam, siquid Latiis fas est promittere Musis,
quantum Zmyrnaei durabunt uatis honores,
uenturi me teque legent; Pharsalia nostra
vivet, et a nullo tenebris damnabimur aevo.

(O sacred toil and great that bards perform!
It cheats death of all victims, and presents
To mortal nations immortality.
Caesar, do not begrudge our holy fame;
For, if our Roman Muses can avail,
As long as Homer's glory shall endure,
Descendants who read me shall read of you;
Our battle of Pharsalia shall live on,
And no age shall condemn us to oblivion.)

Here Julius Caesar has been made to turn aside from his pursuit of
Pompey to visit Troy, presumably so as to bring before Roman
eyes and ears scenes from a part of Asia Minor in which all
educated Romans were interested.[48] This visit causes the poet,
somewhat abruptly at first sight,[49] to apostrophize Caesar as if he
were still alive. The reference is not to Nero, even though Lucan
must have had the literary rivalry between himself and the
emperor in mind. *Pharsalia nostra* was correctly explained by
Housman as 'the battle of Pharsalia fought by you and sung of by
me'.[50] Lucan's poetic idealism has a national trend. The last line
of the opening address (I.66),

tu satis ad uires Romana in carmina dandas,

(Your power alone can sponsor Roman epics)

shows that he is placing himself side by side with Ennius as the
inspired creator of a great Roman historical epic.

Scholars have been too apt to hunt out personal allusions to
Nero and his court where they may not actually exist.[51] Thus it is
very doubtful if III.638ff allude to the manner of Octavia's death
or III.647ff to the attempted drowning of Agrippina.[52] In VIII.673
the reference to executions by whipping off a head alludes not to
Nero[53] but to Gaius, who instituted it (Suet., *Cal.*, 32). The

mention of incest in the Parthian royal family is not aimed at Nero but is a stock-in-trade of rhetorical invective against Eastern morality.

There remains the perplexing question of Nero's great-great-grandfather L. Domitius Ahenobarbus. Domitius is idealized by Lucan at the siege of Corfinium (see page 67 above), omitted in the account of the siege of Marseilles (Book III), and once more idealized at his death in VII.599ff. The idealization in Book II is no doubt, as Menz observes, Lucan's way of deflating Caesar's vaunted *clementia*. The omission in Book III may be due to a desire not to make Domitius fight so soon after having begged Caesar's pardon. The glorious death on the battlefield of Pharsalia accorded him in Book VII is as unhistorical as the presence of Cicero on that occasion: in fact he was killed in the mountains by Antony's cavalry. Clearly this part of the work was written after the quarrel with Nero. But evidently Lucan felt that he could score more off Caesar if he kept to the characterization of Book III, making Domitius a hero to the last, who died with his *libertas* unimpaired, and Caesar a cheap jiber (VII.606f).[54]

In conclusion, Nero himself is flattered in the procemium and never mentioned elsewhere, while the principate and all the house of Caesar are subjected to vitriolic attacks. But these attacks are mild in the first two books (or somewhat milder) compared with the remainder. There can be no doubt in the present writer's mind that the three books said by Vacca to have been published were I–III.[55] If, soon after they appeared, a ban on publication was imposed, Lucan could happily circulate among his friends the remaining books, which attacked not his personal enemy Nero[56] but the enemy of the Stoic opposition, the principate.[57]

ACKNOWLEDGMENTS

I am indebted to my colleague Dr D. C. Earl, for reading through this chapter and making helpful suggestions, and to the General Editor for suggesting additional material.

Notes

1 In addition to the books and articles quoted in this section, see F. Gundolf, *Caesar. Geschichte seines Ruhms* (Berlin, 1924), 32–6; W. H. Friedrich, 'Cato, Caesar und Fortuna bei Lucan', *Hermes* 73 (1938), 391–423; C. Bretscher, 'Caesar und sein Gluck', *Mus. Helv.* 15 (1958), 75–83; and

now A. W. Lintott (n. 57.) Some of the verse translations have been published in O. A. W. Dilke, 'The Battle of Pharsalia: a Verse Translation of Lucan, Book VII', *Proc. of the Leeds Philosophical and Literary Soc., Literary and Historical Section,* 1971, XIV, part vii, 221–68.

2 Most fully covered by P. Tremoli, *M. Anneo Lucano I: L'ambiente familiare e letterario* (Trieste, 1961).

3 N. F. Deratani, 'Bor'ba za svobodu ... v poeme Lukana ...', *Učenye Zapiski Moskovskogo Gosudarstvennogo Pedagogičeskogo Instituta* 32 (1946), 1–15, translated in *Lucan,* ed. W. Rutz, Wege der Forschung CCXXXV (Darmstadt, 1970), 133–48; C. Wirszubski, *Libertas as a Political Idea at Rome* (Cambridge, 1950), esp. 126–9; O. A. W. Dilke, *Lucan, Poet of Freedom,* inaugural lecture, Rhodes University (Grahamstown, 1961); O. Schönberger, 'Ein Dichter römischer Freiheit ...', *Das Altertum* 10 (1964), 26–40; D. Gagliardi, *Lucano, poeta della libertá* (Naples, 1968).

4 For this and the following paragraphs see especially R. MacMullen, *Enemies of the Roman Order* (Harvard, 1967), chs. 1 and 2, with bibliography in notes to these chapters.

5 Tacitus uses the order *Cassius et Brutus,* no doubt to show that Cassius was the first promoter of the conspiracy.

6 W. H. Alexander, 'Cato of Utica in the Works of Seneca Philosophus', *Trans. Royal Soc. Canada* 3rd ser. 40, sect. 2 (1946), 59–74; id., 'Julius Caesar in the pages of Seneca the philosopher', *Trans. Royal Soc. Canada* 3rd ser. 35, sect. 2 (1941), 15–28; Berthe M. Marti, 'The meaning of the Pharsalia', *AJPhil* 66 (1945), 352–76. In Lucan the idealization of Cato is particularly evident in Book IX; cf. M. P. O. Morford, 'The purpose of Lucan's Ninth Book', *Latomus* 26 (1967), 123–9.

7 D., 4.23.4; 5.30.4; *De Benef.,* 2.20.2; 3.24; 5.16.5; *Epp.,* 14.13; 104.29–34. In Seneca's eyes Pompey was just as much a *dominus* as Caesar. For views of Caesar in Silver Latin literature see R. E. Wolverton, 'Speculum Caesaris', in *Laudatores Temporis Acti, Studies in Memory of R. E. Caldwell* (Chapel Hill, N.C., 1964), 82–90.

8 R. Pichon, *Les sources de Lucain* (Paris, 1912).

9 *Les idées politiques de Lucain* (Paris, 1964), 81, cf. 40.

10 Ibid. 86; cf. E. Griset, 'Lucanea III: L'anticesarismo', *Rivista di Studi classici* 3 (1955), 28ff, esp. 56–61.

11 See H. P. Syndikus, *Lucans Gedicht vom Bürgerkrieg,* (Munich/Garmisch-Partenkirchen, 1958), 12ff, 76ff.

12 M. Pohlenz, 'Causae civilium armorum', Ἐπιτύμβιον H. Swoboda (Reichenberg, 1927), 201–10.

13 Brief similes from lightning are found in the *Epic of Gilgamesh* and in the *Iliad* (K154, Λ66); Pindar, in a hymn summarized by Quint. VIII.6.71, had one; but they are not found in extant Latin poetry before Lucan. See P. J. Miniconi, *Étude des thèmes 'guerriers' de la poésie épique gréco-romaine* (Paris, 1951), 192; M. P. O. Morford, *The Poet Lucan* (Oxford, 1967), 55.

14 The first is DDDS, the second and third DDDD, each with a monosyllable followed by three disyllables. For such repeated patterns in Virgil, see G. E. Duckworth, 'Variety and Repetition in Vergil's Hexameters', *TAPA* 95 (1964), 9–65. For an analysis of Lucan's versification

see A. Ollfors, *Studien zum Aufbau des Hexameters Lucans*, Acta Regiae Soc. Scient. et Litt. Gothoburg., Hum. 1 (Stockholm, 1967).

15 *Non in Caesare tantum nomen erat nec fama ducis* (1.143f) probably means 'Caesar did not have as great a name or reputation for leadership [as Pompey with his *cognomen* Magnus]'. M. Annaei Lucani, *De Bello Civili Liber I*, ed. R. J. Getty, Cambridge University Press, 1940, 48.

16 The parallel is pointed out by O. Schönberger, *Untersuchungen zur Wiederholungstechnik Lucans* (Heidelberg, 1961), 59.

17 Thus A. Cattin in 'Une idée directrice de Lucain . . .', *Études de Lettres*, n.s. 8 (1965), 214–23, exaggerates when he writes: 'Le portrait de César . . . est entièrement défavorable' (215).

18 W. Menz, 'Caesar und Pompeius im Epos Lucans', in *Lucan*, ed. W. Rutz, 360–76, believes on the contrary that the week's delay, as usual telescoped by Lucan, was vital to the Pompeian withdrawal.

19 Lucan naturally ignored the cancellation of this *cognomen* by the Emperor Gaius (Suet., *Cal.*, 35).

20 W. Rutz, '*Amor mortis* bei Lucan', *Hermes* 88 (1960), 462–75.

21 W. Blisset, 'Caesar and Satan', *J. Hist. Ideas* 18 (1957), 221–32.

22 This trend is missed by Heitland in the Introduction to Haskins's edition, lvi–lviii. Vivian L. Holliday in *Pompey in Cicero's Correspondence and Lucan's Civil War*, Studies in Classical Literature 3 (The Hague, 1969), argues that Lucan is indebted for his characterization of Pompey to Cicero's letters; cf. V. Ussani, *Sul valore storico del poema Lucaneo* (Rome, 1903), 37ff; Enrica Malcovati, 'Lucano e Cicerone', *Athenaeum* 31 (1953), 288–97. The passages adduced do not offer such close verbal correspondence as those between Livy's excerptors and Lucan, but certainly the portrait of Pompey may be said to progress in each from an almost neutral position to a much franker appraisal, contrary to the view of W. Rutz, who holds that the only development in the poet's characterization occurs at Pompey's death, 'Lucans Pompeius', *Der altsprachliche Unterricht* 11 (1968), 5–22. Cf. Marti (art. cit. n. 6); Lintott (n. 57).

23 This suggestion was made to the writer by Professor E. Wistrand. For the propagandist tracts see P. Jal, *La Guerre civile à Rome* (Paris, 1963), 82ff.

24 M. Rambaud, 'L'Apologie de Pompée par Lucain au livre VII de la Pharsale', *Rev. Ét. Lat.* 33 (1955), 258–96.

25 The *socer-gener* relationship is constantly stressed, and does not spoil the effect of rhetorical poetry in the way that the prosaic English equivalents 'father-in-law', 'son-in-law' do.

26 Cf. Sen., *Cons. ad Marc.*, 25f. The speech on the dead Pompey by Cato in IX.190–214 is a restrained *laudatio funebris*; see S. F. Bonner, 'Lucan and the Declamation Schools', *AJPhil.* 87 (1966), 257–87, esp. 276.

27 Bibliography in M. P. O. Morford, *The Poet Lucan*, 63, nn. 3, 5, 6 (Nigidius is overlooked by R. MacMullen, *Enemies of the Roman Order*, Harvard University Press, 1967). The introduction of Nigidius will not have been an element taken over from Livy: H. P. Syndikus, *Lucans Gedicht vom Bürgerkrieg*, 31.

28 Cf. R. T. Bruère, 'The scope of Lucan's historical epic', *CPhil.* 45 (1950), 217–35, esp. 227.

29 H. Bardon, *Les Empereurs et les lettres latines* (Paris, 1940), 232ff; cf. Brisset, op. cit, 182–4; K. F. C. Rose, *TAPA* 97 (1966), 379–96.

30 P. Jal, 'Images d'Auguste chez Sénèque', *Rev. Ét. Lat.* 36 (1958), 242ff.

31 Cf. Tacitus' portrait of the Germans in *Germ.* 11 and elsewhere.

32 Morford, op. cit., 13–19, with bibliography on 16, n. 1, to which add H. Christensen, 'Alexander der Grosse bei den römischen Dichtern', *Neue Jahrb.* 21 (1909), 107–32; A. Bruhl, 'Le souvenir d'Alexandre le Grand et les Romains', *Mélanges d'archéologie et d'histoire* 47 (1930), 202–31.

33 One feature of this is the insertion of an objection by an imaginary interlocutor. This is found, for example, in x.46, *sed cecidit Babylone sua Parthoque uerendus*, where commentators have failed to recognize the equivalent of a sentence beginning *at enim*.

34 Brisset, op. cit., 208–10; Morford, op. cit., 18–19.

35 For a contrast between Lucan's Cleopatra and the Cleopatra of Augustan poets see J. K. Newman, *Augustus and the New Poetry* (Coll. Latomus, 1967), 33.

36 Chion of Heraclea, ed. I. Düring, in *Göteborgs Högskolas Årsskrift* 57 (1951), no. 5; R. MacMullen, *Enemies of the Roman Order*, Harvard University Press, 1967, 11–13.

37 L. Herrmann, 'Néron et la mort de Perse', *Latomus* 22 (1963), 236–9. It is also unlikely, as argued by A. Pretor, *CR* 21 (1907), 72ff, that the choliambics are a cover-up to protect Persius against Nero's vengeance.

38 *Pharsalia*, the old title, is based on a misunderstanding of ix.985, *Pharsalia nostra*, as if it were a title: Housman has the correct explanation; see p. 77 and n. 50 below. For a different view of the dating see Rose, art. cit.

39 Two scholiasts claim that 1.1–7 were not written by Lucan but were added by Seneca. Enrica Malcovati, 'Sul prologo della Farsaglia', *Athenaeum* n.s. 29 (1951), 100–108, accepts this; E. Griset, 'Lucanea II . . .', *Riv. Stud. Class.* 2 (1954), 185–90, thinks they could have been composed by Cornutus. But we must reflect that the questions in the eighth line, *quis furor . . . quae tanta licentia ferri?*, are likely to have been based on the question in the eighth line of the *Iliad*, τίς τ' ἄρ σφωε θεῶν ἔριδι ξυνέηκε μάχεσθαι; and on that in the eighth line (*quo numine laeso*) of the *Aeneid* if it began *arma uirumque*. G. B. Conte, in 'Il proemio della Pharsalia', *Maia*, n.s. 18 (1966), 42–53, mentions these parallels, and also thinks that the language of Lucan's *proœmium* was inspired by Sen., *Phoen.*, 295–300, 352–6, 414–5.

40 O. Schönberger, *Untersuchungen zur Wiederholungstechnik Lucans*, 102, says that this apotheosis of Nero and that of Pompey in ix.1–18 each occupy 18 lines; but the correspondence is not quite so exact.

41 Among these are E. Griset, 'Lucanea IV: l'elogio neroniano', *Riv. Stud. Class.* 3 (1955), 134–8; Robert Graves, Preface to translation of Lucan; O. S. Due, 'An Essay on Lucan', *Classica et Medievalia* 23 (1962), 68–132.

42 Hor., *Od.*, 1.2.45, *serus in caelum redeas*; Lucan, 1.46, *astra petes serus*. For parallel passages see Getty, op. cit., n. 15, 34).

43 A. D. Nock, 'The Proem of Lucan', *CR* 40 (1926), 17–18.

44 Cf. Alexander Schenk Graf von Stauffenberg, 'Vergil und der augusteische Staat', in *Wege zu Vergil*, Wege der Forschung, Bd. XIX (1963), 177–98.

45 P. Grimal, 'L'Éloge de Néron au début de la Pharsale est-il ironique?', *Rev. Ét. Lat.* 38 (1960), 296–305; cf. Nock, art. cit.

46 As far as Roman history and institutions are concerned, Arnulf (ed. Berthe M. Marti, 1958) was little short of ignorant.

47 Robert Graves, on the other hand, seems to take a delight in retailing all the medieval gossip. He can quote, in support, Suetonius' story (*Vita Lucani*) that Lucan in a public lavatory gave a new twist to Nero's half-line *sub terris tonuisse putes.*

48 Cf. Valerius Flaccus' Troad digression, II.445–578.

49 The connection with the preceding lines is clear enough on reflection. The guide has told Caesar not to walk over the bones of Hector and to pay respect to the altar of Zeus Herkeios. In IX.963 Lucan had spoken of the Greek heroes who fell before Troy as *multum debentes uatibus umbras*, a theme familiar from Hor., *Od.*, IV.9.25ff, *uixere fortes* etc. If Hector and Priam acquired immortality on men's lips through Homer's verse as much as through their own exploits, Caesar would through Lucan's.

50 E. Griset, 'Lucanea 1: le due Farsaglie', *Riv. Stud. Class.* 2 (1954), 109–13, had evidently not read Housman's note. For *Pharsalia* as the name of the battle see J. P. Postgate, 'Pharsalia nostra', *CR* 19 (1905), 257–60; R. T. Bruère, 'Palaepharsalus, Pharsalus, Pharsalia', *CPhil.* 46 (1951), 111–15.

51 Some of these are dismissed by W. E. Heitland, Introduction to Haskins's edition, xxxviii (wrongly numbered xxviii)–xxxix.

52 L. Herrmann, 'Deux Allusions contemporaires dans le livre III du "De Bello Civili" de Lucain', *Rev. Ét. Anc.* 32 (1930), 339–41.

53 As given by Brisset, op. cit., 180.

54 The interpretation of the Domitius episode here given largely tallies with that of Enrica Malcovati, *M. Anneo Lucano* (ed. 1), Milan, 1940, 27ff. In addition to the extract from W. Menz's thesis mentioned in n. 18, there is now printed in *Lucan*, ed. W. Rutz, 257–63, the one referred to in this paragraph. The full thesis was published in typescript (Humboldt University, Berlin, 1952).

55 To imagine that *quales nunc uidemus* can mean anything other than 'in their present arrangement', or that Lucan composed or published books in a different order from this, is surely perverse. All extant Silver Latin poets seem to have composed in the correct order of books; so that historical allusions, where traceable, are consecutive, and unfinished epics of the period, including Lucan's, present a completed portion intended to be continuous.

56 The contrary view is sometimes coupled with the theory that Lucan was deliberately countering Virgil in this; just as Virgil regarded Aeneas as the precursor of Augustus, so Lucan, it is claimed, thought of Caesar as the precursor of his personal enemy Nero: O. Schönberger, 'Zu Lucan. Ein Nachtrag', *Hermes* 86 (1958), 230–9.

57 For the poet's characterization of Caesar, Pompey and Cato, see now A. W. Lintott, 'Lucan and the History of the Civil War', *CQ* n.s. 21 (1971), 488–505.

IV

Lucan and English Literature

O. A. W. Dilke

The influence of Lucan on English literature as a whole has been strangely neglected. Only one work, a German thesis of seventy-five years ago on Shelley's debt to Lucan, even professes to give an outline of the principal English writers indebted to the *De Bello Civili*; and it has many gaps.[1] There is no mention of Thomas Hughes, Samuel Daniel, Michael Drayton and others who should figure prominently in such an account. The latest work on the *Nachleben* of Lucan, likewise in German, suffers from the fact that its author consulted no English works.[2] The present chapter makes no attempt to be fully comprehensive, but it is hoped that others will be induced to take up and advance the research.

The study of Lucan's epic in medieval England is attested by many references. The York library possessed a copy in the time of Alcuin.[3] Joseph of Exeter (Josephus Iscanus), who composed his epic *De Bello Troiano* about 1185, had clearly studied all the available classical Latin epic poets; the very form of his title may have been borrowed from Lucan's. The standard of scholarship on the *De Bello Civili* cannot have been high; English scholars would have no better source generally available than the wordy and ignorant twelfth-century commentary of Arnulf of Orléans.[4] About eighty manuscripts of the poem are known, many of them from the Middle Ages. A great number of medieval writers both in Latin and in the vernacular languages, especially Dante, were indebted to Lucan;[5] he appears in the *Inferno* coupled with Horace and Ovid and following Homer. Apart from the central theme, topics like the poor fisherman Amyclas, the witch Erichtho, the snakes in the Western Desert (Dante, *Inf.* xxv.94f names two of their victims), and the portrait of Cato interested the later Middle Ages. An anonymous French translation appeared in 1380.

In early English literature we find more references to Lucan's poem than borrowings from it. Chaucer has four passages in which Lucan is named.[6] In *The Hous of Fame*, 1497ff (III.407ff), he writes:

> Thoo saugh I on a piler by,
> Of yren wroght ful sternely,
> The grete poet, daun Lucan,
> And on hys shuldres bar up than,
> As high as that y mighte see,
> The fame of Julius and Pompe.

As often in the poem, there is symbolism here: Lucan is not only the great poet of the civil wars but the poet of iron, the stern Stoic who writes of weapons (*ferrum*). At the end of *The Monkes Tale*, Chaucer speaks of Julius Caesar's assassination and adds (B2 3911–12):

> Lucan, to thee this storie I recomende,
> And to Swetoun, and to Valerie also,

the last being Valerius Maximus, who in IV.4.6 recounts Caesar's death. But in *The Tale of the Man of Lawe* (B1 400–3) the lines:

> Noght trowe I the triumphe of Julius,
> Of which that Lucan maketh swich a boost,
> Was roialler ne moore curius
> Than was th'assemblee of this blisful hoost.

make one wonder if Chaucer mistook the catalogue of Gaulish tribes which Caesar's departure left unattended (Lucan, 1.392–465) as a description of Caesar's triumphal procession. There are certainly many references in Lucan to Caesar's expected triumph (II.73–9; IV.358–62; V.328–34; VII.233f, 254–6), but these do not justify Chaucer's words. It has been thought that the apotheosis of Pompey in Book IX inspired the passage where the soul of Troilus ascends to heaven and laughs at the little tragedies of humans.

Lydgate, in his *Fall of Princes*, derives much of his historical material on the fall of Pompey indirectly from Lucan, by way of Laurent de Premierfait's second French translation of Boccaccio's *De Casibus Virorum Illustrium*.[7] Lucan is wrongly associated with the consultation of the Sibylline books before the civil war and the answer R.R.R.F.F.F., interpreted as *regnum Romae ruet ferro flamma fame*. Details are sometimes grotesquely distorted. Thus, although Lydgate mentions a great battle in Thessaly, this pales into insignificance compared with a holocaust by the Nile, a battle in which, he would have us believe, not only Pompey but 300,000 men were killed. However, the burial of Pompey is more faithfully related (VI.2493-9):

> The corps abood withoute sepulture,
> Till oon Coodrus of compassioun
> Aftir the bataille and disconfiture
> Besought(e) hym, of great affeccioun,
> To hide the trunke lowe in the sondis doun.
> Souhte tymbir, and ther he fond but smal,
> To doon exequies with fires funeral.

This description comes from Laurent's much expanded account and originates in Lucan (VIII.712-13), who alone among classical writers gives the name Codrus or Cordus to the burier. Lydgate's introduction of the goddess Fortune, at the beginning of Book VI, to confront Boccaccio has a Lucanic ring.

Skelton, in his *Garland of Laurel*, gives Lucan only a passing mention together with Statius' *Achilleid*.

The *editio princeps* of Lucan came out in 1469, and translations into French and Italian appeared in 1490 and 1492 respectively. Lucan was one of the Latin poets prescribed for lectures at Corpus Christi College, Oxford, founded in 1517; the order of popularity of Latin poetical works sold by the University bookseller in 1520 was Terence, Virgil, Ovid, Lucan, Horace. Yet by the time of the Armada no English translation had appeared. So wholesale appropriation was unlikely to be spotted and must have been practised frequently for ephemeral literature. Norman Douglas claimed that any amount of the use of Greek and Latin classics was permissible.[8] But plagiarism is the only term that can be used of the type of borrowing that we find in *The Misfortunes of Arthur*, by Thomas Hughes.[9] The gentlemen of Gray's Inn performed 'certaine deuises and shewes' before Queen Elizabeth at her Greenwich court in 1588. Much of the performance was in dumb show; but the wars of King Arthur, for which Hughes used Geoffrey of Monmouth as his chief source, were presented in the form of a five-act tragedy in blank verse. For much of the wording of this tragedy Hughes purloined whole sections from Seneca's tragedies and Lucan.[10] Thus in Act IV, sc. ii the *Nuncius*, after a dialogue borrowed from Seneca, relates at length the battle between Arthur and Mordred. The following quotation from this messenger's speech, to which there are many parallels, will show the greatest extent of Hughes's indebtedness:

> Now that the time drewe on, when both the Camps
> Should meet in *Cornwell* fieldes th'appointed place:
> The reckelesse troupes, whom *Fates* forbad to liue
> Till noone, or night, did storme and raue for warres.
> They swarmde about their Guydes, and clustring cald
> For signes to fight, and fierce with vprores fell,
> They onwards hayld the hastning houres of death.
> A direfull frenzie rose: ech man his owne,
> And publike *Fates* all heedlesse flung.
> $\qquad$ (Hughes, IV.ii.34–42, from Lucan, VII.45–52).

In the following scene Conan comments on the results of the battle:

> When Fame shall blaze these acts in latter yeares,
> And time to come so many ages hence
> Shall efts report our toyles and *Brytish* paynes:
> Or when perhaps our Childrens Children reade,
> Our woefull warres displaid with skilfull penne:
> They'l thinke they heere some sounds of future facts,
> And not the ruins olde of pompe long past.
> Twill mooue their mindes to ruth, and frame afresh
> New hopes, and feares, and vowes, and many a wish,
> And *Arthurs* cause shall still be fauour'd most.
> $\qquad$ (Hughes, IV.iii.26–35, from Lucan, VII.207–13).

It must not be thought that the whole of *The Misfortunes of Arthur* is a cento compiled from Seneca and Lucan; some of the play consists of advice intended as applicable to the political situation of the time.[11] But there are cento-like passages and too close imitation, and for these and other reasons the play lacks artistry. If it is true that Hughes's imitation of Seneca has been overstressed, yet his use of Lucan, investigated by J. C. Maxwell, by the present writer, and most recently and fully by G. M. Logan, has been shown to be distinctly servile.

In 1593 the translation of Book I of Lucan by Marlowe was

entered in the Stationers' Register, and it was published in 1600.
It is one of the earliest English poems in blank verse, but Marlowe
restricted his capacity by adhering to a line-for-line translation.
The English line contains only 10 or 11 syllables, whereas the
Latin hexameter with dactylic fifth foot has 13–17 syllables.
Consequently there are some passages where, despite its lack of
inflection, the English line cannot contain all that is expressed in
the Latin; and this is particularly true of Silver Latin, which is
often less diffuse than that of the Golden Age. The shift of the
verbal ending -*ed* to '*d* did, however, help in this direction.

The opening lines of Marlowe's translation are:

Wars worse than ciuill on *Thessalian* playnes,
And outrage strangling law & people strong,
We sing, whose conquering swords their own breasts launcht,
Armies alied, the kingdoms league vprooted,
Th'affrighted worlds force bent on publique spoile,
Trumpets, and drums like deadly threatning other,
Eagles alike displaide, darts answering darts.

Apart from the commendable 'Thessalian' for *Emathios*, the
rendering tends to be too literal: in line 2 it looks as if 'people'
were the object of 'strangling'; in line 4 'the kingdoms league'
(*foedere regni* refers to the First Triumvirate) could hardly be
understood.

The theory has been advanced that Chapman, not Marlowe, was
the translator;[12] but there is no good evidence to support this.
Marlowe's *Tamburlaine* shows a few verbal reminiscences from the
De Bello Civili. So too does Chapman's play *Caesar and Pompey*,[13]
which deals with the theme of the civil wars. Chapman has something of Lucan's pessimistic outlook; but his approach to the
cosmic forces which influenced events is positively medieval. He
makes Ophioneus (a kind of snake-devil to judge from the name)
head of an army of spirits fighting against Heaven, and introduces
a ragged knave, Fronto, who is rescued by Ophioneus. Caesar and
Pompey are unhistorically made to confront each other in argument in Rome at the outset of the civil war; this introduces a
greater measure of historical falsification than we find in Lucan.
Among the probable imitations is a lion simile, transferred from
Caesar (Lucan, 1.206) to Pompey.

The poet Samuel Daniel (1562/3–1619) was called by several

contemporary writers the English Lucan.[14] Turning to the theme of civil war after making his name by writing love poetry, he adopted for his motto Propertius' line *aetas prima canat veneres, postrema tumultus* (let my youth sing of love, my old age war).[15] His work, *The Civile Wars between the Houses of Lancaster and Yorke* ..., was begun in 1594, several times revised, but (a further parallel with Lucan) left unfinished. Its final version ran to eight books.

In his prose preface, addressed to the Countess of Pembroke, Daniel acknowledges his debt to Sallust and Livy for 'that poeticall licence, of framing speaches to the persons of men according to their occasions'. Nowhere in the poem does he mention Lucan, although in the beginning of his eighth book he refers to 'our great Pharsalian field' and to Cato,[16] Pompey and Caesar. But in his prose work *Defence of Ryme* he calls his poem 'my Homer-Lucan',[17] and no one who knew Lucan's opening could fail to recognize the very close borrowing (1.1–3):

I sing the ciuill Warres, tumultuous Broyles,
And Bloody factions of a mightie Land:
Whose people hautie, proud with forraine spoyles,
Vpon themselues turne-back their conquering hand;
Whil'st Kin their Kin, Brother the Brother foyles;
Like Ensignes all against Ensignes band;
Bowes against Bowes, the Crowne against the Crowne;
Whil'st all pretending right, all right's throwne downe.
　What furie, ô what madnes held thee so,
Deare *England* (too too prodigall of blood)
To waste so much, and warre without a foe,
Whilst *Fraunce*, to see thy spoyles, at pleasure stood!
How much might'st thou have purchast with lesse woe,
T' have done thee honour and thy people good?
Thine might have beene what-euer lies betweene
The *Alps* and vs, the *Pyrenei* and *Rhene*.
　Yet now what reason have we to complaine?
Since hereby came the calme we did inioy;
The blisse of thee *Eliza*; happie gaine
For all our losse: when-as no other way
The heauens could finde, but to vnite againe
The fatall sev'red Families, that they

> Might bring foorth thee: that in thy peace might growe
> That glorie, which few Times could euer showe.

Virtually to equate the middle-aged Elizabeth with the youthful Nero might seem to some readers absurd; yet one can imagine that something of the same spirit of enthusiasm was in the air for some years after the defeat of the Armada as in the *quinquennium Neronis*.

The first stanza thus follows very closely the thought as well as the wording of Lucan's opening, while the second and third summarize Lucan, 1.8–20, 33ff. Stanzas 4–7 expand Lucan, 1.63–9, and in the original version Daniel followed Lucan by invoking the monarch as a 'sacred Goddesse' instead of any Muse. In the 1609 version this becomes 'sacred *Virtue*', possibly because he felt that the original wording as applied to Elizabeth had given offence.

After the seventh stanza the tone becomes far more pedestrian, starting with an account of the kings of England from William the Conqueror to the times Daniel is describing. This is not the method of Lucan, who particularly confined himself to a selection of historical events (in Book 1, previous civil wars), and the borrowing accordingly becomes less noticeable. It was thus a just criticism that Drayton made of Daniel:

> Onely have heard some wiseman him rehearse,
> To be too much *Historian* in verse.

But at 1.87ff the more dramatic and imitative approach returns: the personification of England appears to Bolingbroke in his sleep, just as in Lucan Rome appears to Caesar at the Rubicon, urging him to halt, and his speech in reply (1.90.3ff) resembles Caesar's in Lucan, 1.200ff. Similarly Daniel's 'wayling Women', who flock to the temples (1.109) and protest against the civil war, are borrowed from Lucan, 11.28ff; 'the barbarous North' in 1.111.3 is Lucan's *fundat ab extremo flavos Aquilone Suevos Albis*, 11.51f (Let fair-haired Suebi from the furthest North/be sent in hordes by River Elbe . . .); and the prodigies in 11.113.2ff owe something to those in Lucan, 1.522ff.

It is thus possible in Daniel's first book to trace fairly direct borrowing from Lucan's first and the beginning of his second book. But in the remainder of the work no such pattern of borrowing is visible. Since fighting occupies a fairly large part of Daniel's poem, it is not surprising that there are many echoes of Lucan VII. Thus 'no hand of strife is pure, but that which wins' (I.47.8) is a variant on *nulla manus belli mutato iudice pura est* (For, once the judge of war is changed, no hand/Is undefiled), VII.263; the two alternative explanations of Henry IV's forebodings of death (III.62) reflect Lucan's explanations of Pompey's dream (VII.19ff); the rhetorical exaggeration 'new-made hils of bodies slaine' (IV.47.8) is one inspired by Lucan, VI.180f and VII.790f; Daniel's:

> Which, slaughter, and no battaile, might be thought;
> Sith that side vs'd their swords, and this their throat

(VI.110.7–8) comes directly from VII.532f; his

> Com'n is the day, sayd he, wherein who can
> Obtaine the best, is Best: this day must try
> Who hath the wrong, and whence our ills have beene:
> And tis our swords must make us honest men

(VIII.9.5–8) paraphrases VII.254–62; and the leisure after defeat (VIII.30) is from Pompey's thoughts after defeat at Pharsalia (VII.686ff).

Among other reminiscences are II.79.7ff:

> And, with that crie, sinks downe upon the flore.
> Abundant griefe lackt words to vtter more.
>   Sorrow keepes full possession in her heart,
> Lockes it within, stops vp the way of breath,
> Shuts senses out of doore from euerie part,

which comes from Cornelia's collapse in Lucan, VIII.59ff; the isthmus simile at v.89.7–8, from Lucan, I.100ff; and VIII.6, 'What rage, what madness, England, do we see? . . .', which like Daniel's opening comes from *quis furor, o cives, quae tanta licentia ferri?* (Why, citizens, this rage and lust for arms?) (I.8). Apart from such verbal borrowings, there are parallels of situation: the puppet parliament of II.94ff, and Carlisle's protest of III.21ff, which remind us of Caesar's senate and Metellus' defiance; the King's envy of the common peasant, which is somewhat akin to Lucan's envy of the poor fisherman, Amyclas (v.527ff);[18] the apostrophe to France in v.41, reminiscent of those in Lucan VII and VIII; the reference to 'new immortal *Illiads*' (v.5.2),[19] followed by an address to 'great Eliza' (v.9.1), which makes one think of the appeal to Caesar on his visit to Troy (IX.980–6).[20]

The poem of Samuel Daniel falls into two fairly definable types, historical epic and versified history. Of these, it is in the former that the poet imitates Lucan at times, having clearly read him in the original, not, as did Thomas Lodge,[21] in an anthology. His imitation is continuous only in the opening, but visible from time to time throughout the work. He is more impartial than Lucan in his characterization. Coleridge said of him, as some might say of Lucan, 'he must not be read piecemeal'. Yet he was, as Tillyard remarks, a sincere classicizer, who felt truly inspired to imitate.

Francis Bacon quoted from Lucan, and it has been suggested[22] that his now proverbial words in the essay *Of Marriage and Single Life*, 'He that hath wife and children hath given hostages to fortune', may come from Lucan, VII.661–2, where Pompey says:

> coniunx
> est mihi, sunt nati: dedimus tot pignora fatis.

> (I have a wife and children; I have given
> so many hostages to fortune.)

Another work of the same type as Daniel's is Drayton's *Barons Warres*, entered in 1602 and published in 1603.[23] The first five books of Daniel's work had appeared in 1595, and Drayton was evidently moved to rival them for an earlier period of unrest in British history. His preface mentions classical epic not as a source but as a precedent for division into books; here Lucan's work is not among those named, which include the curious entry *Illyricus Argonauticks*. Nevertheless, like Daniel, Drayton begins his first book with a paraphrase of Lucan's opening. His first stanza is:

> The bloudie Factions and Rebellious pride
> Of a strong Nation, whose ill-manag'd might
> The Prince and Peeres did many a day divide;
> With whom, wrong was no wrong, nor right no right,
> Whose strife, their Swords knew only to decide,
> Spur'd to their high speed, by their equall spight;
> Me from soft Layes and tender Loves doth bring,
> Of a farre worse, then Civill Warre to sing.

The causes of the war and the portents are likewise drawn from Book I of Lucan, though fairly freely. Unlike Daniel, who shirks describing battles, he gives several descriptions of arming, battles, and disturbances, and in these one can detect slight signs of Lucan's influence. Thus the 'famous *English* Bowes' which 'yet shun their Ayme' (II.36) come from Lucan, VII.515f. But in general the verbal resemblances are very slight: there is far more reminiscence of Ovid, whom Drayton took as his model for *Englands Heroicall Epistles*. The witch's potions (III.6) are those of Circe, not of Erichtho. The apostrophe at the end of Canto v is of similar type to those at the end of Lucan VII and VIII, yet not modelled on either. Classical mythology is splashed about in a manner totally unlike Lucan's.

Later Elizabethan dramatists avoided the wholesale incorporation to which Hughes was addicted. Kyd, in Act I, sc. ii of his *Spanish Tragedy*, has a battle scene recounted by a general in which the details of woundings are similar to Lucan's, though verbal parallels are slight: thus in III.2.120f:

> The night, sad secretary to my moans,
> With direful visions wakes my vexed soul,

differs materially from Lucan, VII.7f

> at nox, felicis Magno pars ultima vitae,
> sollicitos vana decepit imagine somnos.
>
> (But night, last happy hours of Pompey's life,
> With a false dream deceived his anxious sleep.)

Some borrowings are at second-hand from Garnier. Kyd's play *Cornelia*, covering the period of Caesar's dictatorship, goes back more to Seneca; but it has been shown that his sources were indebted to Lucan.[24] Reminiscent of several lines in Book VII is the passage (Act IV, sc.i, 108–13):

> Egypt, Emathia, Italy and Spayne
> Are full of dead mens bones by *Caesar* slayne.
> Th' infectious plague, and Famins bitternes,
> Or th' Ocean (Whom no pitty can asswage),
> Though they containe dead bodies numberles,
> Are yet inferior to Caesars rage.

The same span of history is covered by five other plays of this and the immediately following period: Sir William Alexander's *The Tragedy of Julius Caesar*, two tragedies of Caesar and Pompey, one anonymous and the one by Chapman already mentioned, Fletcher and Massinger's *The False One*, and Shakespeare's *Julius Caesar*. The history and the character of Caesar in these plays vary. In Alexander's play Caesar is completely autocratic, and the portrait is unsympathetic. *The False One* is about Cleopatra, and the authors 'freely welded into their work much of the glittering metal of Lucan's poetry'.[25] The borrowing in Act I amounts in fact to plagiarism, sometimes incorporating what we may hope is intentional variation, as when *sanguis . . . Achaeus, Ponticus, Assyrius* (Lucan, VII.653f) is rendered 'Pontique, *Punique*, and Assyrian blood'. It also includes the speech by Photinus (i.e. Pothinus) (VIII.484–95), urging the young king Ptolemy to order the assassination of Pompey. The extent of Fletcher's borrowing in one section may be gauged by comparing the speech of Labienus in Act I, sc.i, with Lucan, VII.576–85, 635–7 and other passages in the same book. Shakespeare's play closely follows North's *Plutarch*, and as a result a far more sympathetic picture of Caesar emerges than in the playwrights who follow Lucan.

Ben Jonson[26] was acquainted with Lucan at first hand, and among his plays were two drawn from Roman history, *Catiline* and *Sejanus*. For the first, Jonson was able to draw on Lucan's summaries of earlier civil wars. Catiline and Cethegus in *Cat.*, I.229ff have the same recollections of these as Lucan, II.101–11. In *Cat.*, v.659 'they knew not, what a crime their valour was' is from Lucan, VI.147f. In *Sejanus*, II.178–85 Jonson incorporates a speech from Lucan VIII, a draft of which he had published as a translation: it is the plea of Pothinus, mentioned above as borrowed by Fletcher and Massinger. Sejanus, like Caesar in Lucan, is made to crow at the subordination of the senate. He is punished for his *hybris* (the epilogue starts 'Let this example move th' insolent man/Not to grow proud and careless of the gods'), just as Caesar would have been shown to be in a later book of the *De Bello Civili*.

A contemporary play, John Marston's *The Wonder of Women, Or the Tragedie of Sophonisba*, has a witch named Erichtho after Lucan's, equally unpleasant. In his preface, Marston, evidently hitting at Jonson's *Sejanus*, says 'To transcribe authors, quote authorities, and translate Latin prose orations into English blank verse, hath, in this subject, been the least aim of my studies.' Nevertheless,

there is close borrowing from Lucan, VI.507ff in these lines
(IV.i.101ff):

> Forsaken graves and tombes the Ghosts forcd out
> She joyes to inhabit.
> A loathsome yellowe leannesse spreads hir face,
> A heavy hell-like palenes loades hir cheekes
> Unknowne to a cleare heaven: but if darke windes,
> Or thick black cloudes drive back the blinded stars
> When her deepe magique makes forc'd heven quake
> And thunder spite of *Jove*, *Erichtho* then
> From naked graves stalkes out, heaves proud hir head
> With long unkembed haire loaden, and strives to snatch
> *The Nights quick sulphar*: then she bursts up tombes,
> From half rot searcloaths then she scrapes dry gums
> For her black rites: but when she finds a corse
> But newly grav'd, whose entrailes are not turn'd
> To slymy filth with greedy havock then
> She makes fierce spoile: & swels with wicked triumph
> To bury hir lean knuckles in his eyes
> Then doeth she knaw the pale and or'egrowne nailes
> From his dry hand . . .

The last of Erichtho's unpleasant activities is not only a close but
an accurate translation: Lucan's *excrementa manus* (literally, pro-
trusions from the hand) (VI.543) was understood by Marston, but
wrongly explained by many editors of Lucan before Housman
and ignored by Lewis and Short.

Certainly Lucan was read at school, but not always appreciated:
Sir Thomas Browne[27] wrote later of the lines

> victurosque dei celant, ut vivere discant,
> felix esse mori.

> (The gods conceal from those with life to live,
> To keep them still alive, that death is bliss.) (IV.519f)

'I am much taken with two verses of Lucan, since I have been able
not only, as we do at School, to construe, but understand.'
Shakespeare was one of those who clearly read a selection of Latin
poetry, and it is interesting to find that he borrows from the very

first lines of the *De Bello Civili* in *Julius Caesar*, v.iii.94ff, where Brutus says:

> O *Iulius Caesar*, thou art mighty yet,
> Thy spirit walkes abroad, and turnes our Swords
> In our owne proper Entrailes.

With the translations of Sir Arthur Gorges and Thomas May we come to a period of popularization of Lucan. Before them, the English reader who had difficulty in understanding the Latin had to rely on foreign translations for Books II–X, and these seem for the most part to have been ignored. Sir Arthur Gorges' translation, which appeared in 1614, is in the eight-syllable rhyming couplets which came to be known as Hudibrastic, from Butler's *Hudibras* written some fifty years later. One must admit that they suit such burlesque verse better than the serious epic. Gorges' opening lines are:

> A more than ciuill warre I sing,
> That through th' *Emathian* fields did ring,
> Where reins let loose to head-strong pride,
> A potent people did misguide;
> Whose conquering hand enrag'd rebounds
> On his owne bowels with deep wounds.
> Where Hosts confronting neare alies,
> All faith and Empires Lawes defies.
> A world of force in faction meetes,
> And common guilt like torrents fleets
> Where like infestuous ensignes waue,
> The *Ægle* doth the *Ægle* braue,
> And *Pyle* against the *Pyle* doth raue.

The first four were no doubt in the mind of Sir John Beaumont when he wrote his *Bosworth Field* (1629), which starts:

> The Winter's storme of Ciuille Warre I sing,
> Whose end is crown'd with our eternall Spring,
> Where Roses ioyn'd, their colours mixe in one,
> And armies fight no more for England's Throne.

The remainder of this poem is to some extent inspired by Book VII of Lucan; for example, it starts with a dream of Richard III's, quite different however from Pompey's; the inspection, speech-making and battle are somewhat akin to Lucan's; and certain phrases also come from his poem. Thomas May was an ardent Republican, who made his name not only as poet and dramatist but as historian of the Long Parliament.[28] His verse translation of the whole of Lucan appeared in 1627. Its opening lines are:

> Warres more then ciuill on Æmathian plaines
> We sing: rage licensd; where great Rome distaines
> In her own bowels her victorious swords;
> Where kindred hoasts encounter, all accords
> Of Empire broke: where arm'd to impious warre
> The strength of all the shaken world from farre
> Is met; knowne Ensignes Ensignes doe defie,
> Piles against Piles, 'gainst Eagles Eagles fly.

Evidently not realizing that it had already been used by Gorges, May felt that his rendering of *pila* needed explanation, and wrote: 'If any man quarrell at the word *Pile*, as thinking it scarce English, I desire them to give a better word.' The rendering later found favour with Dryden.[29]

Since Lucan had broken off his poem in the middle of the Alexandrian War, with Caesar in danger of his life, May thought it seemly to add fifty lines, to show that the leader swam safely to his fleet.[30] These additional verses may have inspired him to finish off the poem as he thought it might have ended, and this seven-book continuation, taking the work down to the Ides of March, was published in 1630.[31] It suffers from too strict an adherence to the details of historical narrative. The best part is Cato's suicide in Book IV of the *Continuation*, a death which might indeed have inspired Lucan himself to the top flights of rhetorical poetry. This is the passage in which Cato reads of the soul:

> To whom the Fates present, as now on high
> His thoughts were soaring to eternitie,
> An obiect fit: casting his eye aside
> Diuinest *Plato's Phaedon* he espi'd.
> Oh welcome Booke sent from the gods (quoth he)
> To teach a dying man Philosophy;
> And though thou canst not further, or controle
> The resolution of my fixed soule,

Since Fate has doom'd my end, yet may'st thou giue
Comfort to those few houres I haue to liue.

Ten years later (1640) his Latin version, *Supplementum Lucani*, appeared. It differs in a number of respects from the English, most of these evidently being intended as improvements;[32] thus two references to Caesar's night crossing of the Adriatic were modified, presumably because May realized in the interval that Caesar landed on the same side of the Adriatic from which he started. Similarly the deletion of an encomium of Augustus may be due not so much, as has been thought, to May's increasing Republicanism, as to a realization that Lucan had no particular love of Augustus (see pp. 69–70 above). Cato's dying words are expanded in the Latin version, ending (IV.291–2):

> tua funera saltem
> prosequar, et Stygias liber comitabor ad umbras.

(At least I shall accompany your death
Still free, go with you to the Stygian shades.)

This is copied from Domitius' dying speech (Lucan, VII.612–13):

> Stygias Magno duce liber ad umbras
> et securus eo.

(Free and without a care I go to join
The Stygian ghosts: Pompey is still my leader.)

But May is not always as imitative as this. If Dr Johnson's estimate of him as superior to Cowley and Milton as a Latin poet is perhaps over-generous, Landor was too keen on epigram when he wrote: 'Thomas May indeed is an admirable imitator of Lucan; so good a one, that if in Lucan you find little poetry, in May you find none.'[33] The *Supplementum* came to be regularly appended to Continental editions of Lucan, and was translated into French and Polish. Its first book was actually re-translated into English verse by the Rev. Edmund Poulter (1786), who professed himself dissatisfied with May's English version.

May also wrote plays, including *The Tragedie of Cleopatra Queen of Aegypt* (1639, though acted in 1626), and *Julia Agrippina* (1639). The former gives a more attractive portrait of Cleopatra than we

97

find in Lucan. The germ of it is already to be found in the *Continuation*, where Cleopatra is called 'great' and her affairs with prominent Romans excused on the ground that they were less offensive than the incestuous marriages traditional in the Egyptian dynasties. There are many reminiscences of Lucan, including a mention of the Psylli, introduced in Book IX as experts on snakes. In *Julia Agrippina*, which deals with the intrigues in the imperial house down to the death of Agrippina, Petronius' satire on the *Bellum Civile* is introduced.

Milton was a good classical scholar familiar with much Greek and Latin poetry in the original, capable of good verse composition in those languages, and like Lucan interested in learned digressions on such subjects as astronomy. In composing Latin verse he was skilful at blending his borrowings. The line of his Latin verse most reminiscent of Lucan is in his juvenile poem on Guy Fawkes' Day, line 48:

> iamque pruinosas velox superaverat Alpes;

(Now he had dashed across the hoar-clad Alps . . .)

for Lucan (1.183) has:

> iam gelidas Caesar cursu superaverat Alpes.

(Caesar had dashed across the frozen Alps . . .)

Commentators on *Lycidas* were until recently content to say that the name Lycidas was common in pastoral poetry and to cite examples of this. While it is quite true that in this poem Milton is much indebted to pastoral poetry, and even has verbal reminiscences of it, is it not likely, as has been suggested,[34] that he chose the name Lycidas as especially appropriate to one who perished at sea? In III.635-46, in his description of the naval battle off Marseilles, Lucan has these lines:

> ferrea dum puppi rapidos manus inserit uncos,
> adfixit Lycidam. mersus foret ille profundo,
> sed prohibent socii suspensaque crura retentant.
> scinditur avolsus, nec, sicut volnere, sanguis
> emicuit lentus: ruptis cadit undique venis,
> discursusque animae diversa in membra meantis
> interceptus aquis. nullius vita perempti

est tanta dimissa via. pars ultima trunci
tradidit in letum vacuos vitalibus artus;
at tumidus qua pulmo iacet, qua viscera fervent,
haeserunt ibi fata diu, luctataque multum
hac cum parte viri vix omnia membra tulerunt.

(A grappling-hook, inserting its swift claws
On a ship's prow, pierced Lycidas, who then
Would have been drowned, but friends and swaying legs
Prevented this fate. He was torn apart.
The blood did not spurt out as with a wound:
It fell on all sides from rent arteries.
The circulation to his various limbs
Was cut off by the sea. No other life
Was lost by such a wide gap. Nether parts
Handed to death the limbs that had no life;
But where the swollen lungs lay, where the heart
Was hot still, there the fates delayed for long.
With this part of the warrior they fought hard
Until they won the whole corpse.)

It was thought by Sulpitius that these were the lines which, according to Tacitus,[35] were declaimed by the poet as he was dying. Perhaps rather those were from a separate short poem (*carmen*); but if Milton believed them to be the lines, the passage would have left a lasting impact on his memory.

The influence of Lucan on *Paradise Lost* may be seen partly in characterization, partly in borrowings. Caesar in Lucan's *De Bello Civili* (except for its first third)[36] and Satan in *Paradise Lost* are both noble villains, who to many would seem to have heroic qualities. Caesar can have attributes of the terrible underworld, while Satan (e.g. in *P.L.*, IX.501ff) can possess some nobility of character. The parallelism has been thus summed up:[37]

The Satanic in Lucan's Caesar is plain to see: the continual restlessness and demonic impatience are stressed over and over again; the unhesitating leadership in evil, the impulse of the gambler and allied to that the fascination of the idea of total ruin; the moments of hesitation, remorse and magnanimity which serve only to make more horrifying the defiant impenitence. The Caesarian in Milton's Satan is as plain. Satan is the enemy, as Caesar had been, of quiet and custom and accepted right, he is a tyrant . . .

Verbal reminiscences have sometimes been wrongly attributed. A current work of reference[38] tells us that Lucan was the 'first to use the name Demogorgon (*Phar.*, VI.744)'; in fact this is only Hortensius' explanation of the name in the 1578 Basle edition of Lucan. The name would not, correctly scanned, go into a hexameter[39] and occurs in antiquity, if at all, only in Lactantius on Stat., *Theb.*, IV.516, where *deum Demogorgona* is probably a mistake for *deum demiurgum* (the creator god), as one MS. virtually has. Although *qui Gorgona cernit apertam* may be intended as a pointer to it, Lucan is careful to avoid naming the mysterious super-god: as May's translation has it:

> Will you obey, or shall I him inuoke,
> Whose name the earths foundations euer shooke?
> Who without hurt th' unuailed *Gorgon* sees . . .

Again, *Paradise Lost*, II.592 presumably does not come from Lucan, VIII.539,[40] since Lucan has only one of the three names mentioned by Milton. But there are several strong reminiscences of situation. The most notable is Satan's voyage (*P.L.*, II.890ff), where Milton follows Caesar's attempt to cross the Adriatic in a small boat (Lucan, V.476ff). Verbal parallels are visible in *Paradise Lost*, II.1010ff: 'springs upward' from 'transsiliut', 'into the wild expanse' from 'per vasta silentia', 'Sin and Death amain following his track' adapted from 'sola placet Fortuna comes'; and these two passages present similarities:

> Over the dark abyss, whose boiling gulf
> Tamely endured a bridge of wondrous length
> From hell continued reaching th' utmost orb
> Of this frail world   (II.1027–30)

>   non ullo litore surgunt
> tam validi fluctus, alioque ex orbe voluti
> a magno venere mari, mundumque coercens
> monstriferos agit unda sinus   (V.617–20).

(No other shore witnessed such powerful waves,
Atlantic rollers from a distant world:
Waters that from the boundary of the globe
Drove on these monstrous curves.)

The 'boggy Syrtis, neither sea, nor good dry land' (II.939f) is most directly from Lucan, IX.303f, but the same idea is present in V.484f.

Two other borrowings may be mentioned. In *Paradise Lost*, 1.48 occur the 'adamantine chains' of May's translation of Lucan, VI.801, and this makes one think that Milton knew the translation as well as the original. In *Paradise Lost*, X.458f and 504ff we have borrowings first from Lucan, I.297f, then from the names of snakes in Book IX. Here Milton has not only the commoner names, but amphisbaena, cerastes, hydrus, ellops, and dipsas. The odd one out is ellops (helops), not a reptile but a fish, and not occurring in Lucan: presumably the blind Milton was relying on his memory.

Andrew Marvell[41] composed polished Latin elegiacs, a Sapphic poem in imitation of Horace, and Latin epitaphs, as well as English poems. One brief exercise of his is a re-translation into Latin hexameters of a sentence from Brébeuf's translation of Lucan. In his famous *Horatian Ode upon Cromwel's Return from Ireland*[42] the imitation appears to be of May's translation of Lucan, since there are certain verbal reminiscences: Marvell's 'The forward Youth' (l.1) is inspired by 'His forward Sword' (May's inadequate rendering of *temerando . . . ferro*, Lucan, I.147); 'restless *Cromwel*' (l.9) is from 'restlesse valour' (May's condensation of *nescia virtus stare loco* I.144f); 'like the three-fork'd Lightning, first/ Breaking the Clouds where it was nurst' (ll.13–14) is from May's

> As lightning by the winde forc'd from a cloude
> Breakes through the wounded aire with thunder loude,
> Disturbes the Day, the people terrifyes,
> And by a light oblique dazels our eyes   (I.151–4).

'Much to the Man is due' (l.28) could possibly have its origin in *multum Roma tamen debet civilibus armis* (Even so Rome owes a great debt to the civil wars) (I.44), though the sense is different. Cromwell in this poem is a mixture of Horace's Octavian, Lucan's Caesar and Lucan's Pompey.[43] The dignity and impartiality of the poem are due to Horace, its fire to Lucan. The rapid seizing of arms (ll.5–8) is no doubt taken mainly from Lucan, I.239ff rather than from similar passages in Virgil and Statius.

If Marvell borrowed from May's translation for his own poem, yet when May died in the same year in which the *Horatian Ode* appeared (1650), Marvell wrote an unkind satire, *Tom May's Death*, some of whose lines (21–6) parody those of May's translation and play on the word 'translated' in connection with May's death:

> Cups more than civil of *Emathian* wine,
> I sing (said he) and the *Pharsalian* Sign,
> Where the Historian of the Common-wealth
> In his own Bowels sheath'd the conquering health.
> By this *May* to himself, and them was come,
> He found he was translated, and by whom.

The satire is also indebted to Seneca's *Apocolocyntosis*, especially in the general setting and the phrase 'with foot as stumbling as his tongue'. To explain the difference in tone between Marvell's two poems we need to appreciate, first, that May had changed his allegiance from the Royalist to the Parliamentary side; secondly, that the *Horatian Ode* is purposely impersonal, the skit on May's death extremely personal.[44]

After the Restoration we enter on a period when the study of Lucan seemed less apposite to contemporary life and when the first flush of enthusiasm, brought about by May's translation and continuation and his contemporaries' homage to Lucan, had largely died out. Lines of the poem were quoted in literary works or parliamentary speeches, but there was far less borrowing than hitherto. The first part of Butler's *Hudibras*, published in 1663 (1.ii.493ff), seems to contain a parody of Gorges' translation of Lucan, 1.8ff.[45] Butler's lines are:

> What rage, O Citizens! what fury,
> Doth you to these dire actions hurry?
> What oestrum, what phrenetic mood,
> Makes you thus lavish of your blood,
> While the proud Vies your trophies boast,
> And unreveng'd walks Waller's ghost?
> What towns, what garrisons, might you
> With hazard of this blood subdue,
> Which now y' are bent to throw away
> In vain untriumphable fray?

The 'unreveng'd . . . ghost' is a literal translation of Lucan, but may well be from Gorges' lines in the same metre:

And *Crassus* unrevenged ghost,
Roames wayling through the *Parthian* coast.

Addison's *Cato*,[46] a 'classical' verse tragedy, was performed at the
Theatre Royal and published in 1713, when the succession to the
ailing Queen Anne was being disputed, and when Cato and
'liberty' stood for different ideals to Whigs and Tories. The introduction of the love interest strikes an unclassical note, and the
characters have been criticized as lifeless. There are occasional
reminiscences of Lucan and of May's *Continuation*. Pompey's reported instructions to his sons (Lucan, IX.87–97) to carry on their
father's fight for freedom are varied somewhat in Act III of *Cato*,
where the hero urges his friends to transmit to their sons the
tradition of freedom inherited from their forefathers. Only one
episode from the march through the Western Desert is given
prominence, that of the soldier offering Cato water; this may or
may not have been taken from Lucan. In 1715 Nicholas Rowe
became Poet Laureate, and in 1718, the year of his death, his
verse translation of Lucan appeared; Dr J. Welwood, in the
preface, praises Lucan except for his characterization of Caesar,
caused by the poet's 'smarting under the lashes of *Nero*'s Tyranny'.
The translation was commended by Dr Johnson.

Prose writers have not, on the whole, been influenced by
Lucan; but it has been shown[47] that Samuel Richardson, author
of *Pamela, or Virtue Rewarded*, was acquainted with him. In
Fielding's *Amelia* (1751), VIII.v, Booth speaks of Lucian, where-
upon the bogus scholar thinks he will show his knowledge by
mentioning Rowe's translation. But Booth replies, 'I believe
we are talking of different authors,' and takes the other up on
Lucan, quoting II.387f:

Venerisque hic maximus usus,
progenies: Urbi pater est Urbique maritus,

where Rowe (not there quoted) has:

He sought no End of marriage, but Increase,
Nor wish'd a Pleasure, but his Country's Peace:
That took up all the tend'rest Parts of Life,
His Country was his Children and his Wife.

The bogus scholar, however, takes the last phrase as meaning 'not
only the father of his country but the husband too', and still per-

sists in quoting *Urbis* even when Booth has correctly interpreted *Urbi* as dative of advantage.

If there is one English poet of the nineteenth century whom we can in some way equate with Lucan, it is Shelley.[48] After he had read the first four books of the *De Bello Civili*, he wrote to Hogg (September 1815) that it was a 'poem of wonderful genius, and transcending Virgil'. Later, in *A Defence of Poetry*, he gave a different opinion, but one in which he did not persist: Lucan, he said, was a 'mock-bird' rather than a real poet. In *Adonais*, among those whom he brings forward to mourn for the young Keats[49] are Chatterton, Sydney,

> . . . and Lucan by his death approved.
> Oblivion as they rose shrank like a thing reproved.

No doubt Lucan's lines ix.980–6, ending *a nullo tenebris damnabimur aevo* (and no age shall condemn us to oblivion), occurred to Shelley as he wrote. Shelley, like Lucan, was a lover of freedom and hater of tyranny who also felt he had been ill-treated, so it is not surprising that he found much in common with him and adopted some of his ideas. His early fragment, *The Daemon of the World*, is prefaced by two and a half lines from Book v. Like others, he seems to have been fascinated by the snakes of Book ix: in *Prometheus Unbound*, as Swinburne saw,

> Like him whom the Numidian seps did thaw
> Into a dew with poison   (iii.1.40f)

is from ix.723, 762ff; *The Revolt of Islam* has many snake similes and fables; 'an amphisbaenic snake' in *Prometheus Unbound* (iii.4.119), and 'as with its twine/When Amphisbaena some fair bird has tied', in *The Revolt of Islam* (viii.21), may or may not come from Lucan; in *Prometheus Unbound* (iii.4.18f) we have 'it thirsted/As one bit by a dipsas' (cf. Lucan, ix.737–60). Two main sources can be discerned for the speeches in *Hellas*: the contrast between East and West and between slaves and free men reminds us of Aeschylus' *Persae*; but a number of details clearly come from Lucan, especially from Vulteius' speech in Book iv. In *Prometheus Unbound* Demogorgon (see p.100 and nn.38, 39) appears as a laconic but dominating character. It has been pointed out that the origin of the name Demogorgon is discussed in a note to Peacock's *Rhododaphne*, published in 1818 and written the previous year, when he and Shelley were in constant touch.[50]

Shelley makes his Prometheus enunciate the law, 'Let man be free'. In *The Revolt of Islam*, Canto v, the fourth and fifth stanzas begin 'My brethren, we are free!' This positive approach contrasts with that of Lucan, for whom five hundred years of free republic had been followed by countless years of slavery. Shelley remained an idealist, Lucan developed a cynical approach; yet despite this the two had very much in common.

Whereas Macaulay found Statius 'as bad as ever' on a second reading, his reappraisal of Lucan resulted in an upgrading. First we have his views recorded in 1835 in his copy of the work:[51]

When Lucan's age is considered, it is impossible not to allow that the poem is a very extraordinary one: more extraordinary, perhaps, than if it had been of a higher kind; for it is more common for the imagination to be in full vigour at an early time of life than for a young man to obtain a complete mastery of political and philosophical rhetoric. I know no declamation in the world, not even Cicero's best, which equals some passages in the Pharsalia. As to what were meant for bold poetical flights—the sea-fight at Marseilles, the Centurion who is covered with wounds, the snakes in the Libyan desert—it is all as detestable as Cibber's Birthday Odes. The furious partiality of Lucan takes away much of the pleasure which his talents would otherwise afford . . . Caesar, the finest gentleman, the most humane conqueror, and the most popular politician that Rome ever produced, is a bloodthirsty ogre. If Lucan had lived, he would probably have improved greatly.

One may venture to comment that Macaulay's bias in Caesar's favour is as heavy as Lucan's against him. Today we are perhaps coming towards a better appreciation of political literature.

However, a year later Macaulay wrote from Calcutta:[52]

I am now busy with Quintilian and Lucan, both excellent writers. The dream of Pompey in the seventh book is a very noble piece of writing. I hardly know an instance in poetry of so great an effect produced by means so simple. There is something irresistibly pathetic in the lines:

'Qualis erat populi facies, clamorque faventum
Olim cum juvenis . . .'

(Such was the aspect of the cheering crowd,
Such were their shouts, when long ago, so young . . .)

and something unspeakably solemn in the sudden turn which
follows:

'Crastina dira quies . . .'

(Tomorrow's sleep, ill-omened . . .)

As passages in Lucan 'which surpass in eloquence anything that I
know in the Latin language' he refers to VIII.806ff, a somewhat
prosaic enumeration of Pompey's achievements, and IX.190ff, the
deservedly famous *laudatio funebris* by Cato.

Two English poets have associated themselves with Lucan in
the twentieth century. A. E. Housman's edition *editorum in usum*
appeared in 1926. Its seemingly boastful title has turned out to be
no more than truth; in fact several more recent writers would
have benefited by consulting its laconic Latin notes. But how does
this austere work of scholarship, devoted to authors whose texts
present difficulties, tie up with the poet of *A Shropshire Lad*
(1896)?[53] Housman, as the present writer recollects from lectures
on Ovid, never introduced poetic gifts, general literary criticism,
mythological parallels, or any link between English and Latin
literature into the very minute textual criticism that he passed on
to his audience: in a difficult passage no more than seven or
eight lines might be covered in an hour. The jeers (not always
quite merited) at other scholars in his introduction often make
good reading:

> Other narrators of these events . . . mention the portent of
> bees swarming on the ensigns: Lucan mentions a different and
> supernatural portent, which they do not mention; and he was
> not such a bungler as to mix the two, festooning his sentient
> and prescient standards with clusters of hymenoptera, and
> setting their miraculous tears to trickle through the inter-
> stices of the insects.

But they are not Housman's greatest contribution to studies of
Lucan. His *forte* lies not only in the eradication of mistakes and
misconceptions arising in previous editions, but—and this is not
pedantry—in the establishing of punctuation. A rhetorical poet
like Lucan is ruined if his text is badly punctuated. Centuries of

inadequate punctuation in manuscripts and inferior punctuation in early editions had made much of the text far less pointed than it should be, or even distorted it. The footnotes reveal Housman's ability to weigh up manuscripts, even if he did not examine them himself, and to direct the reader briefly to the right sources of information. We must also not forget the astronomical notes, which are an indispensable part of the edition.

At least there is no doubt that Housman made a valuable contribution to classical scholarship. Whether he did to English poetry is a matter of taste. A recent verdict in an intentionally provocative book is: 'Housman's verse, bad as it is, is not even original to him';[54] the writer adds that he was heavily indebted to Shakespeare, Kipling, the Greek poets and Heine. The link between his poetical and scholarly activities lies not in any reminiscence of Lucan; indeed most of his poems[55] were written in the 1890s, whereas he was working on Lucan in the 1920s. Rather this link is to be found in his meticulous approach: as O. Skutsch puts it,[56] 'Almost every word that Housman wrote, however coolly controlled by the brain, vibrates with the peculiar passion which the passion of truth aroused in him.'

The other poet is Robert Graves, whose prose translation[57] appeared in 1956. In his stimulating, if provocative, introduction he considers Lucan 'the father of yellow journalism' (which is arguable), and admits a distaste for his poetry. Eager to avoid the 'wars more than civil on Emathian plains' type of opening, he starts his translation:

> The theme of my poem is the Civil War which was decided on the plains of Pharsalus in Thessaly; yet 'Civil War' is an understatement, since Pompey and Caesar, the opposing leaders, were not only fellow-citizens but relatives; the whole struggle indeed no better than one of licensed fratricide. I shall here describe how, after the breakdown of the First Triumvirate, . . .

It has often been noted that in the Middle Ages Lucan was looked on more as a historian than as a poet. Here we have a modern poet reverting to this conception, and interspersing what are virtually notes or loose paraphrases in the very pedestrian rendering. Not only have many of the phrases quoted above no actual equivalent in the Latin (though admittedly they are hinted at), but where are the English phrases corresponding to *populumque potentem* and *victrici dextra*? Unfortunately, too, there are inaccuracies in translation, introduction and notes. We are indebted to Robert Graves for making Lucan available to a much wider circle. But Lucan, despite many prosaic passages, is a poet, and one imbued with rhetoric; from Graves' rendering one would not imagine it. Peter Green writes:[58] 'To translate a poet into prose is a completely meaningless act, which implies a gross conceptual fallacy in the translator's mind as to the very nature of poetic expression and poetic logic.'

In conclusion, Lucan appealed to different ages for different qualities. In the Middle Ages he was almost a legendary figure. In early Elizabethan drama he was a quarry for battle scenes. To the writers of the Civil War and Commonwealth periods Lucan's subject was so close that this became the great age of his influence on English literature. Yet even earlier the theme of civil war had its impact, especially on Daniel, himself working on the Wars of the Roses. The eighteenth century respected Silver Latin poetry for its love of epigram. Since then, literature and classical scholarship have tended to part company. Housman belonged to the period when textual criticism was supreme. Today other aspects of the Greek and Latin classics are being increasingly studied, and there is clearly scope for much research on English poetry influenced directly or indirectly by Lucan.

ACKNOWLEDGMENTS

I am particularly indebted to Mr J. C. Maxwell of Balliol College, Oxford, who has made many suggestions. My colleague Dr E. T. Webb was good enough to assist me with the section on Shelley. I am also indebted to Professor D. R. Dudley for his kind help.

Notes

1 R. Ackermann, *Lucans Pharsalia in den Dichtungen Shelleys, mit einer Übersicht ihres Einflusses auf die englische Litteratur*, Progr. (Zweibrücken, 1896).

2 W. Fischli, *Studien zum Fortleben der Pharsalia des M. Annaeus Lucanus* (Lucerne, 1945).

3 *Versus de patribus, regibus et sanctis Euboricensis Ecclesiae*, line 1553, in *Mon. Germ. Hist., Poet. Lat. Aevi Carolini*, ed. E. Duemmler, 1.204.

4 Arnulfi Aurelianensis, *Glosule super Lucanum*, ed. Berthe M. Marti (American Academy in Rome, 1958).

5 Jessie Crosland, 'Lucan in the Middle Ages, with special reference to the Old French Epic', *Mod. Lang. Rev.* 25 (1930), 32–51; A. Belloni, 'Dante e Lucano', *Giorn. Storico della Lett. Ital.* 40 (1902), 120–39; V. Ussani, *Dante e Lucano*, Lectura Dantis (Rome, 1917); R. Newald, 'Nachleben der Antike (1920–29)', *Bursians Jahresber.* 232 (1931), 62; L. Hlaváček, 'Das Bild Caesars in der englischen Litteratur des M.-A.', thesis (Vienna 1958). For the debt of Petrarch's *Africa* to Lucan see R. T. Bruère, 'Lucan and Petrarch's *Africa*', *CPhil.* 56 (1961), 83–99.

6 E. F. Shannon, *Chaucer and the Roman Poets*, Harvard Studies in Comparative Literature 7 (1929), 333–9.

7 *Fall of Princes*, VI.2332ff, esp. 2377–80, 2493–9. Cf. W. F. Schirmer, *John Lydgate, a Study in the Culture of the fifteenth century*, trans. Ann E. Keep (London: Methuen, 1961), ch. 21. See A. Hortis, *Studi sulle opere latine di Boccaccio* (Trieste, 1839), 646ff; J. Raith, *Boccaccio in der englischen Litteratur von Chaucer bis Painters Palace of Pleasure*, Aus Schrifttum u. Sprache d. Angelsachsen 3 (Leipzig, 1936), 71–3. Boccaccio, *De Casibus Virorum Illustrium*, translated and supplemented by Laurent de Premierfait (Bruges, 1476 and Paris, 1483); the fall of Pompey is given in both editions, sometimes in the same words, sometimes in different.

8 *Old Calabria* (first pub. 1915), London: Secker, 1956 ed., 174.

9 *Early English Classical Tragedies*, ed. J. W. Cunliffe (Oxford, 1912), xc–xci, 217–96, 326–42.

10 The borrowings from Seneca are mostly mentioned by Cunliffe, but not those from Lucan, as pointed out in the review by G. C. Moore Smith, *Mod. Lang. Rev.* 8 (1913), 219–20; see also J. C. Maxwell, 'Lucan's first translator', *Notes & Queries* 192 (1947), 521–2, and 206 (1961), 397; O. A. W. Dilke, 'Thomas Hughes, Plagiarist', ibid. 208 (1963), 93–4; G. M. Logan, 'Hughes's use of Lucan' in *The Misfortunes of Arthur*, RES n.s. 20 (1969), 22–32. For early English dramas inspired by Seneca see B. R. Rees, 'English Seneca: a Preamble', *Greece and Rome* n.s. 16 (1969), 119–33.

11 W. Clemen, *English Tragedy before Shakespeare*, trans. T. S. Dorsch (London: Methuen, 1961), 85ff (the writer ignores the borrowings from Lucan); E. Walker, 'A possible interpretation of the *Misfortunes of Arthur*', *J. Engl. & Germanic Phil.* 24 (1925), 2.

12 L. C. Martin, 'Lucan-Marlowe? Chapman', *RES* 24 (1948), 317–21.

13 J. E. Ingledew, 'The date of composition of Chapman's *Caesar and Pompey*', *RES* n.s. 12 (1961), 144–59, writes (151): 'Chapman certainly had Lucan in front of him when writing certain scenes of the play, but only 28 lines out of a total of 2,085 can be attributed to him as a source.'

14 Edition of *The Civile Wars* by L. Michel (Yale, 1958); Joan Rees, *Samuel Daniel* (Liverpool, 1964)—does not mention Lucan; E. M. W. Tillyard, *The English Epic and its Background* (London, 1954), 322–37; L. F. Bell, 'The background of the minor English Renaissance epics', *ELH* 1 (1934), 63–89; G. Gregory Smith, *Elizabethan Critical Essays* (Oxford, 1904),

11.316; H. Nearing, *English Historical Poetry 1599–1641* (University of Pennsylvania, 1945).

15 Prop., 11.10.7. Thomas Freeman's comment on this is:

> Know, here I praise thee as thou wast in youth;
> *Venereous*, not mutinous as now.

16 Wrongly referred by Michel to the elder Cato.

17 See Tillyard, op. cit., 253, 322.

18 The fearlessness of Amyclas when Caesar knocked at the door impressed Dante, who alludes to it in *Par.*, xi.67–9.

19 Tillyard, op. cit., 324–5.

20 *Caesar* in Lucan fairly certainly refers to Julius Caesar; but Daniel may, like others, have understood it as referring to Nero.

21 R. W. Condee, 'Lodge and a Lucan passage from Mirandola', *Mod. Lang. Notes* 63 (1948), 254–6.

22 C. S. Brown, 'Lucan, Bacon and Hostages to Fortune', *Mod. Lang. Notes* 65 (1950), 114–15.

23 Michael Drayton, ed. Kathleen Tillotsen and B. H. Newdigate, vols. 2, 5 (Oxford, 1941).

24 H. Baker, *Induction to Tragedy* (Louisiana State University, 1939), 75; W. Blisset, 'Lucan's Caesar and the Elizabethan villain', *Stud. in Phil.* 53 (1956), 553–75, esp. 567; *The Works of Thomas Kyd*, ed. F. S. Boas (Oxford, 1901).

25 Sir A. W. Ward, *A History of English Dramatic Literature* (London, 1875), 11.223. For this and following plays see E. Köppel, *Quellenstudien zu den Dramen Ben Jonsons, John Marstons u. Beaumonts u. Fletchers*, Münchener Beitr. zur roman. u. engl. Philol. 11 (1890); *id.*, *Quellenstudien zu den Dramen George Chapmans, Philip Massingers u. John Fords*, Quellen u. Forschungen zur Sprach- u. Culturgesch. 82 (1874). The play, published about 1620, is most conveniently consulted in *Beaumont and Fletcher*, ed. A. R. Waller, vol. 3 (Cambridge, 1906), 300ff.

26 Ed. C. H. Herford and P. Simpson (Oxford, 1925–52); W. Blisset, 'Lucan's Caesar and the Elizabethan Villain', *Stud. in Phil.* 53 (1956), 553–75, esp. 571ff.

27 *Religio Medici*, I. xliv.

28 A. G. Chester, *Thomas May, man of letters, 1595–1650* (Philadelphia, 1932).

29 *The Hind and the Panther* (1687), ll.160–1.

30 R. T. Bruère, 'The Latin and English versions of Thomas May's *Supplementum Lucani*', *CPhil.* 44 (1949), 145–63, with text on 147.

31 *A continuation of the Subject of Lucan's Historicall Poem, till the Death of Julius Caesar.*

32 Bruère, art. cit., considers the internal evidence for the priority of the English version very fully. Some of the discrepancies could point the other way, but added to the external evidence some of the internal seems decisive in favour of his argument. In any case the chronology points strongly this way.

33 *Lives of the English Poets*, ed. B. Hill (Oxford, 1905), 1.13; Southey and Landor, 'Second Conversation', *Works* (London, 1846), II.170.

34 E. E. Duncan-Jones, '"Lycidas" and Lucan', *Notes & Queries* 201 (1956), 249; cf. Milton, *Poems*, ed. J. Carey and A. Fowler (London, 1968). There is a third Lycidas (Sannazaro, *De partu Virginis*, III.185ff) who is not wholly irrelevant.

35 *Ann.*, xv.70: *recordatus carmen a se compositum, quo vulneratum militem per eiusmodi mortis imaginem obisse tradiderat, versus ipsos rettulit.*

36 See pp. 62–9 above.

37 W. Blisset, 'Caesar and Satan', *J. Hist. Ideas* 18 (1957), 231. See also A. Thierfelder, 'Der Dichter Lucan', *Archiv f. Kulturgesch.* 25 (1935), 1–20, esp. 15: 'Es handelt sich bei Lucan mit einem Worte um ein Epos, welches Satan zum Helden hat, eine Verkörperung schlechthin des bösen Prinzips, die mit den geschichtlichen Julius Cäsar nur noch wenig Ähnlichkeit aufweist'; C. M. Bowra, *From Virgil to Milton* (Oxford, 1945), 220ff.

38 E. S. Le Comte, *A Milton Dictionary* (London, 1961). The name Demogorgon, evidently picked up from Lactantius' commentary by Conradus de Mure (c 1281), was introduced into Renaissance literature by Boccaccio, *Genealogia deorum*. English writers who use it include Spenser, Milton (*Prolusio* and *Paradise Lost*), Peacock and Shelley. See H. Fletcher, 'Milton's Demogorgon', *J. Engl. & Germanic Phil.* 57 (1958), 684–9, and for Shelley pp. 104–5 above.

39 Incorrectly scanned in both Conradus de Mure, *Fabularius seu repertorium vocabulorum* (Basle, c 1470), 4: *Demonibus gorgon hoc est terror demogorgon*; and Robert Greene, *Orlando*, 1164: *tuque, Demogorgon, qui noctis fata gubernas*, . . .

40 *Columbia Index* to *Paradise Lost*.

41 *The Poems and Letters of Andrew Marvell*, ed. H. M. Margoliouth, 2 vols (Oxford, 1927 and reprint); J. M. Wallace, *Destiny his Choice: the Loyalism of Andrew Marvell* (Cambridge, 1968); W. Blisset, 'Caesar and Satan', *J. Hist. Ideas* 18 (1957), 221–32.

42 R. H. Syfret, 'Marvell's "Horatian Ode"', *RES* n.s. 12 (1961), 160–72.

43 A borrowing from Sallust, *Catiline*, has also been noted: L. Proudfoot, 'Marvell, Sallust and the Horatian Ode', *Notes & Queries* 196 (1951), 434.

44 Syfret, art. cit., 171.

45 See I. Jack, *Augustan Satire* (Oxford, 1952), 23, n. 3; for Gorges' translation see p. 95 above.

46 F. Smithers, *The Life of Joseph Addison*, 2nd edn (Oxford, 1968).

47 E. Poetzsche, *Samuel Richardsons Belesenheit*, Kieler Studien zur englischen Philologie n.F.4 (Kiel, 1908), has not been seen by the present writer.

48 R. Ackermann, *Lucans Pharsalia in den Dichtungen Shelley's*, Progr. (Zweibrücken, 1896).

49 The only phrase of Keats' poetry thought to stem from Lucan is 'a shadow of a magnitude', which may have come from Shelley's 'his name that shadow of his withered might' (*Hellas*) rather than direct from *magni nominis umbra*. See P. Shorey, 'Keats and Lucan', *CPhil.* 22 (1927), 317.

50 R. Ackermann, 'Studien über Shelleys Prometheus Unbound', *Englische Studien* 16 (1892), 19–39; *Shelley: Poems published in 1820*, ed. A. M. D. Hughes (Oxford, 1910), 175; M. Castelain, 'Démogorgon, ou le barbarisme déifié', *BAGB* 36 (1932), 22–39; Shelley, *Prometheus Unbound*, ed. L. J. Zillman (University of Washington, Seattle, 1959), 313–20.

51 G. O. Trevelyan, *The Life and Letters of Lord Macaulay* (London, 1883), 1.467 n.1.

52 Ibid., 1.466–7.

53 For an outline of Housman's poetic and scholarly activities see I. Evans, *English Poetry in the Later Nineteenth Century*, 2nd edn (London, 1966), ch. 19 and bibliography, 466–7.

54 Brigid Brophy and others, *Fifty Works of English Literature we could do without* (London: Rapp, 1967), 102.

55 Including many of those in *Last Poems* (1922) and *More Poems* (1936).

56 *A. E. Housman* (London, 1960).

57 *Lucan, Pharsalia: dramatic episodes of the Civil Wars* (Penguin).

58 *Essays in Antiquity* (London: Murray, 1962), 209–10.

V

Structure in the Satires of Persius

Sarah Grimes

According to the *Vita*[1] ascribed to Probus, A. Persius Flaccus was born in A.D. 34 at Volaterrae in Etruria of an equestrian family, and died in A.D. 62. From the age of twelve he was educated at Rome where he came into contact with a number of distinguished men active in literature, philosophy and politics: Servilius Nonianus, the orator and historian whom the elder Pliny described as *princeps civitatis* (*N.H.*, XXVIII.29), consul in 35, and a member of one of the most illustrious families to have survived this far into the empire, is said to have been cherished as a father by Persius (*Vita*, line 18); Persius' acquaintances Lucan and Seneca were both members of the Stoic group whose opposition to Nero grew stronger as his reign advanced. There is no need to mention Seneca's major role in politics until A.D. 62, and the fact that Lucan enjoyed the Emperor's friendship from A.D. 60.[2] Both perished in the Pisonian conspiracy of A.D. 65. Thrasea Paetus, Persius' kinsman through marriage, was also a central figure in the opposition. Consul in 56, he wrote a life of the younger Cato (Plutarch, *Cato*, 25; 37) which, in the circumstances, could only be inflammatory; in the senate he insisted on the right to free discussion (Tacitus, *Ann.*, XIII.49; IV.48f; XV.20f) and on the occasion after Agrippina's death when Nero convened the senate to damn her name (Tacitus, *Ann.*, XIV.12.1) Paetus firmly condemned the motion by walking out; in A.D. 66, after some years of conspicuous absence from the senate (Tacitus, *Ann.*, XVI.21ff), he was accused of treason and allowed to choose his own death. The Stoic group was held together by family ties as much as by philosophical tenets, and Paetus was married to Arria, the daughter of the famous A. Caecina Paetus who had opposed Claudius; Arria was related to Persius and it was through this

relationship that Persius enjoyed almost ten years of close friendship with Paetus and accompanied him on journeys (*Vita*, lines
30–2).[3] Even Persius' revered teacher, L. Annaeus Cornutus, was
later exiled by Nero, in A.D. 65, for speaking too freely (Dio,
LXII.29); it is not known how close he was to Nero and how active
his opposition was during Persius' lifetime.

Yet in spite of such committed company, Persius makes no
political criticisms or allusions in his satires, and avoids all
references to specific contemporary events, institutions or celebri-
ties. The only exceptions are the mention of Caligula's *ovatio* after
his 'victory' over the Germans and Britons, in Satire VI.43ff, an
event which took place when the poet was five years old; less
precisely, the mention of Judaism in Satire V.179ff; and the quotations of bad contemporary poetry in Satire I.[4] Elsewhere, social
institutions are treated in very broad terms so that the satirical
point is directed rather at the general tenor of human life than
at the particular society which produced it. For example, patronage in Satire I, religion and superstitious practices in Satire II,
and legal freedom in Satire V.73ff, are not given a historical
setting with a wealth of proper names or illustrations taken from
contemporary or recent events—as is Juvenal's technique—
but are related to a moral point and are illustrated by invented
details.

Whether because of legal restraint and fears of public hostility,
as Horace, Persius and Juvenal all take care to stress,[5] or by the
conventions of the genre, Roman satire after Lucilius was not
poetry of invective and it is not strange that Persius avoids it. But
the point in question here is much broader than simply the lack of
invective. For both Horace and Juvenal draw their material from
the society around them and the world depicted in their poetry is a
social, and sometimes a political world: Horace introduces his
friends (and enemies, though less exalted men) by name, by
describing 'personal' details of his life in the high circle of
Maecenas, the bustle of Rome, and the quiet spirit of his home;
Juvenal depicts the notorious of the previous generations to
create a picture of a society corrupt from top (Domitian and
Messalina) to bottom (freedmen and *graeculi*).

There is no equivalent in the satires of Persius. Named contemporaries are rare. Macrinus, Caesius Bassus and Cornutus
appear in the frames of the poems—the first two as addressees of

Satires II and VI respectively, the third as a dramatic character in Satire V—but not as elements in the poems' world which give it its particular colouring and subject matter. Glyco, a tragic actor who was manumitted by Nero, is mentioned at Satire v.9; Attius Labeo (1.4,50), Masurius (v.90) and the *magni Messalae lippa propago* (i.e. L. Aurelius Cotta Messalinus, II.72) were perhaps contemporaries or were recently dead;[6] of Staius (II.19 and 22) and Vettidius (IV.25) nothing is known. Attempts were made to find allusions to Nero: the *Vita* (lines 56–60) records that Cornutus, as literary executor, amended line 121 of Satire I, which read *auriculas asini Mida rex habet*, to *auriculas quis non habet* because he feared that the allusion would be too pointed. Also, the Scholia attribute the examples of bad poetry quoted at Satire 1.93–5 and 99–103 to Nero. Such assertions cannot be finally verified or refuted, but are in a high degree improbable[7] and would seem to have been prompted by some uneasiness at the lack of contemporary point in Persius' work.

Otherwise personal proper nouns, which are the most obvious device for evoking a specific historical society, are relatively infrequent, and the worlds they refer to are too remote from the poet's own times and from each other to help create a coherent picture of a society. We are referred to the far distant past with Cincinnatus (*Quinti*, 1.73), Cato (III.45) and Ennius (VI.10), and to the Greek past with Arcesilas (III.79), Solon (III.79), and the whole setting of Satire IV. Other names are mythical (e.g. Brisaeus, 1.79) or purely fictional (e.g. Publius, v.74; Pulfennius, v.190; Tadius, VI.66). A substantial number of personal names are literary, at one remove from the real world: Davus, Chrysis and Chaerestratus (v.161ff) come from Menander; Pedius (1.85), Nerius (II.14), Natta (III.31), Dama (v.76) etc. from Horace's Satires.[8]

The nature of these references, the rarity of named contemporaries, the absence of particular social or political references, make it clear that the material of the poems is not drawn from the fabric of a specific society. And consequently the world depicted and interpreted in them is far from being that of an integrated, well-grounded society, let alone the society of contemporary Rome or provincial Italy.

It is not my purpose to account for this choice of material— which could only be done by investigating the personality of the poet or the social and political circumstances of his time—but to see whether or not it is coherently worked out in the poetry.

The argument of Satire 1 is essentially *anti*social, and thus complements the avoidance of social and topical material. The main character of this dramatic poem vigorously rejects the literary standards of the people and asserts his own, much higher, ones. He will have few readers for his works, the poem continues, but this is no cause for regret since the general run of society has no judgment but thinks in terms only of praise and fame. Such thinking is both absurd, since praise and fame are in the long term valueless, and false as a measure of artistic merit, since the patron-client relationship creates ulterior motives. There follows an attack on contemporary literature—smooth-sounding trivia, barbarous confusions of archaisms, affected conceits in place of solid argument (language is no longer a means of communication with the style determined by the particular situation, but is an instrument for display), and flaccid bombast. Finally, satire is defended by precedents and for its qualities of sharpness and integrity. Thus the main speaker in the poem is characterized by an individualistic disposition, and his withdrawal from the scramble for popularity is fully justified by the corruption of those who confer it.[9]

The point is made decisively in the vivid dialogue with which the poem opens:

> o curas hominum! o quantum est in rebus inane!
> 'quis leget haec?' min tu istud ais? nemo hercule. 'nemo?'
> vel duo vel nemo.   'turpe et miserabile.'   quare?
> ne mihi Polydamas et Troiades Labeonem
> praetulerint? nugae.   (1-5)

> (O the troubles of humanity! How great a void there is in life.
> 'Who's going to read that?' Are you asking me that? Why,
> no one. 'No one?' Or one or two at the most. 'How shameful and disgraceful.' Why so? Because Polydamas and the
> Trojan women might prefer Labeo to me? Nonsense!)

Here we have a dramatic situation involving two speakers (although this has been questioned),[10] one in the character of a satirist justifying his work,[11] the other his critic. Something of their attitudes and their interrelationship is economically conveyed through the aggressive and forceful expressions of the satirist character, peremptory in his dismissal of the shallow and conventional responses of surprise and regret which the weaker interlocutor puts to him. It is clear from the weighty style and sense of the opening line[12] and from the question which follows it that the one character is reading his poetry and is interrupted by the other: thus the characters are not presented in a void but are placed in particular circumstances; and, moreover, circumstances which are appropriate to occasioning the harangue which forms the rest of the poem, treating the decline of literary standards and the general lack of judgment shown by writers and supporters of literature alike. This setting is, however, only suggested and not developed: it is not revealed, for example, whether the two are speaking in private, or whether the interrupter is one of an audience present at a public recitation.

The function of a dramatic structure is not an easy thing to describe. We may think of a poem in general terms as being a verbal act, thereby entailing a speaker (or writer, in an epistolary poem) and a listener or reader. These 'fictional' speakers and listeners are said to form the poem's 'fictional' or 'dramatic situation' (and are sometimes introduced by the device of a 'frame', as in Satire i—a short passage at the beginning, and sometimes also at the end of a poem explaining the who, what, why and where). Immense variations in the roles they play and in the degree of overtness with which they appear in the poem are possible. In most secondary epic poetry, for example, the listeners are almost entirely latent, perhaps because it tends to the universal, and even the speaker—in the role of a story-teller—is generally concealed behind his narrative, appearing in the poem only in the form of sympathy or empathy influencing a description (and in such editorial passages as *arma virumque cano*). Dramatic poetry is characterized by the fact that both speaker and listener are brought fully and overtly into the body of the poem; the dramatic poem, that is, does not lie in a more or less implicit situation, but the situation is overtly contained in the poem. The effect of this is that the dramatic poem is a much denser structure than its non-dramatic counterpart, in the sense of its being a move away from the relatively open-ended position in which we, the readers, are overhearing a speech, towards an enclosed situation which, by its self-containment, creates an illusion of full-scale activity, of things happening. So we are not just eavesdroppers over the shoulder of a somewhat shadowy and intangible fictional listener, but spectators, so to speak, of an inward-looking whole, complete in itself. Style, tone, development of thought, and the point of view from which descriptions are taken are all provided with a concrete reference, namely the characters. This has already been seen in the first lines of Satire 1, where the varying tones and sequence of ideas have been located in the attitudes of the two speakers and in their interrelationship. Lack of such concreteness in poems like Persius', which treat of formal ethical themes, or develop as arguments (as opposed to a story or a description), would probably have led to an abstract generalizing spirit which most satirists tried to avoid because it was removed from the business of everyday life. Or it could create a sermon which easily becomes diffuse when it is not felt to relate to a particular occasion: the dramatic poem avoids this by bringing the fictional listener fully into the poem so that the moral themes are expressed, as it were, for his benefit and thus are integrated into the poem rather than referring outwards with the pragmatic aim of converting someone.

Finally, the dramatic structure aids the development of the argument by putting the question and answer process of thought into an external form, which is more accessible to the imagination. The personality or attitude of the interlocutor can provide further arguments, if he is sympathetic to the main character's views; or stand as living proof of the satirical contention, if he is hostile or himself corrupt; or expose and ridicule the main character if the positions are reversed; or simply put questions and draw out the main speaker, if he is neutral.[13]

In the first satire the adversary is not thoroughly defined and it could hardly be said that he plays any of these parts. He tends to be manipulated by the satirist character, who invests him with contemptible views and faults of judgment which the adversary has not himself expressed or shown. W. S. Anderson[14] relates this to Stoic doctrines, seeing the satirist character as 'the steady incarnation of *sapientia*' whose sardonic, contemptuous attitude towards the adversaries and illustrative examples which he cites is an expression of the absolute distinction made by Stoics between the *sapiens*, who has all the virtues, and the *stulti*, who have none. After the swift interchange with which Satire 1 starts, the satirist character at once assumes the dominant role with an un-interrupted speech which lasts until line 24, while the illusion of a dialogue is maintained through the second person singular verbs (*accedas*, 6, *castiges*, 7 and *te quaesiveris*, 7) which recall the presence of the interlocutor. In lines 13ff the speaker gives a description of a recitation, beginning with the first person plural *scribimus inclusi*. G. L. Hendrickson[15] calls this a 'satirical exaggeration', a tech-nique in which the satirist includes himself among the objects of his criticism for an effect of urbanity (or, I would suggest in this case, an effect of sarcasm). The technique can clearly be seen in the preceding lines where the speaker's act of perception is put in the singular, *aspexi* (10), and the objects of his perception in the plural, *facimus* and *sapimus* (10–11); the plural then carries over by association to the listener, *ignoscite* (11).

The generalized introduction *scribimus inclusi* suggests that the description is to be of an illustration of a common type of be-haviour (in the style of 'this is the sort of thing we do'), conceived in the speaker's imagination for the benefit of the adversary; and the following words continue the same generalizing spirit—'We shut ourselves away to write—this one verse, that one prose.' Then, however, as the details of the recitation emerge, there comes a change of spirit whereby the illustration's explanatory function with respect to the speaker's argument becomes subordinate to the description itself:

> grande aliquid quod pulmo animae praelargus anhelet.
> scilicet haec populo pexusque togaque recenti
> et natalicia tandem cum sardonyche albus
> sede leges celsa   (14–17)

(Something sublime for a copious wind-bag of a lung to wheeze out. All spruced up and white in a new toga and sardonyx birthday ring, you will read this to the people at last, from a lofty seat.)

After the introduction the tense moves to the future (*leges*, 17) which denotes a more positive view of the topic—treating it, that is, as something precise that *will* happen rather than something that could happen or happens as a general rule. A further degree of intensification follows with the use of present tenses preceded by *tunc* (*intrant* and *scalpuntur*, 21, *colligis*, 22): the occasion of the recitation is, in the speaker's imagination, brought down the time scale from the future to the present. Similarly, there is a change in the subject, from the general 'we (all)' to 'you' (singular: *leges* and *colligis*) with the effect of narrowing the general down to the particular and of converting the hypothetical into the physically present—namely, the interlocutor. It is almost as if the speaker were describing his own surroundings and what his interlocutor is doing.

What seems to have determined the form of this description is that as the speaker builds up the details of the picture—the prima donna-like lung capacity, the clean new toga and the birthday ring—there is a progression in which these details, because they are depicted with such precision, assume a substantiality which gives them a more 'real' status than that of thoughts in the speaker's mind. The syntactical structure therefore cannot remain that of the hypothetical and general, because the recitation is no longer viewed in this light.

All the details are concrete and their particularity draws attention to the description itself and away from what it contributes to the argument, which is that literature is being debased to the level of vanity, sensationalism and titillation. We do not shut ourselves away to write 'something grand to recite', nor 'something grand to pour forth with pride', but 'something grand which the lung overswollen with breath (or spirit) wheezes out' (*grande aliquid quod pulmo animae praelargus anhelet*, 14). Further, the line gains added force from the double meaning of *animae* (cf. Horace, *Od.*, 1.XII.37f, *animaeque magnae prodigum*); from the use of a rare word, *praelargus* (Lewis and Short cite only one other instance of its use, by the early fourth-century poet Iuvencus); and from the metrical position of *anhelet* so that accent and ictus both fall on the aspirated vowel, thus making sound echo sense. The subject of the illustration is described by pinpointing two details of his appearance, each of which is particularized: he is not just 'dressed in a new toga' but is 'spruced up' (*pexus*) and 'white' (*albus*) 'in his new toga', while his *natalicia . . . sardonyche* is significant by its being such a small thing to be described. In each case the entity to be described is not treated abstractly for its artistic or ethical qualities—the *grande aliquid* is not described as turgid or bombastic; the reciter is not described as proud or as inadequate to his job—but the abstract quality is conveyed metaphorically by means of physical objects. Further, these are so fully described that their literal value as pure description has greater weight than their value as imagery, particularly since the tenor of the image (bombast, pride etc.) is nowhere explicitly stated. The texture is made so dense by graphic minutiae that the imaginary status of the objects is obscured amongst the mass of closely observed appearances.

Thus by emphasis on the substantive detail the concrete force of the description surpasses its setting in the speaker's imagination and assumes a strength of reality equal to that of the dramatic frame itself. The structure of the image and the overall dramatic structure no longer reflect the same illusion; a tension exists between them which both creates a quality of tautness and complexity, and hints at an exposure of the dramatic illusion. For the illustration has created a slight doubt as to which is the more important, in which area of life the dramatic action is to take place—within the main speaker's mind, or between the main speaker and his interlocutor; whether, in fact, any distinction obtains between these two areas of experience.

After being denounced the interlocutor makes an attempt at self-defence (24ff) with the argument that learning is useless unless its product—poetry—is made known to others.[16] The main speaker dismisses this with contempt and the interlocutor takes up the lamer defence that it is 'nice' to be pointed out as a famous man and to have one's work learnt by schoolchildren, to which the main speaker replies with an illustration of a bloated amateur poet at a party, written in the third person, *hic aliquis ... eliquat* (32–5). It is not, however, introduced as a hypothetical instance (in the manner of 'For example, suppose that someone does such-and-such . . .'). Instead, the speaker creates a picture which he holds up for inspection:

> ecce inter pocula quaerunt
> Romulidae saturi quid dia poemata narrent.   (30–1)

(Behold the bloated sons of Romulus asking over their cups what heavenly poesy has to report.)

This introduction avoids the didactic analytical approach of the hypothetical form, where the moral point is all too obvious. In fact, the liveliness of this form becomes very apparent when the affronted poet of the illustration rises from the party, so to speak, and reproves the speaker for his hostile criticism:

> 'rides', ait, 'et nimis uncis
> naribus indulges. an erit qui velle recuset
> os populi meruisse et cedro digna locutus
> linquere nec scombros metuentia nec tus?'   (40–3)

('You're mocking', he says, 'and you're too ready to curl up your nose. Is there anyone who would deny that he wants to have earned a place in people's talk; who would deny that, when he has spoken things which deserve cedar oil, he wants to leave behind him work that won't fear to become the wrapping paper of mackerels and incense?')

The main speaker is quoting his creation's views almost as if the latter were present in the dramatic frame and could hear what was being said about him (but only almost, since the main speaker reports the speech—as *ait* indicates—and thus the creation does not become entirely independent of his creator).[17]

The idea which this illustration of the dilettantes' party expresses is, basically, that praise is trivial and not worth pursuing when life is viewed in its entirety, as an interval of time ending in death. In addition a comment is made on the present state of literature because in this particular case the praise given to the poet is undeserved since, first, his poetry is bad, and, second, social circumstances make praise obligatory. This implied social criticism is subtly conveyed in the two parallel clauses with their slight difference in degree of affirmation—*adsensere viri* (36) and *laudant convivae* (38)—the poet's compeers just give approval while the clients praise.[18]

His disapproving attitude towards the mincing poet involves the speaker in the illustration, thus permitting a closer point of view than the imaginary existence of the scene warrants. This is expressed partly in the quality of description, mainly in the form of the whole. When the poet is first picked out from his company, one precise visual detail is given to characterize him, *cui circum umeros hyacinthina laena est* (32), and then attention is focused on his manner of speech which is evoked with great immediacy by drawing on sound values (particularly in *Phyllidas, Hypsipylas, vatum et plorabile siquid/eliquat ac tenero subplantat verba palato,* 34–5).

Yet the quality of description has less density and concrete force than the earlier recitation scene, for it is interspersed with comments and mocking analyses so that the line of argument and the ideas illustrated in the passage are kept in mind, rather than allowing the scene and characters depicted to exist as independent beings. This interpretative element is seen in the explicit judgment of *rancidulum* (33), in the terms *tenero* and *subplantat* (35) which are weighted with adverse criticism, and in the two sarcastic questions (36–7 and 38–40) which draw a conclusion from the group's behaviour. The general form of the illustration—introduced by *ecce* and concluding with the poet's reply to the speaker—does give a sense of present immediacy, the idea that the speaker's imaginary world is of a strength to equal the external 'real' position in which he is placed in the situation of the dramatic frame. By expressing the internal viewpoint this form complements and deepens the non-social outlook of the theme which rejects public opinion as a standard of judgment and, by implication, replaces it with a personal assessment—for which the speaker is accused by the poet of excessive austerity, of lacking consideration for natural feelings: that is, his isolation is emphasized.

The suggestion, the general tone and balance of this and the earlier illustration, which function to confuse distinctions between the imagined and the actual, prepare the way for an explicit disruption of the dramatic illusion, which occurs immediately after the party illustration:

quisquis es, o modo quem ex adverso dicere feci,   (44)

(Whoever you are, you whom I have just made to speak for the opposition.)

If *quisquis es* refers to anyone at all, it must be either the dramatic adversary or the poet figure of the *exemplum*. Whichever we choose (although the form of the line makes a choice unnecessary) the external dramatic situation has been absorbed into the speaker's thought process. For if we take the first possibility, then the words *quem ex adverso dicere feci* make the adversary a creation of the main character, and this breaks down the externalized dramatic illusion of two independent characters with which the poem began. If *quisquis es* refers to the poet figure, it follows that the interlocutor of the rest of the poem is this same poet who originated from the main speaker's imagination; for the lines following, with their wealth of imperatives and questions, are strongly dramatic and therefore the subject of line 44 continues as a dramatic character. Either way, then, there has been a progression from an externalized situation with spatial illusions to the expression of thoughts dramatically, and then to the use of this dramatic level in the dialogue structure.

After such an admission the dramatic fabric will inevitably be ambiguous. Thus, as the speaker progresses in his consideration of the value of praise, discovering that it is bestowed irrespective of literary merit but according to the poet's social status, the adversary gradually assumes the form of a poetaster patron (53-7) who expects flattery in return for his patronage. The speaker disregards the power and social position of the patron and tells him the real truth about himself, a truth that is far from flattering (You're a fool, old bald-head', 56), so that once again the speaker is in opposition to his society. Whether the patron is an imaginary creation invented for the occasion, or whether he is the ambiguous interlocutor forced into a role, is an irrelevant question since the distinction between the two worlds has broken down. The identity of the second character is lost and what remains is the main speaker and his ideas, which are given life by being set in a dramatic form.

The poem continues in dialogue form as particular literary faults are treated: first the contrived effect caused by poet's being motivated by a desire for fame rather than by self-expression, then excessive smoothness and lack of vigour. In line 88 we have a shift from third to second person:

> quippe et, cantet si naufragus, assem
> protulerim? cantas, cum fracta te in trabe pictum
> ex umero portes? (88-90)

(And if a shipwrecked sailor comes begging with a song am I to pull out a penny? You sing do you, when you carry from your shoulders a painting of yourself in a shipwreck?)

This shift in person should be distinguished from the traditional apostrophe, for there is a difference in the degree of dramatic development. With the apostrophe there is no genuine feeling that the subject is present to the dramatic speaker; it is just a device by which attention is drawn to a point by treating it in a slightly more emotional manner than a third person description or comment. In the case of the sailor turned professional beggar, the second-person concrete description of his physical appearance gives some illusion of presence because it suggests that the speaker is describing what he is seeing. In lines 53–7 the illusion is even stronger since the subject addressed is made to speak. (Lucan very often apostrophizes Caesar, but he does not make Caesar reply.) Persius does use the apostrophe on occasions and the difference between it and his more idiosyncratic dramatizations is clear: for example, at 58, *o Iane*, or 61, *vos, o patricius sanguis . . . posticae occurrite sannae*, where in each case, there is little or no development; or at 125 where the speaker apostrophizes his possible reader, *aspice haec, si forte aliquid decoctius audis*, and then goes on to speak of him in the third person.

In summary, Satire 1 is constructed on a dramatic basis, although the place in which the conversation takes place is not particularized. Nonetheless, the frame provides a set of references in the characters and their literary activities which serve to integrate the style, themes and mode of argument by providing a base for them. Thus the poem becomes dense and self-sufficient. Then, as the dialogue advances, this basic illusion is undermined through the manipulation of the adversary by the main speaker, so that the dramatic unity is felt to lie in the latter's imagination creating all the objects of his derision. This is made explicit by the line *quisquis es, o modo quem ex adverso dicere feci*: on the one hand, the interlocutor, whoever he is, is shown to have been created by the speaker, instead of being an independent character of the same standing as the speaker; on the other hand, he is *treated* as an independent dramatic character by being addressed, questioned and even made to reply. The poem remains dramatic, but its setting seems to be the main speaker's imagination, rather than any physical 'real' world. This is prepared for by the surface density, both in the nature of the descriptions and imagery, and in the rich variety of dramatized illustrations which are presented not with the potential subjunctive, but with the indicative second person as of something present in the dramatic setting.

The change in illusion expresses structurally the attitude of the speaker and the implications of the themes. The principal line of thought running through the poem is that the writers and supporters of literature are corrupting that same literature with their bad motives of ambition and desire for glory, fame and praise. These motives are created or nourished by the social climate—in particular, the decline of recitations into an occasion for titillation (13–23); the system of patronage with its attendant vices of flattery (30–40) and self-deception (49–57); and in general, the lack of sincerity (85–91) and manliness (103–6). All this is attacked and condemned by the main speaker. In the satire's 'positive' part[19]—which is significantly short (123–34) and expressed negatively (*non hic qui . . . nec qui . . .*)—he defines the reader who would enjoy his work: the man who also enjoys Greek Old Comedy; not the man who mocks at Greek sandals; nor the one who shouts 'One-eyed' at a one-eyed man[20] and has an exalted opinion of himself because he has the authority of a minor and provincial official position; nor the man who ridicules Greek learning and philosophy. The negative form in which the readership is defined, the implication that the rejected categories cover a large section of society, recalls the opening expectation of the number of readers, *vel duo vel nemo* (3). It can be deduced from the nature of the criticism that the basis of this rejection, both here and throughout the poem, is the perversion of values found in and caused by the society, the disregard for the inner qualities of integrity and respect for truth and knowledge. With this basis the dramatic structure harmonizes, since, in undermining the interpersonal relationship of the two characters and replacing it with the dramatized ideas of one of them, it gives the effect of subordinating the external social world to the thoughts, feelings, values—in short, the mental life—of the individual. The structure, then, constitutes an undercurrent of suggestion which complements the stated arguments and views of the satire. And finally, there is harmony of tone, as well as of implication, between the two levels: the device of disrupting the illusion is a violent one which dislocates one's orientation and upsets one's belief in how the poem is set; equally violent is the speaker's strongly felt rejection of almost all that he sees around him.[21]

Satires II and VI are not dramatic poems, for only one character speaks and the other is addressed by name in a fairly formal manner which implies a written, not a spoken, form of communication.

Satire VI has been described as the most Horatian of Persius' works, in verbal allusions, in its themes, and in the persona of the writer.[22] It is interesting for our purpose as an exception, a contrast. In the introductory frame the geographical situations of the fictional writer and reader are described in such a way that it is made clear, by the distance between them, that the form is epistolary. The statement of place creates an epistolary illusion of considerable strength, which is increased by the 'personal' details which the writer develops from the introduction:

> hic ego securus volgi et quid praeparet auster
> infelix pecori, securus et angulus ille
> vicini nostro quia pinguior, etsi adeo omnes
> ditescant orti peioribus, usque recusem
> curvus ob id minui senio aut cenare sine uncto (12–16)

(Here I am safe from the crowd and from what the calamitous south wind might have in store for the herd, safe also from fretting because that corner of our neighbour's is more fertile than ours. Even if every low born upstart were to grow rich, yet still I would refuse to be bowed down and grow old before my time or dine without oil on account of this.)

From here it is an easy generalization to moral topics, the value and right use of material wealth, and thence to a discussion of inheritances.

As with Satire I, the various aspects of the poem are closely integrated with the fictional situation, so that the illusion of the latter and the unity of the former are strengthened: style, tone, imagery are such as a letter-writer might use, and therefore the impression that it is a letter lasts beyond the explanatory frame; and because these qualities are all rooted in the epistolary situation they have a unifying base. For example, the recurring image of land and sea[23]—which is variously used to express the security of true possessions as opposed to the hazards of acquisition for its own sake, and the manly and stable qualities associated with the countryside as opposed to foreign extravagance—is already introduced in the scene descriptions of the frame. Bassus has withdrawn from winter to the warmth and security, it is implied, of his Sabine hearth:

admovit iam bruma foco te, Basse, Sabino? (1)

(Has winter already sent you to your Sabine hearth, Bassus?)

And the writer's Ligurian retreat hints at a contrast to be developed later of land (warmth) to sea (cold):

mihi nunc Ligus ora
intepet hibernatque meum mare (6–7)

(For me the Ligurian coast now grows warm and my sea is wintering.)

Similarly, the relaxed tone of one communicating with a friend is maintained more or less consistently through the fluid development of thought and the expansive expression of ideas. The progression from describing his location to describing his feelings about it is a natural one; and an easy transition from this to the generalizations which follow is provided by the statement *discrepet his alius* (18). The admission is almost benevolent. It creates, by its sense and by its simplicity and syntactical isolation, a reflective pause and a link between the thought which gave rise to it and that which follows from it, reading as a sympathetic hesitation to apply one's own views too widely. It leads to the consideration of two extremes, the parsimonious and the spendthrift, and then the middle way: *utar ego, utar* (22). The idea that wealth is to be used, not hoarded, is then justified by an appeal to common sense—there is another harvest in the fields. An objection is raised (as the particle *at* (27) signifies) that one should keep something in reserve for emergencies, a friend who is shipwrecked, for example, and loses all his property. The writer turns this argument against the objector with the conclusion that, in this case, one should give him some of one's land (*caespite vivo*, 31). But this raises the further objection that one is giving to another what belongs to one's heir, who will then begrudge the funeral expenses. The theme of inheritance occupies the rest of the poem: the writer is prepared to test his heir for signs of rapacity, and if he fails the test another heir can easily be found, for all men are brothers if one traces ancestry back far enough; inheritance is a gift whose sum is all that remains on the giver's death and not what he possessed, and perhaps spent, during his life. The final plea is to live freely, without the ambition to be richer than everyone else.

Two points emerge from the consideration of the themes: first, there is a development of ideas rather than an expansion of one single idea or a collection of unrelated points; second, the development is associative and fluid. The two together promote a coherent thematic level so that there is one continuous thread running from the setting up of the frame to the final line. The theme is not intensely or abstractly argued, but, because it is associative and unified and without the violence of leaps of thought or of juxtaposed disparities, the thematic level is located in the relaxed, contemplative mood of one withdrawn from the winter and writing a letter to a friend.

Similarly, the imagery on the whole avoids the highly-wrought involvement which was so marked in Satire 1. For example:

> at vocat officium, trabe rupta Bruttia saxa
> prendit amicus inops remque omnem surdaque vota
> condidit Ionio, iacet ipse in litore et una
> ingentes de puppe dei iamque obvia mergis
> costa ratis lacerae;   (27–31)

(But duty calls: a friend's ship has been wrecked, destitute he clings to the Bruttian rocks and the Ionian sea has buried all his possessions and his unavailing prayers; he lies on the beach together with the huge gods from the stern and the ribs of the torn ship which are now attracting the sea-gulls;)

The description is conceptual and visual: it does not include for example, the friend's agony or fear as he clings to the rocks, nor are there obviously empathetic details (such as rags or tear-stained face). This lack of emotional delineation avoids a sense of close involvement. Also, the point of view from which the description is taken is a distant one: there are no *small* details of the friend's appearance as he lies on the shore, and the proper names *Bruttia* and *Ionio* also convey a sense of distance by placing the scene in its geographical context. The effect is to create a clear picture of setting and circumstances with the feeling more of reportage than of immediate presence. If the description is compared to the recitation scene in Satire 1.13–23, the qualities of the former will become more apparent: there, each point to be described is some aspect of physical appearance and is made un-usually specific by the addition of concrete details; here, each of the main nouns has but one qualifying adjective, and not neces-sarily one that adds to the concrete image—the friend is *inops* (which describes his plight, not his physical being) and he loses *omnemque rem* (not, for example, his full coffer and every single one of his fine pots and pans). In the recitation scene the word order is convoluted and the imagery complicated with the mixed meta-phors *liquido cum plasmate guttur/mobile conlueris* and *auriculis alienis colligis escas*; in the shipwreck scene the word order is simple to the point of severity, particularly in the first two lines where each adjective is placed next to its noun, so that line 28, after the first word, consists solely of this pattern; and the only complexities of figure are the zeugma *remque omnem surdaque vota/condidit Ionio*, the transferred epithet *surdaque vota*, and the metonymy *dei* for *deorum effigies*—none of which does violence to the sense. They do not create a picture whose force lies in some disturbing physical per-version, but suggest the ironical point that the man's prayers are unheard and drowned, while the gods themselves are washed up safely onto the shore: they enliven the description by their im-plicit comment on the disaster without obscuring its significance for the argument. The conceptual element in the details *inops* and *remque omnem* also points clearly to the illustration's purpose and its place in the themes. Furthermore, the description does not stand isolated from its context: the conclusion drawn from it continues the image:

> nunc et de caespite vivo
> frange aliquid, largire inopi, ne pictus oberret
> caerulea in tabula. (31–3)

(Now break off a piece of your fertile land, bestow it on the destitute man to prevent him from having to wander around with a painting of himself on a sea-green board.)

and the argument continues on the same particular level (because of such generosity the heir will not provide a proper funeral, and so on). The illustration is not a metaphor but fits smoothly into the narrative on its literal meaning as a particular case of an emergency.

For all these reasons—the strongly built-up frame and the continuation of its illusion through the tone, the expression of themes, the quality of the description and the continuity they have with their contexts—the epistolary illusion is strong enough to contain the dramatic element of the dialogue which the writer sometimes uses to develop his argument. Moreover, this dramatic element remains fairly embryonic, as the following analysis will show. The result is that there is no disruption of the original fictional situation in the manner of Satire I. (This is not to imply, I should stress, that one is therefore a better poem than the other. The difference is one of kind, not value; and in each poem the structure is in harmony with the general tone.)

A singular imperative is used at line 25: *messe tenus propria vive.* Because it follows a passage of ethical argument, it has the rhetorical effect of imparting a more urgent note to the recommendation than an impersonal passive would do. The second person implicit in the imperative is taken up in *quid metuas* (26) and then in *frange aliquid, largire inopi* (32), and a rudimentary question and answer sequence follows. There is no characterization to establish the identity of an adversary and no suggestion of a change in the circumstances by means of descriptions, which would give scope for fully dramatic dialogue. In line 41 the heir is introduced:

> at tu, meus heres
> quisquis eris, paulum a turba seductior audi.   (41–2)

(But you my heir, whoever you may be, come a little away from the crowd and listen.)

While some illusion of his actual existence is perhaps implied in the spatial quality of *a turba seductior*, the qualification *quisquis eris* gives him a hypothetical standing; and while the rest of the poem is addressed to him, he does not himself answer back: words and reactions are attributed to him by the writer, the latter thereby remaining in charge.

Finally, by the nature of its illusion, the letter form can sustain without confusion this type of imaginary conversation more easily than can the dramatic form. For in the dramatic poem the main character is a performer within the illusion that the poem is composed of a conversation between himself and another; if he then starts creating his own characters with whom to talk, one's belief in the scene between the two characters is undermined. In the epistolary poem, on the other hand, the main 'character' has the role of a writer setting thoughts on paper; if *he* then creates his own illusion of a conversation or argument and characters to take part in it, there is no contradiction between the epistolary illusion and the illusion of the dialogue, since both illusions are set in—or at least derive from—the writer's mind.

Satire II is different. It opens with a formal address, *hunc, Macrine, diem numera meliore lapillo*, and continues with an honorific description of Macrinus. The formality suggests a written, as opposed to a conversational, communication; and the address and description suggest that the poet is motivated by the wish to honour Macrinus. The frame does not establish the relative positions of writer and recipient, the circumstances which gave rise to the desire to honour Macrinus or how well they know each other, or much about their characters—only that it is Macrinus' birthday (1–2) and that he is an honourable man (3–4). The fictional situation of the communication is barely disclosed, with the result that there is no strong illusion in the frame of a concrete source for theme and style.

After addressing Macrinus, the writer builds up an illustration of the hypocrisy typical of many people:

> haut cuivis promptum est murmurque humilisque susurros
> tollere de templis et aperto vivere voto.
> 'mens bona, fama, fides', haec clare et ut audiat hospes;
> illa sibi introrsum et sub lingua murmurat: 'o si
> ebulliat patruus, praeclarum funus!'   (6–10)

(Not everyone is prepared to get rid of muttering and low whispers from the temples and to live by audible prayers. 'A sound mind, reputation and credit'—this loudly, such that a stranger might hear. But underneath his breath he mutters secretly to himself, 'Oh, if only my uncle would give up the ghost—what a splendid funeral!')

The type illustrated here is then addressed as an adversary in a one-sided dialogue by the writer, who fires a rapid succession of questions, suggests answers, replies to them and, in the process, exposes the absurdity of the other's position. After this, another type of person, exhibiting a similar superstition, is illustrated in a third-person *exemplum* with dramatized details and introduced, like the party illustration of Satire 1.30–43, by *ecce*. Then there is a return to the one-sided dialogue form. Here the character of the adversary, while not incompatible with the adversary of 15–30, has no obvious identity with him. The latter is a man who secretly prays for wealth and is shown to have no understanding of the nature of him to whom he prays; the former is, first, a man who prays for strength and good health but whose rich diet contradicts his prayer; and, second, a man who prays for prosperity and fertile herds but who denies the cogency of his demand by slaughtering his cattle for sacrifices and, ironically, exhausts what wealth he does already have by such lavish offerings. The adversaries are characterized only by the moral point they illustrate, so that when this point changes there is nothing to maintain a unity of person over the interruption of the semi-dialogue form at 31–40. The semi-dialogue is continued as the theme is elaborated in its more general significance: the reason why the aid of the gods is invoked with material bribes—gilding the statues of the gods—is that it is gold which men value above all. Having, as it were, reached a thematic climax in establishing this connection, the writer apostrophizes the cause:

> o curvae in terris animae et caelestium inanis,
> quid iuvat hoc, templis nostros inmittere mores
> et bona dis ex hac scelerata ducere pulpa?   (61–3)

(Oh you spirits bent down to the earth, empty of divinity,
what use is it to introduce our morals into the temples and
to deduce the gods' desires from this corrupt flesh?)

The crediting of the gods with materialistic values is both immoral and ineffectual, the writer continues, appealing to the high priests, *at vos/dicite, pontifices, in sancto quid facit aurum?* (68–9). After a 'satirical exaggeration' (*quin damus id superis*, 71),[24] the poem ends on a personal note and a suggestion, not of what we should pray for, but of what we should offer to the gods:

> conpositum ius fasque animo sanctosque recessus
> mentis et incoctum generoso pectus honesto
> haec cedo ut admoveam templis et farre litabo.   (73–5)

(A sense of duty and right, deep-seated purity of mind and a
heart imbued with noble integrity. Give me these to take to

the temples and I will gain a favourable hearing with an offering of spelt.)

We have seen that in Satire VI a coherently constructed epistolary setting contains within it a dramatic mode of expression which gives vigour to the ideas without overthrowing the original illusion. In Satire II the fictional situation is weakly defined, with the result that the dramatic mode used later in the poem would seem not to be located in a known character placed in particular circumstances which a dialogue structure, by its nature, would seem to demand. The fact that it is Macrinus' birthday has only an incidental connection (birthdays being a time for prayer) with the theme dealing with the nature of religion and its corruption into superstition;[25] whereas the withdrawal from winter to the countryside is closely associated with the moderate enjoyment of life's pleasures that Satire VI advocates, and the association is further enhanced by the motifs of land and sea, the countryside and its produce. Also in Satire VI the writer is established at the beginning as being in a contented, reflective mood (which is also connected with his situation), so that the argument has him as its source, both for subject matter (contentment as one's aim in life, moderation as the means of achieving it), and for the manner of presentation (the logical flow, with adversaries introduced gently and without strong presence, just enough to fulfil their function as aids to the thought process). In Satire II little of the writer's character emerges—only an impersonal definition, his ethical standpoint.

Yet it is clear from the foregoing analysis that the theme of Satire II is not argued with the abstract detachment which would reflect this definition of the writer, but with dialogues, *exempla*, and apostrophes, which express a sense of strong feelings and engagement with the subject. This is seen most strikingly in the change at 8–15 where a type of person is first described in the third person and then addressed and questioned in the second person (from *murmurat*, 9, to *poscas*, 15), which implies that the speaker has started descriptively, impersonally, with the intention of analysing, but then, as his first example unfolds and the vice is revealed, he becomes involved to the extent that he must argue. And so he engages the subject of his example in a rush of questions to force him out of his blindness and hypocrisy:

> heus age, responde (minimum est quod scire laboro)
> de Iove quid sentis? estne ut praeponere cures
> hunc—cuinam? cuinam? vis Staio? an scilicet haeres?
> quis potior iudex puerisve quis aptior orbis?   (17–20)

(Come now, tell me—it is only a small point I want to know
—what do you think about Jupiter? Is it that you would care
to place him above—above whom? Whom? Staius perhaps?
Do you hesitate? But what better judge is there, what more
suitable guardian for orphans?)

The writer's strength of conviction is also expressed in the concrete mode of exposition, which builds up a sense of immediacy
and force in descriptions by investing an idea with objects of
material existence, as, for example, with the second adversary:

> poscis opem nervis corpusque fidele senectae.
> esto age. sed grandes patinae tuccetaque crassa
> adnuere his superos vetuere Iovemque morantur. (41–3)

(You demand strength for your sinews and a body faithful in
old age. Well, granted; but your huge dishes and heavy
sausages forbid the gods to grant them and hinder Jupiter.)

The image has, as it were, a greater degree of density than the
shipwreck scene in Satire VI: the overall form is that of a particular case illustrating a general point (the practice of making
prayers a substitute for effort or self-denial); but within this form
precise, concrete terms are used to express an abstract concept
and these are given a further degree of self-sufficiency by the
addition of specific details: we have, not 'gluttony', nor 'too much
rich food', but 'huge dishes and heavy sausages'. The description
is full enough to provide them with their proper status as material
objects, and the fact that the abstract concept, gluttony, is not
itself brought into the image permits them to retain this status.[26]
In short, the style and the manner of argument throughout the
poem are given a definite source in the writer's conviction, which
partly offsets the rudimentary nature of the frame. The fictional
situation does remain weaker than those of Satires I and VI, since
in Satire II there is a character but in no expressed situation, and
he is conveyed in a more implicit, less demonstrative manner. For
whereas in the other poems the fictional situation was established

first in the frame, and then used to contain the narrative or exposition, here the fictional situation, such as it is, is created *by* the exposition. Therefore there is a difference in balance: the base by which the poem is ordered into a unified whole plays a less dominant part, with the result that there is not the same strong sense of presence or activity, of the poem being a self-contained act, complete in itself. This does not detract from the poem but, rather, finds its corollary in the implications of the ethical views propounded.

In Juvenal's tenth satire, which also deals with prayers, the question asked is not whether the request made to the gods is itself a wholesome one, but whether the consequences of its being granted bring the desired happiness.[27] A long series of examples shows that the consequences are invariably disastrous: wealth, political power, eloquence, military glory, long life, and beauty all bring destruction or misery, generally because society envies, and therefore overthrows, any eminence.[28] This theme is expressed by means of descriptions of certain situations in life, but these are not closely analysed to discover underlying causes; nor, except for a brief concession to virtue at the very end (363–5), is the theme explicitly related to a moral criterion—people are not condemned for praying for what they think will bring happiness, only for being misguided. One can deduce from this that the principle underlying the satire, although never openly expressed, is that of the pursuit of happiness guided by reason, which is a relative principle (relative to particular circumstances of one's life). Persius, on the other hand, treats the value of prayer in terms of an absolute moral standard which is derived from the nature of divinity and discoverable as inner virtue. For what the writer attacks is the spiritual corruption revealed by prayers for riches or power or even health, regarding these as evidence of materialistic values and condemning them because they are incompatible with the gods' values (which, by definition, are the true values). This line is analytical rather than descriptive, and concerns itself with the individual's soul, not with his physical existence and his existence in society. In all these—the absolute standard, the analytical approach, the concern with the 'inner man'—there is harmony with the poem's structure in which the role of adversary is not allowed to assume independence and create an interpersonal situation; the character of the writer is not placed substantively in an external physical context; and the setting virtually consists of just an attitude, a strongly felt belief.

Satire III, treating the themes of moral awareness and the achieving of this by means of a philosophical education, is a dramatic poem whose structure has features more like those of Satire I than of II or VI. In one respect, however, it is the reverse of Satire I, for in the introductory frame the place and circumstances are fully described while the distinction between various characters is left ambiguous. This is a difficult passage, and it seems best to start with a literal translation (I have avoided assigning speeches, which would anticipate the analysis):

> Yes, these habits *are* common.[29] Already the clear morning is entering the windows and widening the narrow cracks with its light. We are snoring enough to work off indigestible Falernian wine, while the shadow reaches the fifth line of the sun-dial. Hey, what are you doing? For some time now the mad dog-star has been baking the harvest dry and all the cattle are under the broad elm (6), a friend says. Is it true? Is it so? Someone come quickly! No one? Glassy bile begins to swell: I am ready to burst, so you would suppose the herds of Arcadia were bellowing. Now the book, the two-tone parchment with the hairs removed (10), paper and knotty pen have come to hand. Then we complain because the ink is heavy and clots on the pen. But when water is added the black ink grows pale, we complain that the pen makes double watery blots. O unhappy man, always ever more unhappy, have we come to this (15)? Ah, why do you not rather ask for scraps to nibble like a tender dove or like rich men's children, and pettishly refuse to let nanny sing you to sleep? Am I to study with such a pen? Who are you trying to fool? Why do you whimper such evasions (20)?

The situation is clear: someone is oversleeping, he is awakened, shows signs of panic and irritation, finds excuses for not settling down to his studies, and a derisive reprimand follows. The difficulty is whether the oversleeping and the reprimanding are performed by one and the same or by two different characters. Attempts have been made to resolve the problem by appeal to biographical parallels, but these are found to cut both ways; and furthermore this method of inquiry is founded on the doubtful assumption that the main character in the poem must represent Persius himself.[30] It is, rather, the first-person plural verbs which cause the difficulty, and any interpretation of the passage will depend upon what the subject of these is taken to be.

G. L. Hendrickson argues the view that there are two characters, a tutor, who is identified with the friend mentioned in line 7, and his student; and in addition an impersonal narrative level.[31] The plural verbs, he maintains, have as their subject 'we all': 'the subject of the description, though individualized, is nevertheless one of a class large enough to admit the satirical exaggeration of all mankind' (p. 336). That Persius uses this 'satirical exaggeration' has already been noted, but the context here does not support the interpretation. It is one thing to say 'we are all fools, or sinners, or hack-writers', but quite another to say 'in such-and-such a room on such-and-such a day we all oversleep, we are all woken by a friend, we all cry out, etc.' The individualizing quality, that is, precludes the generalizing. A closer parallel, in its personal and particular context, would seem to be with Satire v:

> secrete loquimur. tibi nunc hortante Camena
> excutienda damus praecordia, quantaque nostrae
> pars tua sit, Cornute, animae, tibi, dulcis amice,
> ostendisse iuvat.   (21–4)

(We speak in private. Urged by the Muse we now give you our heart to be thoroughly shaken out, and it is a great delight to show you, Cornutus, how great a part of our soul is yours, dear friend.)

Loquimur might have as its subject Cornutus and the speaker, but the subject of *damus*, and the person of the possessive adjective *nostrae*, must be I, and only I.[32]

The well-known interpretation of A. E. Housman[33] starts from the assumption that the verbs do have a singular subject. From this he argued that there is only one character—apart from the friend mentioned in line 7—who narrates, speaks, and acts the whole. In lines 15ff, where a dialogue evolves, the character divides into a higher and a lower self as an internal conflict arises between his conscience and his laziness. From this point the higher self develops the argument against the lower until line 62, when his theme expands to take in a wider audience.

This interpretation is well-founded and coherent—perhaps too much so, for in failing to acknowledge ambiguity and blurred edges it imposes a slightly false neatness. It should be recognized that between *hucine rerum/ venimus* of lines 15–16 and *a, cur non potius . . . poscis* of 16–18 there is a change of stance or viewpoint which *could* indicate a change of speaker (for example, the *unus comitum* breaking in to interrupt the other's complaints and vapid contrition—as *o miser inque dies ultra miser* might be interpreted). Housman's analysis is immensely valuable in showing that no change of speaker is explicitly indicated or demanded by the sense, but it is perhaps unnecessary to be dogmatic about a singleness of speaker, since this is not explicit either. There is, then, a genuine ambiguity lying not only in the identification of speakers, such as has been met in the other satires (1.40 for example), but also in the very existence of different speakers. There is a flow of thought and action, shifting viewpoints and differing outlooks, but these are not embodied in clearly distinguishable characters.

A static narrative description sets the scene, creating a leisurely pace and giving a strong concrete substance to the fictional illusion. Once inside the bedroom, the description is taken up by a character within it, one who describes both himself and his surroundings (*stertimus . . . dum linea tangitur umbra*, 2–3; the paradox of describing oneself asleep is permitted by the Latin historic present); the point of view is no longer overhead but internal to the narrative. This static descriptive mood is disrupted by the friend's speech (5–6),[34] which introduces a dramatic element, although it is still contained within the narrative mould by the rubric *unus ait comitum*. But then follows speech or thought expressed directly, with no narrative intervention: *verumne? itan? ocius adsit/ huc aliquis. nemon?* (7–8). The directness reflects the situation: as the character is awakened by his friend, he casts off the narrator's role, ceasing to *describe* what he is doing, and just acts. And the rapid flow of elliptical command and questions convey a mood of panic and haste after oversleeping. When the time for study approaches, the pace once more slows down to static description of book, parchment, paper, pen and temperamental ink. Again the description is made in the first person (*querimur*, 12 and 14), and is expressive of the character's mood through the impersonal syntax—*inque manus chartae nodosaque venit harundo*, 11, rather than, for example, 'I pick up the pen . . .'—which reflects

his detachment from his working materials, and thereby his unwillingness to work; and through the particularity of description,
which suggests that his indolence prevents him from actually
using the objects and so, instead, he just looks at them. Then
from this failure to settle down to work reflection on his inaction
arises (15–16), and reflection leads naturally to criticism and rebuke (16ff).

The frame, then, is set in the form of a narrative, with a
sequence of events and actions described and performed by the
first-person narrator. The place and the time are given so that the
dramatic illusion does not lie solely in the characterization but is
reinforced by being placed in particular surrounding circumstances. In addition to his behaviour, the narrator's feelings are
also depicted, both explicitly (as in 8–9 and 15–16) and implicitly
in the style of description. There is a liveliness in the flow of action
and the variations of pace, a vividness in the graphic quality of
description, both of which help to consolidate the scene as the
basis of the rest of the poem. It is an exceptionally firm basis: the
rebuke which begins at line 16 is part of the narrative picture,
drawn from observation of the activities already depicted and
following on naturally from the preceding expression of contrition (whether the tone of this be plaintive or remorseful). And
this rebuke, developed and expanded and continued to the end of
the poem, forms the poem's argument and contains its themes.
Thus the poem as a whole is effectually driven along by its
dramatic situation.

In this story presented in the frame, there is the one blurred
point—the number of characters present. As I mentioned above,
it is not possible to determine whether the one who criticizes is
the same character as the one who is criticized, the late sleeper,
and to attempt to do so is to miss the point. For the ambiguity, the
lack of distinction, serves the same function—although fulfilling
it in a less violent, more gentle and suggestive way—as the disruption of the dramatic illusion in Satire 1: it allows the poem a
dramatic structure, with all the concreteness and the strong sense
of density and coherence which is inherent in such a structure,
while avoiding an interpersonal situation which would be dis-
cordant with the basic individualism of the poem's material and
the main character's attitude.

In this satire the individualistic attitude is expressed in the importance given to self-awareness in the themes. The argument presented is that moral well-being cannot be achieved unless you have first learnt to recognize your own faults, just as a sick man has no hope of being cured unless he acknowledges that he is sick and in need of treatment.

The speaker of the critical part which begins at line 16 reproaches and censures with considerable vehemence the indolent character of the introduction. He condemns the latter's social pretensions and contrasts these with his inner being:

> ad populum phaleras! ego te intus et in cute novi.
> non pudet ad morem discincti vivere Nattae   (30-1)

(Take your trappings to the mob! I know you inside, within the skin. You're not ashamed of living in the style of dissolute Natta.)

Thus the speaker establishes the subject of his argument—not the externals of fashionable ancestry and social status, but the inner soul, the seat of moral existence. He then draws a contrast (made clear by the connective *sed* and the emphasizing pronoun *hic*) between his interlocutor and Natta[35] who is described as *stupet hic vitio . . . caret culpa, nescit quid perdat* (32-3). Natta, that is, is not a moral being, because he has lost all sense of responsibility and awareness of his condition: the implication is that the interlocutor, by contrast, does have some awareness. This implication is not stated, but it provides the link with the next section which is a prayer emphasizing the gravity of the consequences of moral corruption, the torture of remorse which attends the comprehension of virtue when it can no longer be achieved. If the prayer is to have any sense in its context,[36] we must see it as following not from the description of Natta, who is emphatically beyond all possibility of remorse (*nescit quid perdat, et alto/ demersus summa rursus non bullit in unda*), but from the unspoken description of the interlocutor who is in danger of falling into this state of living damnation. For his inaction depicted in the frame does not portray a vicious criminal, nor even a hardened sinner, but one who oversleeps yet is disconcerted by having done so, who cannot settle down to work yet deplores the fact. Furthermore, the lack of explicit differentiation of characters links sinner with censor and suggests that the denunciatory lecture which forms most of the poem is itself a sign of self-awareness. It is only a suggestion and should not be exaggerated, but it does mean that the ambiguity of the characterization is not only harmonious with the theme of self-awareness as a precondition of morality, but also contributes to the expression of that theme.

It is also significant that the thought process draws on a fairly searching analysis of the actions depicted in the frame, on the feelings and reactions of the character, and this helps to bring out the depth and complexity of the frame and therefore of the dramatic illusion. And the fact that the speaker takes for granted the connection between lines 32–4 and 35–43 and does not spell it out compels the reader to return to the frame and appreciate it afresh. The dramatic setting, therefore, informs the poem to a marked degree.

After the prayer, the distinction between amorality and immorality, which was touched upon but not fully explained in the contrast between Natta and the interlocutor, is expanded in a second contrast (44–62). The speaker recalls his early schooldays, pointing out that his avoidance of lessons by feigning illness was not reprehensible, was even justifiable (*iure*, 48), since he had no sense of right and wrong but was absorbed in games. Against this he sets the interlocutor, making the contrast direct by keeping to the subject of education: the interlocutor has had all the advantages of a Stoic training (*sapiens . . . porticus*, 53–4) yet he still lives a dissolute life with no aim, no sense of purpose. By thus contrasting the education of both (although at different stages, corresponding to primary school and university, which helps to avoid differentiating the identities of critic and criticized) he implicitly develops the theme to introduce the idea of a philosophical training being the means of achieving moral awareness and understanding. This forms the subject of the rest of the poem, but first there is a recall to the frame:

> stertis adhuc laxumque caput conpage soluta
> oscitat hesternum dissutis undique malis. (58–9)

(Still you're snoring, yawning off yesterday, head drooping and its joints slackened, jaws torn apart in all directions.)

The recall, stressed by the echo of *stertimus* in line 3, strengthens the dramatic illusion by directing attention to the situation in which the speech is taking place and by which it is motivated. It is important, since a few lines later the speaker changes to a second person plural as if he were addressing a large audience (63ff). The apparent change of listener is justified by the material: the theme broadens to treat the need and value of philosophy in general and forms the positive part of the satire—the cure of the fault which has been analysed in the first half of the poem. The use of a plural addressee expresses the idea that the point has universal application, and, by its oratorical style of addressing the world, sets a tone of impassioned exhortation suited to the expression of an ideal.[37] The passage begins with a negative example of behaviour, and proceeds with its positive counterpart:

> elleborum frustra, cum iam cutis aegra tumebit,
> poscentis videas; venienti occurrite morbo,
> et quid opus Cratero magnos promittere montis?
> discite et, o miseri, causas cognoscite rerum:
> quid sumus et quidnam victuri gignimur, ordo
> quis datus, aut metae qua mollis flexus et unde,   (63–8)

(You might see men demanding hellebore when it is too late, after their skin is already sick and swollen. Meet the disease at the first onset, and what need is there to promise Craterus great mountains? Learn, wretches, and understand the causes of things: what we are and for what life we have been born; what place has been assigned to us, or how we should make a smooth turning round the goal, and when we should take it.)

This view continues until line 76 with the further philosophical problems of the correct quantity and the true value of money, just desires, one's debt to family and to country and one's part in divine and human spheres; the section ends with an appeal to place these philosophical inquiries above material considerations. Half-way through (71), the second-person verbs and pronouns revert to singulars to reaffirm the dramatic setting, and thus the effect of the plurals is held in check, expressing the strength of the speaker's beliefs but not extending so far as to undermine the basic dramatic illusion.

Then the justification for advocating this course of study is developed in three distinct stages forming a pattern of objection, reply, and conclusion. First, a centurion is quoted mocking philosophers for wasting their time and health in useless, unpractical speculations, and his speech is given a favourable reception in the market place (77–87). Next comes a dramatized *exemplum* of a sick man who ignores the advice of both doctor and friend to rest and undertake a cure, and as a result ends up being buried (88–106). Finally, in reply to the interlocutor who takes this *exemplum* literally and therefore objects that it does not apply to him, that he has no symptoms of illness, the main speaker points out that avarice, lust, fastidiousness, fear, and anger create in him palpitations or ulcers or change in temperature or signs of madness (107–18). The implication is that moral corruption is no different from physical disease: both need to be recognized and acknowledged first and then treated if they are not to cause disaster.

As regards the dramatic structure, lines 77–106 proceed with fairly self-contained illustrations, and the reader's sense of the dramatic illusion is lessened until the process of argument between the main speaker and interlocutor is resumed in the concluding section. The centurion is presented, by means of an indefinite pronoun and a potential subjunctive, as a hypothetical case (*hic aliquis de gente hircosa centurionum| dicat*, 77–8) which gives him the status of an idea thought up to serve the argument. But at the end of his speech, when his audience's reactions to it are described, the mood changes to the indicative and thus gives a stronger sense of reality (*his populus ridet, . . . torosa iuventus| ingeminat*, 86–7). This is by now a familiar technique, whereby an illustration becomes too vivid to keep to its place as part of the argument but comes to exist in its own right. Here the indicative description is not developed far enough to subvert the dramatic illusion—to suggest, that is, that the scene is no longer set in the indolent character's study, but in a busy market place—but it does draw attention away from the illusion, particularly since the main speaker makes no direct comment on it, which would reassert the setting of main speaker arguing with interlocutor. Instead, it is at once followed by the second illustration, of the sick man. This is set in the present indicative and forms a complete story, with a sequence of events and dramatic treatment, recording the man's words to his doctor and the dialogue between him and his friend. It thus forms a parable or allegory, since the metaphor of physical illness to denote moral corruption has already been established (*elleborum frustra* . . . 63–5), and therefore doctor and patient are transparently representative of philosopher and student. It is not just this, however, because the story is told with such richness of description, as for example:

> turgidus hic epulis atque albo ventre lavatur,
> gutture sulpureas lente exhalante mefites.
> sed tremor inter vina subit calidumque trientem
> excutit e manibus, dentes crepuere retecti,
> uncta cadunt laxis tunc pulmentaria labris.
> hinc tuba, candelae, . . . (98–102)

(He goes to his bath bloated after a good meal, his stomach white and sulphurous vapours oozing slowly from his throat. But as he is taking his wine a trembling seizes him and shakes the warm tumbler from his hands; his teeth are laid bare and chatter; the rich morsels fall from his sagging lips. Hence trumpet and candles, . . .)

The description ends on an ironical note: he is laid out for the funeral but—as if this compensated for dying—his newly freed slaves (in gratitude) will carry him off in proper style. Moreover, the relationship between morality and physical condition is by this time more complex than that of interchangeable equivalents. The image was first established implicitly in descriptive details (e.g. 9, 32),[38] then explicitly as a parallel in 63ff; but here and in the concluding section a causal connection is made: the interlocutor is taught that moral faults bring on physical symptoms of illness.

The physical illness motif, that is, works on more than one level, which results in a greatly increased richness of texture. The poem's surface is an argument made jagged by the suppression of logical connections and, in the second half, expressed solely by means of rich, vivid illustrations and of dialogue continued within the framework of the illustrations. But if this descriptive richness and the prickly vigour arising from the avoidance of smooth logical analysis form the surface, they also give a sense of depth: the complexity of the way in which the imagery functions and in the way it relates to the argument, and the lack of logical clarity in the presentation of the argument force us to question and to search beyond the superficial. The danger of such density is that it could lead to incoherence and a breakdown of unity. These are avoided, however, on the one hand by the continuity of the sickness motif which is present even in the introductory frame; and on the other, by the substantiality of the dramatic illusion: the setting is fully described, as we have seen, and is organically related to the argument which develops from it.

The surface ruggedness and vigour are perhaps the most immediately striking quality of this and the other satires. They are worth reading for the imagery alone, where even a yawn can turn into a horrific disintegration of the face (58–9). It is worthwhile, as a conclusion, to look at one such image in detail, and then to see how it interacts and harmonizes with other aspects of the poem.

The main speaker of Satire III starts his censure with a contemptuous description of his interlocutor:

> . . . sonat vitium percussa, maligne
> respondet viridi non cocta fidelia limo.
> udum et molle lutum es, nunc nunc properandus et acri
> fingendus sine fine rota. (21–4)

(A jar of ill-baked green clay echoes a flaw when struck and gives back a surly sound. You are damp soft clay, now now you should be hastened and moulded endlessly on the sharp wheel.)

The image can perhaps be understood more easily if it is compared to a similar one by Lucretius:

> intelligit ibi vitium vas efficere ipsum
> omniaque illius vitio corrumpier intus
> quae collata foris et commoda cumque venirent;
> partim quod fluxum pertusumque esse videbat,
> ut nulla posset ratione explerier umquam;
> partim quod taetro quasi conspurcare sapore
> omnia cernebat, quaecumque receperat, intus. (VI.17–23)

(He then realized that a pot forms its own fault and everything, however beneficial, that is collected outside and placed within, is contaminated by the pot's fault. He grasped this partly because he saw that it was leaky and cracked so that in no way could it be filled; partly because he perceived that it defiled, as it were, with a bitter taste, whatever was put into it.)

The comparison of a man with a vessel was a philosophical commonplace (cf. Horace, *Epist.*, 1.2.54 and Plato, *Gorgias* 493A–493D), a useful one because it contains within it both the idea of man as a passive receptacle of ideas and the idea of man as an active creator and destroyer of values. Persius puts the stress on the former (since he is dealing with the formation of character); Lucretius puts it on the latter and expands the metaphor analytically in a study of all the ways in which a pot can corrupt or fail to contain its contents. The analytical quality is present in the nature of the description: the physical being of the *vas* is not described, the contents are not characterized—except in one vivid flash, *taetro quasi conspurcare sapore*—but both are treated abstractly and the logical connections are precisely defined (*partim quod . . . videbat, ut nulla . . . ratione, partim quod . . . cernebat, quasi*). Any graphic quality in the image is further weakened by the two explanations which are given (that the pot leaks, and that it has the power to defile) because they are physically contradictory. Everything is directed at amplifying those apsects of the image's vehicle (the pot) which pertain to its moral significance, and at each point a straightforward similarity with the tenor (man) can be understood. All is reasoned, there is no tension between similarity and disparity of vehicle to tenor. With Persius' image almost the reverse is true. The pot itself is described with much closer attention to physical details, *viridi . . . limo, non cocta fidelia, udum et molle lutum* and *percussa* where the action of striking evokes a tangible presence; the elisions of the first half of line 23, *udum et molle lutum es* convey the softness and malleability of clay, *nunc nunc* is slow and heavy, and therefore urgent, followed by the quick *properandus et acri*, so that the sensuous qualities are conveyed by directly sensory means. When the clay is overtly identified with the man (*lutum es*) we are led to consider what kind of similarity and disparity do hold, in a way that Lucretius, by suppressing the tenor, does not lead us to do. Further, the difference between clay and man is more extreme than that between Lucretius' abstractly conceived pot and man, and it is emphasized by describing the clay and the pot in sensuous and concrete terms, in the very area, that is, where disparity exists. Thus the image is not limited to the obvious and expressed comparison of man and pot to become just a symbol: both pot and man maintain their separate identities (to which the delay in introducing the tenor contributes by enabling the description to be taken first on its literal value). This has the poetical function of making the texture dense, by preserving the substantive quality of what is described and refusing to allow objects to become merely representative of ideas and thus to be submerged in the argument. It also expresses a sensibility attracted by the appearance and working of physical objects, the intricacies and details of experience, but not ordered so as to convey a belief in a latent design in the world—the element of disparity in the image is too strong for that; nor examined scientifically and with detachment—which would demand a closely followed through simile. Rather, Persius delights in creating an image whose violence is seen in the intimacy with which human and inanimate are blended and identified.

Violence was endemic in Silver Age literature, most evidently in the tragedies of Seneca and the epics of Lucan and Statius; it is basic to the whole structure of Persius' satires. In Satire i the dramatic illusion is disrupted and in Satire iii it is made ambiguous (a less extreme technique, as befits this poem's rather more positive and hopeful themes). Violence is reflected on another level in the imagery and descriptions, which are violent in structure or in horrific details, or both, and in the harshness, the lack of logical ease or smoothness with which the argument unfolds. Together these reinforce or express the themes, which all—except for those of Satire vi—in varying degrees of intensity imply an attitude of extreme individualism manifested in rejection and absolute standards: no concessions are made to human frailties; only contempt is shown for easiness, smoothness, softness. In Satire iii this attitude is combined with the stress laid on self-awareness, in Satire ii with the definition of virtue as a purely spiritual quality, in Satire i with the call to assess and produce literature without regard to the extrinsic rewards bestowed by society.

Thus style, tone, and themes form a unity, which is given a concrete base in the dramatic structure. The circumstances or situation in which the verbal act takes place is brought fully into the poem to become a recognizable part of the expression, with the themes and style rooted in the characters and their setting. Hence a sense of self-sufficiency—which is needed to contain all the violence, forcefulness, and vigour.

ACKNOWLEDGMENTS

I am extremely grateful to Professor K. J. Reckford, Professor D. R. Dudley and Mr and Mrs I. M. LeM. DuQuesnay for their many and searching criticisms and suggestions during the various stages of this essay's composition.

Notes

1 Included in W. V. Clausen's edition, *A. Persi Flacci Saturarum* (Oxford, 1956), which I have used throughout this essay. J. Conington's edition (Oxford, 1893) offers valuable notes and translation. As a work of reference, O. Jahn's exhaustive Prolegomena and Notes (*A. Persii Flacci Satirarum Liber Cum Scholiis Antiquis*, Leipzig, 1843) are still invaluable.

Recent studies, particularly from America, rejecting the biographical and romantic criticism prevalent in the nineteenth century and the first part of this century, have brought a deeper understanding of Persius' poetry and a higher estimation of its merits. K. J. Reckford, 'Studies in Persius', *Hermes* 90 (1962), 476–504, has analysed patterns of unifying imagery and the underlying themes which these express. C. S. Dessen, *Iunctura Callidus Acri* (Illinois Studies in Language and Literature 59, Illinois, 1968) has developed Reckford's ideas with further analyses of the style and overt themes. She provides an extensive bibliography which I will not repeat here, but attention should be drawn to two excellent articles by W. S. Anderson: 'Part versus whole in Persius' fifth Satire', *PQ* 39 (1960), 66–81, and 'Persius and the rejection of society', *Wiss. Zs. Univ. Rostock* 15 (1966) *Gesellsch. u. Sprachwiss. Reihe*, heft 4/5, 409–16.

2 Cf. *PIR II*, A 611; and K. F. C. Rose, 'Problems of Chronology in Lucan's career', *TAPA* 97 (1966), 379–96.

3 How much the opposition to Nero was Stoic opposition, and how much it was a family tradition which was later embellished by Flavian biographers, is debatable. For a recent discussion, see Oswyn Murray, 'The Quinquennium Neronis and the Stoics', *Historia* 14 (1965), 41–61.

4 But see n. 7 below for authorship of these. While he does discuss in this satire what are, presumably, faults of contemporary literature, his treatment of the matter is general rather than topical. For example, a poetic recitation is described (13–23) in a purely fictional form; Juvenal, in the comparable passage (VII.83–9) manages to work the poet Statius into the example.

5 Horace, *Sat.*, I.iv.21–38 *et passim*; *Sat.*, II.i.1–2, 21–3, 60–2 *et passim*; Persius, *Sat.*, I.107–10; Juvenal, *Sat.*, I.150–70. But note that Horace does not relinquish the right to censure, while Persius and Juvenal do, at least, partially—the one will dig a hole and bury his secret (I.120), the other will speak only of the dead (I.170–1). How much these assertions and denials of the freedom to criticize can be taken at their face value, however, is another question.

6 For Attius Labeo, see scholia on Satire 1.4.49 and 50; and *PIR II*, A 1358.

For Masurius Sabinus, see Gaius, *Inst.*, 11.218, where it is said that he lived up to the time of Nero, and *PIR I*, M 271. Cotta Messalinus flourished in Tiberius' reign and is last mentioned in A.D. 32 (Tacitus, *Ann.*, VI.5): see *PIR II*, A 1488.

7 Against them stands the fact that the one contradicts the other: why should Cornutus have been so cautious as to delete a slanted reference while letting stand a direct criticism of Nero? Moreover, the Scholia give incompatible interpretations: line 93, *non autem sunt Persii, sed poetae nescio cuius graecissantis . . . et dicit hos versus Neronis in haec nomina desinentes*; and line 99, *Hi versus Neronis sunt . . . Ipse autem Persius finxit hos versus*. Which incompatibility suggests that there was no certain historical evidence for the authorship. But see H. Bardon, *Les Empereurs et les lettres latines*, Paris, 1940, 203–6, where Neronian authorship is accepted.

8 And as with the names of people, so with geographical place names. The frame of Satire VI is the only one which gives specific locations for its characters—the Sabine countryside and the Ligurian coast. Elsewhere, place names are rare and not closely particularized. Several of them are used to signify a type—*canis Apula*, 1.60, or *Tuscum fictile*, 11.60, or *Arcadiae pecuaria*, 111.9, or *Siculi iuvenci*, 111.39—where, in each case, the epithet is almost inseparable from its noun and therefore tends to lose its geographical reference (like Yorkshire pudding). Rome is mentioned twice, in Satire 1 at lines 5 and 8, and further details are given in *Tiberino in gurgite* (11.15), in *Licini in campos, . . . Crassi . . . aedis* (11.36), and in *Subura* (V.32). Italian references also occur (Umbrians and Marsians in 111.74 and 75; Cures in IV.26, and the Bruttian rocks and Ionian Sea in VI.27 and 29), as do foreign references. But this is all: there are no walks around or surveys of Rome or travels across Italy such as Horace and Juvenal treat us to.

9 See also K. J. Reckford, art. cit., 500 ('The reverse side of this *indignatio* is a very modern isolation') and his analysis of the *Prologus*, 501ff.

10 By G. L. Hendrickson, 'The first Satire of Persius', *CPhil* 23 (1928), 97–112.

11 The concept of a *persona* is by now so widely accepted that it is hardly necessary to emphasize that a first person character is not the same as the author. However, the term is often, but wrongly, used as if it were an optional device, something that a poet chooses whether or not to employ and whose presence the critic deduces from biographical parallels and internal consistency. Thus, for example, C. S. Dessen can say at the end of her study: 'it should by now be evident that Persius does not speak directly in his poems but instead assumes a variety of personae. As evidence one may cite the fact that the speaker varies according to the subject of the Satire and that when Persius includes autobiographical material, as in Satires III and V, he selects details which will enhance his particular persona' (op. cit., 93). The implication being that one has to *prove* that the device of the persona has been employed. I say that this is a misuse of the term because the concept has a valuable ontological meaning which should not be lost by treating it merely as a term of rhetoric: it distinguishes the empirical being from the imaginary being created in the

poem's words; the persona of the writer is a representational object in a representational medium, i.e. a character in a poem.

12 Traditionally this first line is a quotation from the first book of Lucilius' satires. The tradition derives from the Scholia, whose comment, however, is on line 2, *quis leget haec*. For a full discussion, see F. Marx's note on Lucilius 1.9 in his edition, *C. Lucilii Carminum Reliquiae* (Leipzig, 1904–5).

13 For further points on dramatic structure as used in satire, see J. M. Aden, 'Pope and the satiric adversary', *Stud. Eng. Lit.* 2 (1962), 267–86, and M. C. Randolph, 'The structural design of the formal verse satire', *PQ* 21 (1942), 368–84.

14 Art. cit. (1966), 412–13.

15 'The third Satire of Persius', *CP* 23 (1928), 335–6.

16 This defence is usually taken to mean that poetic inspiration cannot be suppressed. See, for example, G. G. Ramsay's note and translation (Loeb, 1965), and R. G. M. Nisbet's comment in his article, 'Persius', *Critical Essays on Roman Literature: Satire*, ed. J. P. Sullivan, (Routledge & Kegan Paul, 1963), 44. The terminology used in the defence certainly suggests this (*hoc fermentum et quae semel intus/ innata est rupto iecore exierit caprificus*) but the syntax undercuts it (*quo didicisse, nisi . . . exierit: for what purpose* is it to have studied, *unless* this yeast and wild fig-tree . . . might spring forth?') It is an economist's argument, assessing the wages appropriate to one's labour: the bursting forth of the poetry is the reward of studying, not an inescapable necessity. Is it too fanciful to suppose that the adversary *intends* to present the argument of irrepressible poetic inspiration (and hence the *fermentum* and *caprificus*), but gets it wrong?

17 But see Dessen (op. cit., 31) who takes the subject of *ait* as the adversary of the dramatic situation. The third person, she argues, is used to prepare us for the revelation of the adversary's imaginary status in line 44. Perhaps the significant point is the ambiguity which permits two interpretations, just as the identity of the subject of line 44 is open to two interpretations.

18 And see O. Jahn's Prolegomena, p. xlvi, '*assensere viri* quod epicam gravitatem spirat, et alterum quod magis commune: *laudant convivae*'.

19 On this term see Randolph, art. cit., who sees as a general characteristic of verse satire a bi-partite division into the negative part (destructive attack on or exposure of vice, folly etc.) and the positive (statement of the opposing virtue). It is usual for the negative to outweigh the positive.

20 The meaning of these two characteristics is far from clear: in the first case, is it Hellenophobia specifically, or general chauvinism, that the speaker rejects? In the second case, is it the rudeness, or the stupidity of stating the obvious, that comes under attack?

21 Violence in technique is also found in such mixed metaphors as *liquido cum plasmate guttur/ mobile conlueris* (17–18), or *hoc fermentum et quae semel intus/ innata est rupto iecore exierit caprificus* (24–5). This one is particularly striking not only for its structural violence (i.e. in combining the human and the vegetable so intimately), but also for the horrific idea it expresses. For violence in syntax and metre, see Anderson, art. cit. (1966), 414–15.

22 Dessen, op. cit., 78ff.

23 See Reckford, art. cit., 498, and Dessen, loc. cit.

24 See p. 119 above. But with the examples in Satire 1.10–13 (*facimus, sapimus* and *scribimus*) the 'exaggeration' lay in the inclusion of the self with the crowd: where one might have expected a 'they' because the action described is dishonourable, one finds a 'we'. The example in Satire 11.71 (*damus*) described an honourable action—the action which the writer is advocating as desirable—and therefore the 'exaggeration' lies in the inclusion of the crowd with the self. The effect is to avoid a self-righteous tone which an assertion of superiority could create. But see p. 138 below and n. 32 where first person plurals are discussed more fully.

25 But see Dessen (op. cit., 41ff) who rightly argues that there is a *thematic* connection with the frame and the rest of the poem: that Macrinus' honest and open manner of prayer provides a contrast to the vices attacked in the body of the poem; and the introduction and conclusion are linked in that both present the positive part of the satire (a form of 'ring composition'). This thematic pattern, however, does not enhance the fictional situation—either by increasing our understanding of it, or by making it influence the style, tone and treatment of themes in the way that the settings of Satires 1 and vi clearly do—since the motivation for the contrast between Macrinus and the general run of society is insufficiently established.

26 If there is a pun in *Iovemque morantur*—i.e. Jupiter is so gorged on all this heavy food that he is slow to respond; as Conington puts it, the *tucceta* 'clog the gracious purposes of Jupiter'—then the concrete terms have an extra internal function in the vehicle of the image, thereby increasing the quality of density. The existence of the pun depends upon whether the *grandes patinae tuccetaque crassa* can be interpreted as sacrificial offerings as well as the glutton's own diet. Jahn's note on these lines gives some support for this view.

27 This is stated at the beginning of the poem, and the answer to the question is anticipated:

> quid tam dextro pede concipis, ut te
> conatus non paeniteat votique peracti?
> evertere domos totas optantibus ipsis
> di faciles   (x.5–8)

28 The causes are not inevitably found in the corruption of society: longevity brings misery in the form of the obscenities of senility, in the loss of loved ones whose time span is normal, and in the destruction of all one's hopes (188–288). But in the treatment of the other prayers, the criticism moves naturally from ethical to social.

29 This first sentence, *nempe haec adsidue*, is a problem in itself. *Nempe* recalls the beginning of Horace's Satire 1.x (*nempe incomposito dixi pede currere versus/ Lucili*) where *nempe* draws attention to the reference back to Satire 1.iv. Persius' usage does not have any such specific reference, so that it functions purely within the poem it introduces and suggests that there is some previous thought, discussion or activity lying behind the poem and giving it its motivation. What this would be depends on how we take *adsidue*. It could have the sense of something taking place over a long

period of time, either in the context of the poem's themes (the faults to be attacked are an everyday occurrence), or of the dramatic picture of the opening section (Conington: 'Is this always the order of the day, then ?'). Alternatively, it could mean 'busily', as G. L. Hendrickson argued: 'Our young sluggard has assured his friend and mentor that he is working hard—*assidue sum versatus in studiis.* This is the presumptive background which the real fact (introduced by *nempe*) unmasks. Persius' opening places the reader at the moment of an unexpected visit from his tutor, and what does he find of this vaunted assiduity? hard sleeping instead—*nempe haec assidue*, with emphasis on *haec*' (art. cit., 333–4). I do not know which is the more probable interpretation, although Hendrickson's is certainly attractive.

30 See, for example, the series of articles beginning with J. Tate's 'Was Persius a "Micher"?', *CR* 42 (1928), 63–4, which was answered by G. B. A. Fletcher, 'Was Persius Not a "Micher"?', *CR* 42 (1928), 167–8, and defended by J. Tate again, 'Persius No "Micher"', *CR* 43 (1929), 56–9.

31 Art. cit., 332–42. His interpretation can most easily be set out by quoting the whole section with explanatory rubrics:

Tutor: nempe haec adsidue. *Narrative:* iam clarum mane fenestras
intrat et angustas extendit lumine rimas.
stertimus, indomitum quod despumare Falernum
sufficiat, quinta dum linea tangitur umbra.
Tutor: en quid agis? siccas insana canicula messes
iam dudum coquit et patula pecus omne sub ulmo est,
Narrative: unus ait comitum. *Student:* verumne? itan? ocius adsit
huc aliquis, nemon? *Narrative:* turgescit vitrea bilis:
Student: findor, *Narrative:* ut Arcadiae pecuaria rudere credas.
iam liber et positis bicolor membrana capillis
inque manus chartae nodosaque venit harundo.
tum querimur crassus calamo quod pendeat umor.
nigra sed infusa vanescit sepia lympha,
dilutas querimur geminet quod fistula guttas.

Presumably, although Hendrickson does not specify, the tutor takes up from here—

o miser inque dies ultra miser, hucine rerum
venimus? a, cur non potius teneroque columbo
et similis regum pueris pappare minutum
poscis et iratus mammae lallare recusas?

—and continues for the rest of the poem. There is no explanation for the change from first person *venimus* to second person *poscis*.

32 Other examples of the first person plural used where the subject is evidently singular, are *temptemus* (III.113) and the possessive adjective *nostro* in VI.14 (quoted above, p. 117). I have not been able to find any instance of Persius using the first person plural for second person singular, as G. Némethy, *A. Persii Flacci satirae* (Budapest, 1903) suggested for Satire III.

33 'Notes on Persius', *CQ* 7 (1913), 12–32.

34 Both J. Conington and G. G. Ramsay (Loeb, 1965) give the whole of 1–6 to the friend. But this demands that we take *stertimus* as equal to *stertis*— see n. 32 above. Moreover, there is a change of style at line 5, marked by the interjection *en* and developed in the more forceful quality of the description, which suggests a different viewpoint from that of 1–4. Hendrickson says of lines 1–4: 'That this is narrative, and not words addressed to the young slothful by the rebuking friend and mentor, is clear from the repetition which follows . . . The lateness of the morning hour is thus explained first descriptively to define the situation for the reader or audience; thereupon in the mouth of the tutor it is repeated in language of vehement rebuke' (art. cit., 334).

35 A character from Horace, Satire ii.vi.124.

36 Hendrickson, art. cit., suggests that it should be moved to follow after line 57. This would make a smoother reading, certainly, but I doubt whether it is quite legitimate to tamper with the text in so radical a manner. The reading as we have it is not as unintelligible as Hendrickson suggests.

37 For the stylistic devices used in the passage to communicate a sense of solemnity, see E. V. Marmorale, *Persio* (2nd edn Florence, 1963), 46.

38 For a full analysis see Reckford, art. cit., 489, and Dessen, op. cit., 52–7.

VI

On Translating Petronius

J. P. Sullivan

The *Satyricon* of Petronius has attracted many translators in the twentieth century,[1] not merely because of the challenge offered by an author who uses both prose and verse, but also because of the varied critical and literary problems he presents. His comparative neglect by earlier translators was, of course, due to his reputation as a surreptitious classic, a reputation that seems scarcely deserved, if one considers what is available in English literature itself. Nevertheless one remembers Cyril Connolly's story in *Enemies of Promise* of the black-bound copy of Petronius that he kept in chapel as 'rather a gesture' and the evocation of Petronius' reputation by J. K. Huysmans in *À rebours*. As a consequence of this reputation, apart from the inevitable literal translation in the Bohn Library, by Walter Kelly, there were, until this century, no accessible versions in English after Burnaby's translation of 1694.[2]

Another reason for Petronius' attraction for modern translators, now that there are no extraneous barriers against an unexpurgated version, lies perhaps in the strange, and perhaps overly seductive air of modernity he wears. Although the reasons for his choice of form and the principles governing the work are very different, the *Satyricon* is the one piece of ancient literature which most closely resembles that most popular twentieth-century art form, the realistic novel. The Greek romancers, even Apuleius, have far too much of a fairy-tale atmosphere to stand such a comparison, and so Petronius remains the classic that strikes the twentieth-century reader as modern in the way, for instance, John Donne appeals to us and Spenser does not. Of course, as T. S. Eliot said of Donne, 'There are two ways in which we may find a poet to be modern: he may have made a statement which is true everywhere and for all time . . . , or there may be an accidental relationship between his mind and our own.'[3] The latter seems the case with Petronius, although it is difficult to define the elusive but certain feeling of modernity that impresses the reader. Some obvious similarities suggest themselves: like the works of such modern masters as Joyce, Pound and Eliot, the *Satyricon* is highly literary in a thoroughly contemporary way, that is to say, Petronius has a critical, rather than a reverential attitude to the Graeco-Roman literary tradition. Again, the tone of the work is one of ironic detachment, with a careful and sophisticated separation between the author himself and his narrative vehicle, the 'anti-hero' Encolpius, who is himself an emotional and volatile Felix Krull; this recalls the twentieth-century technique, common in poetry and the novel, of the *persona*, a narrator who is in varying degrees distinguishable from the actual writer. Of course, for the strong vein of realism, even of morbid sexuality, in the work it would be idle to cite modern parallels.

This feeling of modernity, however, may be too seductive for the translator. It may lead him to accept Petronius without critical examination because of his contemporary appearance; consequently the real qualities and originality of the *Satyricon* may go unappreciated, and certain parts of the work may seem vaguely unsatisfying, because they do not exhibit Petronius' more usual and striking realism. The tone may therefore seem uneven and the novel-reader may object to the mixture of prose and verse, or to the excessive use of coincidence, or to the author's tearing of the veil of verisimilitude by an inappropriate aside to the reader (*Satyricon*, 132.15). To dispel these doubts in the reader's mind and to reproduce the subtler qualities of Petronius' style and achievement, the translator needs both an understanding of the literary and historical background of the *Satyricon* and, based upon that, a coherent critical view of the work. For Petronius does not require a radical 'creative' approach in the manner of Ezra Pound, but rather a variety of techniques to deal with the differing aims and tones of the various episodes. The *Cena Trimalchionis*, for instance, is based on different literary premises from Eumolpus' critique of contemporary historical epic and his exemplary poem on the civil war (*Sat.*, 118ff), and the atmosphere of the episodes set in the *Graeca urbs*, which is probably to be identified with Puteoli, is very different from the more fantastic atmosphere of the events at Croton (*Sat.*, 124.2ff).

Before offering my own evaluation of the *Satyricon* and the reasons why so many detailed decisions have to be made by the translator, it may be helpful, in order to give some idea of the variety
of the work, to set down first a summary of the extant narrative
and a reconstruction of the missing parts of the story. As far as
we can judge, the *Satyricon* was a lengthy work; there is some evidence that part of the extant narrative belongs to Books XIV and
XV. The circumstances of composition and publication may explain this and also the fact that many of the episodes—the *Cena
Trimalchionis*, for instance—are self-contained digressions: that is
the point of them.

The narrator, Encolpius, is what we nowadays term an 'anti-
hero': he is young, well-educated, emotional, cowardly, and immoral; and his sexual ambivalence is a factor around which much
of the story revolves. He is not the omniscient or disinterested
narrator familiar from many modern novels, but rather a main
part of the plot. The starting point of the work has been plausibly
set in Massilia. Servius on Virgil's *Aeneid*, III.57 (fr. I) tells us that
in Petronius there was an account of how the inhabitants of Massilia took measures against a plague. One of their poorer citizens
would become a voluntary scapegoat; he would be maintained for
a whole year at public expense, living on special food. At the end
of that time, after proper ceremonies to bring the ills of the city
down on his head, he would be cast out. The fifth-century Bishop
of Clermont-Ferrand, Sidonius Apollinaris, mentions Petronius in
two lists of great Latin writers, the second reference being:

> et te Massiliensium per hortos
> sacri stipitis, Arbiter, colonum
> Hellespontiaco parem Priapo
> *(Carm.*, 23.155–8 = fr. IV)

(And you, Arbiter, worshipper of the sacred stump,
Amid the gardens of Massilia,
A match for Priapus of the Hellespont.)

Finally, various passages in the narrative hint that Encolpius is
hounded by the Wrath of Priapus (*gravis ira Priapi, Sat.*, 139.2),
and there are dark allusions to the nature of his offence against
him (*Sat.*, 133.3). The most persuasive interpretation of all these
hints is that Encolpius, on at least one occasion, was involved in

the worship of Priapus, who was usually represented by a tree-trunk, rough-hewn into a body with a large phallus; such figures often stood in gardens. What exactly the offence against the god was (*facinus*, *Sat.*, 133.3) is impossible to ascertain. Perhaps the robbery and violation of a temple (*Sat.*, 133.3), or the betrayal of some secret (*proditio*, *Sat.*, 130.2); or he may even have impersonated Priapus himself, for Encolpius seems to be well-endowed physically (*Sat.*, 130.13) and the words of Sidonius—*Hellespontiaco parem Priapo*—might well allude to this.[4] Indeed his extenuating plea—*non toto corpore feci* (*Sat.*, 133.3)—might be interpreted as a delicate euphemism. If, as was also suggested by Cichorius, the work opens with a plague, then Petronius would seem to be using both the *Iliad* and the *Odyssey* for his structure, just as his admired Virgil did. Of course the *Reiseroman* would provide a more promising framework for the sort of episodes Petronius had in mind to display his literary versatility, and this explains why there are more allusions to the *Odyssey* in the course of the surviving narrative.

The basic structure then is a parody of epic; the spring of the plot a comic variation on the Wrath of an Offended Deity; and much of the humour consists of treating low life personages and their shady adventures with all the careful style and literary allusiveness that were customary for more elevated themes. This comedy of contrast between style and content is nowhere better seen than in the case of Eumolpus, whose lofty views on the decadence of the age and the arts, expressed in elaborate rhetoric (*Sat.*, 83.8ff), are immediately followed by the scandalous story of his seduction of his host's son at Pergamum.

Encolpius' travels from Massilia would naturally continue in the direction of Italy, and the drift of his movements seems southwards. He moves in the extant narrative from Puteoli to Croton, after an earlier set of adventures in Baiae. In Italy he runs foul of the law. Perhaps it was here that he robbed a temple. Certainly fragments VIII, XIV and possibly XII, hint at a trial scene, but we know he escaped his obvious fate in the arena (*effugi iudicium, harenae imposui*, *Sat.*, 81.3,9; cf. fr. VIII). While he is in the *ergastulum*, however, he meets the young, effeminate, and fickle Giton, with whom he falls in love (*Sat.*, 81.5). Giton escapes with him and becomes Encolpius' lover and travelling companion. The next recoverable episodes take place in Baiae, the notorious Roman watering-place near Naples. Two distinct adventures may be made out from later references, although their sequence is purely conjectural.

The pair fall in with a notorious courtesan named Tryphaena. Her initial interest in Encolpius is soon replaced by a deeper affection for Giton. Their situation seems very comfortable but Encolpius' jealousy forces them to move, although not before Encolpius brings about Tryphaena's public disgrace (*Sat.*, 106.4). This jealousy of Encolpius over Giton recurs frequently and is a mainspring of the mechanics of the plot. The situations that lead to it may be part of Priapus' vengeance.

Encolpius' other entanglement in this area is with the rich merchant-captain, Lichas, and his wife Hedyle. Lichas was on very intimate terms with Encolpius (*Sat.*, 105.5, 108.6), but the relationship ends with Encolpius' seduction of Hedyle and his theft of a valuable sacred rattle and robe of Isis, the tutelary deity of Lichas' ship. Adding insult to injury, before departing, Encolpius commits some outrage against the captain in the colonnade of Hercules at Baiae (*Sat.*, 106.2).

Still in the same area, the pair fall in with Ascyltos, an aggressive young homosexual, who may have been living with a certain Lycurgus (*Sat.*, 81.4). This episode presumably revolved around another jealous incident, this time involving Giton, Encolpius, and Lycurgus. Encolpius apparently kills Lycurgus by stealth and the trio rob his villa and escape. The proceeds of this robbery, some gold pieces, are sewn up in an old tunic and entrusted to Encolpius.

The next set of adventures overlaps with part of our extant text. It would seem that somewhere in the country near Baiae and Puteoli, the three commit another crime. They steal a cloak, but in leaving the scene they are separated, and Encolpius loses the tunic with the gold pieces. Although Encolpius sees the countryman who finds it, he dares do nothing about it. The trio, once united, witness and disturb some ceremonies in honour of Priapus, which are being held, we discover later, by the priestess Quartilla. It is not impossible that the cloak stealing and the sacrilege are part of the same episode, as Quartilla speaks of robbery (*latrocinia*, *Sat.*, 17.4) as well as sacrilege.

The episode of the cloak and tunic culminates in our narrative with an attempt to sell the cloak and the unexpected recovery of the tunic with the gold pieces (*Sat.*, 12–15). This is immediately followed, if the sequence of our fragments is correct, by the grotesque episode with Quartilla, who has tracked them down to avenge herself for their sacrilege. Despite the fragmentary text, the general import of the episode is clear enough. On the one hand it is a further instance of Encolpius' continual and painful brushes with the resentful Priapus; on the other, Quartilla is the first of the strong, libidinous women whom we meet in our extant narrative, although not the first in the original work (apart from the mysterious Doris of *Sat.*, 126.18, there have also been Hedyle and Tryphaena). Such women are a standard target of ancient satire, and Petronius was forced by his choice of a satiric *form* to adopt certain conventional satiric subjects—the riggish female would be a natural choice for a work entitled *Satyricōn libri* or *Books of Satyric Matters*. The contrast between the low sexual content and the delicacy of the style and the parodic but still poetic colouring is part of the humour.

On the details of the punishment inflicted on the trio and the orgy that intermittently accompanies it we need not elaborate. The peaceful close of the scene is followed by a gap. And with the *Cena Trimalchionis* we revert to the less orgiastic sequence of adventures in Puteoli. Before the trio had tried to sell the cloak and had been captured by Quartilla and her followers, our narrative had opened with a speech delivered by Encolpius, attacking in an elaborate rhetorical parody the low level of contemporary rhetoric. Encolpius is addressing Agamemnon, a professor of rhetoric. They are in Agamemnon's school, and no doubt Encolpius and Ascyltos had scraped an acquaintance with him for their own ends. Agamemnon's defence is friendly and complimentary, and although Encolpius slips away to pursue Ascyltos, whose intentions towards Giton he strongly suspects, it is through the offices of Agamemnon that the three are invited to dinner with Trimalchio (*Sat.*, 26.7ff), the high point of our *Satyricon*. Before we reach this section, there is an attempted rape of Giton by Ascyltos. A jealous quarrel follows, in the course of which Encolpius tries to end their association in order to have Giton to himself once more. The *Cena* and the episodes involving the cloak and Quartilla[5] serve as interruptions in the steady decline of the relationship between Encolpius and Ascyltos.

From 26.7 onwards, however, the sequence of events is clear enough. Encolpius becomes more of a detached narrator, drawing for us a would-be satiric portrait of the great vulgarian Trimalchio, one of the self-made freedmen so common in first-century Rome. Oddly enough, the comic creation involved in this character, for all the sarcastic comments of Encolpius, leaves the reader in the end with a sympathetic impression of Trimalchio. It is the novelist rather than the satirist in Petronius that finally gets the upper hand. There is no need to enumerate the different incidents as the text has survived with almost no lacunae in the Trau MS. (*H*), but the literary devices deployed are worth noting. We are given Trimalchio in the round, first by Encolpius' description of his physical appearance and environment, then by the realistic reportage of his freedman friends at dinner, then, more dramatically, by Trimalchio's own speeches and general behaviour, culminating in his quarrel with his wife and his long, boastful description of his rise to fortune. The sources Petronius drew upon for this elaborate portrait are many and varied. Plato's *Symposium* and Horace's *Cena Nasidieni* (*Satires*, 2.8) supplied the literary framework and some of the incidents; a keen observation of the manners, appurtenances, and ways of speaking in this *milieu*, supplied most of the matter; and for the great portrait of the host Petronius drew extensively and imaginatively on Seneca's writings.[6] Yet this parodic motive in no way interferes with the creative power of the characterization. Trimalchio is self-subsistent and the *Cena* again illustrates the Petronian method of blending a realistic subject-matter with a highly literary treatment: the humour of the episode is the same as the humour of the whole work, although it may be argued that here Petronius surpassed himself.

After the three escape from Trimalchio's house, we return to the quarrel between Ascyltos and Encolpius, but to the latter's surprise Giton abandons him for Ascyltos. A new figure now enters to take Ascyltos' place, the lecherous old poet Eumolpus, whose two invectives against the moral decay of the age and the arts contrast comically with his story of the Boy of Pergamum, an amusing *conte* of which Eumolpus is made the hero. At the end of this episode in the picture gallery, Eumolpus recites, apparently impromptu, sixty-five iambic senarii on the Fall of Troy. The poem is a free reworking of part of Book II of the *Aeneid*, and its aim, as far as we can see, is pastiche or parody of Senecan tragedy. The problems it presents for the translator may be deferred for the moment.

The poet and his new friend visit the baths, where Encolpius discovers Giton, and the two lovers are reunited. But Encolpius finds that in Eumolpus he has simply substituted one rival for another and his jealousy shows itself in the usual emotional ways. Peace, however, is made at last and the new trio take ship for Tarentum. Unfortunately the ship belongs to Encolpius' old enemy Lichas, and carries another old enemy and rival, the courtesan Tryphaena. For all their ingenious attempts to escape detection, Encolpius and Giton are flushed from hiding—another intervention of Priapus. A mock-epic battle ends in some sort of reconciliation, which provides further occasions for Encolpius' jealousy to show itself.

This peace is followed by a real storm: Encolpius, Eumolpus, and Giton manage to escape. Lichas is drowned and the discovery of his body next day provides another opportunity for Senecan parody. The three now proceed to Croton, and on the way Eumolpus delivers himself of a long poem on the civil war—the so-called *Carmen de Bello Civili*, which was, incidentally, the first piece of Petronius ever to be translated into English.[7]

The last episode of the work as we have it consists of two narrative strands: the deception of the legacy hunters of Croton by Eumolpus and Encolpius' affair with the aggressive and demanding Circe. The humour of this last depends mainly on the contrast between the realities of sexual passion and impotence and the romanticism of the elegiac style of the narration—Ovid is heavily drawn upon for the parodic effects. Priapus of course is still the divine harasser of Encolpius and frustrates him in his attempt to achieve 'the right true end of love'. Fortunately the romantic note and the note of sexual realism come over easily into English and the only problems for the translator presented by this episode are purely tactical.

The work ends abruptly with a confrontation between Eumolpus and the legacy hunters. No doubt they had grown suspicious and Eumolpus seems to be attempting to lull their suspicions by pretending to be on the point of death. He also imposes such difficult conditions in his will—the beneficiaries must eat his corpse, for example—that one may surmise that he hopes to put them off and make his escape. One may also surmise that Encolpius does not return to favour in his lady's eyes, but that she joins the legacy hunters in their final vengeance. Eumolpus perhaps met his end in Croton, but Encolpius and Giton presumably escaped, perhaps with the help of Circe's maid, Chrysis (cf. *Sat.*, 139.4). What further adventures befell Encolpius can only be guessed at. No doubt there was some comic resolution of the main plot, the Wrath of Priapus, which alone could end Encolpius' wanderings. This is suggested by analogies, whether drawn from the *Odyssey*, the Greek novel proper, the *Reiseroman*, or even from the only comparable Latin work, Apuleius' *Metamorphoses*. The fragments suggest a possible episode in Egypt, where scenes from the later Greek novels were often set, and allusions to Isis through the extant narrative (e.g. *Sat.*, 114.5, 117.3) afford some food for speculation. The mother of the gods might play a comic role in the *Satyricon* as she plays a serious role in Apuleius' novel.

Of course this bald summary is liable to give a misleading impression, an impression merely of a picaresque romance or a bawdy adventure story: it does not do justice to the tone and spirit of the work. The plot as we have it involves many digressions, excurses on literary, philosophical, and social themes, long verse sections, and short stories. No doubt in the vanished portion of the narrative these were as common as they are in the extant fragments, although we cannot guess at their nature and extent as we can at the incidents of the plot proper.

What must be stressed is that, for all its picaresque plot, the *Satyricon* is a highly literary work, which, despite the doubts of centuries, was written specifically for the amusement of Nero's court circle, itself a highly literary group which, at different times, included Seneca, Lucan, Petronius and others: Nero's own artistic interests are of course notorious. The author of the *Satyricon* was almost certainly the T. Petronius described by Tacitus (*Annals*, 16.18)[8] as Nero's *arbiter elegantiae*, for it is unlikely that in a circle of such a sort his taste would be confined to court etiquette and the connoisseurship of wine (cf. Pliny, *Natural History*, 37.20). Some of Tacitus' remarks are relevant to the historical understanding of the *Satyricon* and deserve being repeated:

> illi dies per somnum, nox officiis et oblectamentis vitae transigebatur: utque alios industria, ita hunc ignavia ad famam protulerat, habebaturque non ganeo et profligator ut plerique sua haurientium, sed erudito luxu. ac dicta factaque eius quanto solutiora et quandam sui neglegentiam praeferentia,

tanto gratius in speciem simplicitatis accipiebantur. pro consule tamen Bithyniae et mox consul vigentem se ac parem negotiis ostendit. dein revolutus ad vitia seu vitiorum imitatione inter paucos familiarium Neroni adsumptus est, elegantiae arbiter, dum nihil amoenum et molle affluentia putat, nisi quod ei Petronius approbavisset . . . neque tamen praeceps vitam expulit, sed incisas venas, ut libitum, obligatas aperire rursum et alloqui amicos, non per seria aut quibus gloriam constantiae peteret. audiebatque referentes nihil de immortalitate animae et sapientium placitis, sed levia carmina et faciles versus. servorum alios largitione, quosdam verberibus affecit . . .

(Petronius . . . was a man who spent his days sleeping and his nights working or enjoying himself. Industry is the usual foundation of success, but with him it was idleness. Unlike most people who throw away their money in dissipation, he was not regarded as an extravagant sensualist, but as one who made luxury a fine art. His conversation and his way of life were unconventional with a certain air of nonchalance, and they charmed people all the more by seeming so unstudied. Yet as proconsul in Bithynia and later as consul, he showed himself a vigorous and capable administrator. His subsequent return to his old habits, whether this was real or apparent, led to his admission to the small circle of Nero's intimates, where he became the Arbiter of Elegance. In the end Nero's jaded appetite regarded nothing as enjoyable or refined unless Petronius had given his sanction to it . . .)

Tacitus' description of Petronius' death through the machinations of Tigellinus refers to his literary tastes:

Not that he was hasty in taking leave of life. On the contrary he opened his veins and then, as the fancy took him, he bound them up or re-opened them. Meanwhile he talked with friends, but not on serious topics or anything calculated to win admiration for his Stoicism. He listened to their contributions—not discussions about the immortality of the soul or the views of philosophers, but simply gay songs and light verse. He gave some of his slaves rewards, some whippings . . .

As is clear from Tacitus' description of Petronius' downfall, there were personal rivalries at work around Nero, but it is also clear from the *Satyricon* that, as might be expected, there was literary rivalry also. The *Satyricon* in fact has a number of scarcely veiled and easily recognizable attacks on contemporary Neronian writing, not in the serious manner of Persius' first satire, but in the form of amusing parody and *ad hoc* literary criticism. For instance, the critique put in the mouth of the disreputable poet Eumolpus (*Sat.*, 118) is clearly directed at Lucan: Eumolpus criticizes the rhetorical taste for unassimilated *sententiae* in poetry and strongly opposes the abandonment of the traditional divine machinery of epic used by Virgil and now replaced by more Stoic modes of the supernatural in the *Pharsalia*. The poem that follows, with its constant allusion to, and retreatment of Lucanian material, is a sort of Virgilianization of Lucan's theme. Similarly, the *Troiae Halosis* (*Sat.*, 89), the poem on the sack of Troy also delivered by Eumolpus, is a hostile imitation of Seneca's style in his tragedies, as the verbal allusions and reminiscences—particularly of the *Agamemnon*—make clear.

Less commonly appreciated, however, is the fact that much of the philosophical and social moralizing put into the mouths of Eumolpus and the equally disreputable Encolpius is comic parody of the subjects, sentiments, and phrasing of Seneca's philosophical works, particularly of that near-contemporary work, written towards the end of Seneca's life, the *Epistulae Morales ad Lucilium*. The echoes and reminiscences of Seneca found in Petronius must be taken as parody because the contexts in which they occur are uniformly humorous or ironic. A couple of examples will perhaps suffice. In the elaborate and, at least initially, satiric portrait of Trimalchio, he is given an absurd and drunken speech on the common humanity of free men and slaves (*Sat.*, 71.1). This strongly resembles the Stoic doctrine on the subject expounded by Seneca in *Epistulae Morales*, 47. Trimalchio is not obviously kind to his slaves elsewhere in the *Cena*, and Encolpius criticizes the confusion caused by Trimalchio's tasteless invitation of his slaves to the table. This therefore constitutes an aesthetic, and Epicurean, criticism of the social consequences of such Stoic themes. Petronius' own attitude to his slaves was based on justice, not equality (Tacitus, *Annals*, 16.19). Again, Encolpius' extravagant and rhetorical exclamations over the body of his dead enemy

Lichas (*Sat.*, 115.9ff) read like nothing so much as a pastiche of Seneca's numerous remarks on the uncertainty of fortune, the unimportance of burial, and the futility of human planning.[9] It should be added that Petronius' veiled attacks may not have gone altogether unanswered. The later books of the *Epistulae Morales* contain attacks on a certain section of Neronian society, the *turba lucifugarum*, which, to judge from Tacitus' description of Petronius' nocturnal habits and general way of life, must surely have included the courtier. What else are we to conclude from such remarks as these?

> sunt qui officia lucis noctisque perverterint nec ante diducant oculos hesterna graves crapula quam adpetere nox coepit . . . interrogas quomodo haec animo pravitas fiat aversandi diem et totam vitam in noctem transferendi? omnia vitia contra naturam pugnant, omnia debitum ordinem deserunt; hoc est luxuriae propositum, gaudere perversis nec tantum discedere a recto sed quam longissime abire, deinde etiam e contrario stare . . . post prandium aut cenam bibere vulgare est; hoc patres familiae rustici faciunt et verae voluptatis ignari . . . non oportet id facere quod populus; res sordida est trita ac vulgari via vivere . . . causa autem est ita vivere quibusdam, non quia aliquid existiment noctem ipsam habere iucundius, sed quia nihil iuvat solitum, et gravis malae conscientiae lux est . . . praeterea luxuriosi vitam suam esse in sermonibus dum vivunt volunt . . . quomodo cultu se a ceteris distinguunt, quomodo elegantia cenarum, munditiis vehiculorum, sic volunt separari etiam temporum dispositione . . . (*Ep.*, 122 *passim*)[10]

(There are those who confound the duties of daylight and dark, and do not open their eyes, still heavy from yesterday's hangover, before night begins to come on . . . Do you want to know how this moral depravity begins of shunning the day and transferring the whole of one's living to the nighttime? All vices fight against nature and they all abandon the proper order of things; this is the settled aim of high living, to enjoy what is perverse, and not merely to depart from what is right but to fly from it as far as possible, and then even to take up the opposite position . . . Drinking after lunch or dinner is vulgar: respectable country folk do this and people who have no idea of true pleasure . . . One must not do what ordinary people do; living in the usual vulgar way is sordid . . . The reason however why some live in the way I described is not because they think that night-time itself offers any more fun, but because nothing normal pleases them, and light is a burden for a bad conscience . . . Besides those who live high want their lives to be talked about while they are living it . . . Just as they set themselves apart from the rest by their appearance, by the tastefulness of their dinner parties, and the elegance of their chariots, so they wish to be set apart also by the disposition of their time . . .)

The *Satyricon* then is a much more topical and, in a sense, *opportunistic* production than has sometimes been realized. The suggestion that it was written to be recited by a trained voice—presumably to the court circle—is a useful one.[11] Such serial presentation would not only explain the possible length of the work, and its dramatic shifts and changes of tone, but also its episodic nature; it would also give more point to what might strike us as rather topical criticism or parody of the authors, such as Lucan and Seneca, whom Petronius for some reason disliked. If Petronius had such varied aims in mind, then it would be natural for him to choose as his literary vehicle Menippean satire, the mixture of prose and verse, which would allow him to display his artistic versatility, deploy his literary criticism, and through the medium of only semi-serious satire, exhibit his most characteristic quality, his insolent and daring good taste—even at the expense of certain court worthies.[12] Menippean satire, developed from Cynic diatribes by Menippus of Gadara into a literary form, had been introduced into Latin literature by Varro: that it was still a viable genre is suggested by the extant *Apocolocyntosis* of Seneca, which, whether that is its true title or not, must have been written at the beginning of the Neronian period, in A.D. 54. This work is of course just a short political squib; much of Petronius' originality consisted in expanding the possibilities of such fictional narrative, adding a flexible plot, and making some at least of the episodes into elaborate and imaginative set-pieces.

The nature of the audience may also explain what is perhaps the most striking feature of the *Satyricon*, the combination of low characters, vulgar milieux, and sometimes bizarre sexual incidents, with a terse, artistic narrative Latin, constant literary allusions, and occasional ornate passages of a more elevated style, sometimes serious, sometimes parodic, but always carefully polished. And it is noteworthy also that, in the words of M. Baillard, 'jusque dans ses pages le plus érotiques, Pétrone s'interdit constamment les gravelures et crudités de mot si familières à Catulle, à Martiale, et même à Horace.' Of course this is the basic comic impulse of the work: the refined, literary, and ironic treatment of uniformly disreputable personages and sordid ways of living in a Latinity which, when it is not reproducing vulgar speech, is remarkably pure by the Attic canons of the plain style, the *genus tenue*. Even Petronius' literary sophistication reinforces this underlying source of humour. The Wrath of Priapus against Encolpius which seems to have sent him off on his wanderings and which is responsible for many of his misfortunes in the extant narrative is, as we have seen, a parody of the Wrath of Poseidon against Odysseus, as several Homeric allusions remind us; and a pastiche of Virgil is introduced to describe, of all things, Encolpius' limp sexual organ (*Sat.*, 132.11). The artistry is perfectly understandable in the light of the high degree of literary culture during the Neronian period, but the choice of such subject matter, even for humorous treatment, has to be explained by a certain *nostalgie de la boue*, which not infrequently goes hand in hand with material and intellectual refinement. It was perhaps the same *nostalgie de la boue* that sent Nero the *artifex* wandering in disguise through the lower quarters of Rome like a seventeenth-century rowdy or an imperial Dorian Gray (Suetonius, *Nero*, 26). Certainly some such impulse must be invoked to explain both the detailed observation in the *Cena* of a milieu and a speech that one would imagine were foreign to an arbiter of elegance and also the peculiar range of sexual scenes which Petronius chose to depict.

Obviously a number of factors interacted in suggesting to Petronius the subjects, the treatment and the form of the work, and it would not be easy to determine which was logically or temporally prior to which. Petronius' decision to choose for his vehicle a form of *satura*, which, with such kindred forms as epigram, represented the earthy, more Italian strain in Roman literature and provided Quintilian with one of his more justified literary judgments (*satura quidem tota nostra est*), was a critical decision. It did not of course entail that a stern moral purpose must underlie his creative work: satire, whatever we now think of it, was an art form like any other, not versified sermonizing. Juvenal's protests of *saeva indignatio* and *difficile est saturam non scribere*, are as conventional as the epic poet's invocation of the Muse, and will not stand up to a scrutiny of the essentially artistic motives for his writing. The moral positives, such as they are, are there for the sake of the poem, not the other way round. Similarly, Petronius is not a satirist in any high moral sense of the word: he is an artist developing the potentialities of certain traditional satiric themes. For instance, our final feeling for that impressive comic creation, Trimalchio, is one of sympathy and amusement, not disgust— and Petronius has carefully led us to this by undercutting the moral and aesthetic criticisms of Encolpius; Encolpius inadvertently reveals himself as a rather timorous, impressionable and gauche commentator on the action. The choice of form, however, would suggest certain themes and subjects, and others would be suggested by his predecessors in satire: Trimalchio owes something to Horace's Nasidienus; libidinous women like Quartilla, Tryphaena and Circe had been satirical butts throughout antiquity; and legacy-hunting (*captatio*), a very Roman vice, had a fascination for the Roman satirists which it does not have for us.

These and other subjects had respectable antecedents, as indeed had sexual themes of a more forthright sort, and Petronius could defend his work on the grounds that such writing represented reality, or what really happened, as opposed to unreal rhetorical exercises, philosophical moralizing, or the mythological poems that Martial and Juvenal so despised.[13] Moreover, in contrast to Stoic writers such as Lucan and Seneca, Petronius was an Epicurean and his work is clearly based on Epicurean principles. Unlike Stoic literary theory, Epicurean theory, as we know it from Philodemus and others,[14] did not take literature to be the servant of morality; literature's purpose was pleasure. So on both counts Petronius' well-known defence of his work (*Sat.*, 132.15) has to be taken seriously, and it both disposes of the constant attempts to make him out some sort of moralist as opposed to a pure artist, and also reveals most clearly the basic intention of the work.

The defence is put in the mouth of Encolpius, the narrator, just after he has been chiding his sexual equipment for having failed him with Circe: the humour of the episode in no way undermines the validity of the defence, for all of the episodes in the *Satyricon*, other than some of the literary discussions, are meant to be humorous. The passage runs as follows:

> Quid me constricta spectatis fronte, Catones,
> damnatisque novae simplicitatis opus?
> sermonis puri non tristis gratia ridet,
> quodque facit populus, candida lingua refert.
> nam quis concubitus, Veneris quis gaudia nescit?
> quis vetat in tepido membra calere toro?
> ipse pater veri doctos Epicurus amare
> iussit, et hoc vitam dixit habere τέλος.

A paraphrase would run something like this: the work you are now hearing no doubt provokes the usual strictures from the more censorious who believe that in accordance with Stoic literary theories a work of art should be instructive and moral, not least in the narrowest sense of that term. Such critics will condemn this work, which is a reaction against our present high-flown modes of writing and old-fashioned puritanism, and which has its own literary and stylistic intentions. Its pure Latinity has one end: to charm you, not to instruct you. My subject is human behaviour and the narrative is realistic and humorous, although *honest* might be a better way of describing it. No one is unaware of the important place sex has in ordinary life. Does anyone take a moral stand against harmless and natural sexual enjoyment and comfort? As an Epicurean I could even invoke philosophical principles in their defence and point to Epicurus' doctrines about its supreme importance.[15]

The poem of course does not embrace all the aspects of the *Satyricon*; the literary allusiveness, for instance, and the topical parody are not mentioned, but it does stress what we know from other sources such as Macrobius (*In Somnium Scipionis*, 1.2.8), that there were large areas of sexual matter in the work, and the basic plot, a comic and sexual *Reiseroman*, is properly represented by its original title, *Satyricōn libri*, namely, *Books of Satyric Matters*. The poem also brings out that Petronius was an Atticist in style, Epicurean in his philosophy and literary theory, and a realist strongly opposed to the writers of moral tracts and far-fetched declamations. (The latter had already been bitingly condemned by Encolpius in the opening chapter of the work.) We know from

Eumolpus' critique of Lucan that Petronius was also a traditional-
ist in his literary taste.

From this critical view, certain conclusions for the translator
naturally follow. The narrative style of the work, which belongs
to the *genus tenue*, is an educated, plain, rhythmical Latin; it should
therefore be represented by a spare but elegant English with un-
forced speech rhythms. Arguably the very vigorous and racy colloquial American used by one of the most successful of Petronius'
translators, William Arrowsmith, does some injustice to the tone
of the original by increasing its tempo. Similarly, Petronius' careful avoidance, in accordance with Attic principles, of the large
Latin vocabulary of obscenity, even when he is dealing with quite
bizarre sexual incidents, is lost in certain other translations that
conceive the work merely as pornography and which try to bring
out that aspect of it by a crude, if not vulgar, heightening of the
language of some of the episodes.

But the basic tone modulates at times into ironic or high-flown
parody of contemporary writing: for instance, in Encolpius' fake
moralizing on the uncertainty of life over Lichas' corpse (*Sat.*,
115.9ff), and perhaps also in the opening chapters, where Encolpius, in a suitably ornate style, delivers himself of an elaborate
criticism of contemporary declamation. Here the language of the
translation must be suitably shrill and forced, and the translator
should use the rhetorical and exclamatory style that he would find
appropriate for a translation of Seneca's philosophical works. Too
restrained an English might lose the mocking and parodic tone
of the original. Here is a brief example:

'ubi nunc est' inquam 'iracundia tua, ubi impotentia tua?
nempe piscibus beluisque expositus es, et qui ante iactabas
vires imperii tui, de tam magna nave ne tabulam quidem nau-
fragus habes. ite nunc mortales, et magnis cogitationibus
pectora implete. ite cauti, et opes fraudibus captas per mille
annos disponite...' (*Sat.*, 115.12–14)

('Where are they now,' I cried, 'all your anger and your greatness? But two little hours ago you boasted of your pride of
power and your manhood's strength and yet, what are you
now? Food for the fish, for every crawling creature in the sea.
Of all that mighty ship you once commanded, not one poor

saving spar is left you in your utter shipwreck. And yet we scheme and hope, stuffing our foolish hearts with dreams, scrimping and saving, hoarding the wealth we win by wrong, planning our lives as though we had a thousand years to live! . . .') (*Tr.* Arrowsmith)

The considerable departures from the original here are justified by the substitution of a modern, more American (and wordier) rhetoric. The *ite nunc* formula, variations of which are common in Seneca,[16] is dropped, but satisfactorily replaced by the more modern device of piling up a succession of florid adjectives. Such techniques that make use of *equivalences* rather than literal translation have to be constantly borne in mind by the translator of Petronius, otherwise the complex surface of the work is reduced to monotony and flatness.

The question of parody immediately brings up two difficult problems that face the translator: the *Troiae Halosis* and the *Bellum Civile*, two long poems of 65 and 295 lines respectively, which describe the capture of Troy and the causes and opening events of the Civil War. As I stated earlier, the first bears an obvious relation to Seneca's tragedies and the second to Lucan's *Pharsalia*; a straightforward modern translation of them both will misrepresent Petronius' intentions by offering dull, undistinguished poetic versions; the reader then is likely to take them as two unsuccessful poems seriously intended by Petronius, and he may be left with a low estimate of the writer's—or the translator's—taste and competence. He may take them, at best, as deliberately mediocre, as a way of concretely presenting to us the poverty of Eumolpus' talent. But in fact Eumolpus is not the target here, and he does show elsewhere intellectual enthusiasm, literary appreciation and critical insight (e.g. at *Sat.*, 118); the consistency of his character is sacrificed temporarily to Petronius' local aims, which are to attack Seneca and his nephew Lucan.

Now clearly there is no well-known and accepted twentieth-century translation of Senecan drama that could be utilized to represent adequately what Petronius is doing. One might imitate the language of the great Elizabethan translator of Seneca, Thomas Heywood, and then the poem would at least impress the reader as an imitation of Elizabethan drama, which is closer to what is needed. Other possibilities are perhaps a parody or pas-

tiche of Pope's language in his translations of Homer. Certainly
some sort of artificial language is necessary. If a contemporary
solution is desired, one might suggest a parody or imitation of the
loose iambic lines and melancholy language of the plays of T. S.
Eliot. My own solution, which was to imitate Anglo-Saxon al-
literative poetry somewhat in the manner of Pound's translation of
an early English poem *The Sea-Farer*, I am no longer satisfied with.
The idiom is too alien to reproduce the effect Petronius intended.

The solution to the critical imitation of Lucan is much easier.
No translation of Lucan can play the host to this parasite: this
would be far too unreal. A straight translation would be insuffer-
ably dull—the *Bellum Civile* is in itself a dull and, linguistically, a
not very poetic treatment of Lucan's subject. For Petronius'
audience the interest would lie predominantly in catching the
interwoven echoes and reminiscences of Lucan and Virgil. Now
there is one obvious modern poet whose style, technique, and
language would be instantly recognizable—Ezra Pound, particularly the Pound of the *Cantos*, the nearest thing the twentieth century has to an epic poem. If the *Bellum Civile* were translated into
a pastiche of the *Cantos*, then its function as a literary exercise, with
a definite relationship to an original, would be immediately seen;
the poem would then perhaps provide some interest for the reader
conversant with the techniques of modern poetry. A brief sample
will suffice:

> quare tam perdita Roma
> ipsa sui merces erat et sine vindice praeda.
> praeterea gemino deprensam gurgite plebem
> faenoris illuvies ususque exederat aeris.
> nulla est certa domus, nullum sine pignore corpus,
> sed veluti tabes tacitis concepta medullis
> intra membra furens curis latrantibus errat.
> arma placent miseris, detritaque commoda luxu
> vulneribus reparantur. inops audacia tuta est.
> hoc mersam caeno Romam somnoque iacentem
> quae poterant artes sana ratione movere
> ni furor et bellum ferroque excita libido?
>
> (*Sat.*, 119.49–60)

The sentential—and Stoic—character of this passage, like the
whole poem, is meant to remind us of Lucan's *Pharsalia* and its

rhetorical style of writing. Petronius' criticism of the *Pharsalia* consists of Virgilianizing the style and reintroducing the divine machinery of epic which Lucan, perhaps rightly, dropped in favour of a more Stoic (and therefore more modern) vision of the interaction of the numinous with the world of men. But clearly the parasitic nature of this piece of *vers d'occasion* is lost on the English reader if it is translated in a straightforward manner, as it was by Fanshawe, whose version reads as follows:

> here then lyes
> *Rome* her own *Merchant* and own *merchandise.*
> Besides now *use* on *use*, men's *principals*
> So swell'd, it overwhelm'd them. No man calls
> His house his own. None uningag'd: but *debt*
> Like to a lingering disease, doth fret
> Into their barking bowels, being pain'd
> They cry to *Arms*: and wealth with *ryot* drayn'd
> Must heal with *wounds*: safe *Want sets on fire.*
> Cast in this *sleep*, and rowling in this *mire*
> What reasons can wake *Rome*, but *war* and *blood*:
> Which till th'are felt, are never understood.

What is lost is clearly the subtle parody of the poem. What is needed is some modern equivalent to play host to the English translation. Both Arrowsmith and I independently hit on the idea that the only twentieth-century poem that would offer the appropriate resonance for the average reader was the *Cantos*. The passage of the *Carmen de Bello Civili* now in question does in fact bear a striking resemblance to *Canto XLV* ('With usura hath no man a house of good stone . . .'). Arrowsmith's version accordingly ran like this:

> self-betrayed, self-sold, self-prey and quarry made.
> Whence no avenger rose.
>   And usury, a rot:
> the people drowning in a double sea, by debt pulled down,
> by usury,
>   a filth.
>   With usura hath no man a house;
> no man's body but by debt is bound, in mortmain; hard
> of usura,

the rot within, the impostumé in the guts,
foetor-infestation that flameth the blood to fever,
that bays the body down.
                    Usura, a ruin,
whence springeth war, whence revolution breaketh;
whence desperation taketh arms, and profligate and pauper
make cause together. Beggary hath daring.
O Rome,
            in such a sewer sunk, in such a sleep,
what surgery could cure, what skill could waken into life,
but war, the rage of war, the passion of the steel?

The actual quotation from Pound fits perfectly and recalls the frequent local imitations of the *Pharsalia* that abound in Petronius' verse.

There is another incidental advantage in adopting the verse techniques of the *Cantos*: the translation may be as free or as close as one wishes, provided the basic rhetoric is preserved. In the case of the above passage, Arrowsmith chose to expand, but roughly the same length may be preserved if the translator wishes, as this alternative version shows:

Rome a lost city,
                    merchant and merchandise,
                    plunderer and plundered.
A vile vortex, a gaping whirlpool
The people drowning.
    With *Usura*
    Merdery in the absolute rottenness,
    With usura hath no man a house
    With usura hath no man a hand free
    A canker born in the hidden marrow,
    A madness raging in the limbs of the body politic
    And wandering with its sorrows
    Like a pack of hounds.
    And out of this revolution
    Revolution from poverty.
War tempts the poor.
Dissipated finances are recouped by murder,
Boldness with nothing has nothing to lose.
Drowned in this filth, sodden with this sleep,

What practitioner's skill can rouse Rome surely?
Furor militaris
None but the soldier's, *furor militaris*,
       desire pricked by the sword.

                   (*Tr.* Sullivan)

    The other verse insertions in the work present little difficulty. None of them are particularly ambitious, although they are sometimes amusing and function in their context very adequately as *vers d'occasion fictive*, sometimes to illustrate the situation, sometimes as displays of poetic versatility, sometimes as general literary parody. At one point, for instance, Trimalchio steps a little out of his character as a pretentious and ignorant freedman in order to recite some lines which he alleges are by Publilius Syrus. Although most of the language is suitably archaic, some anachronistic touches suggest that this is in fact a display of Petronius' facility for verse imitation. (And after all, if the lines were really Publilius', their insertion would be no great feat and the inconsistency in Trimalchio's character would be rather pointless.) Here a suitably archaic diction imitating the highly alliterative language and clotted rhythm of the original is not difficult to achieve, and this would achieve an effect equivalent to the original in its context.

    It may be added in passing that many of the smaller difficulties that face the translator of Petronius are simply problems that face any translator of a work which involves poetry and elaborate verbal wit. The wide diversity of metres employed in the shorter poems has to be reproduced somehow in English. Naturally any attempt to imitate the actual metres themselves has to be eschewed: the genius of English versification is quite different from that of Latin (as translators who use six foot stress lines to reproduce the Latin hexameter so frequently forget). The translator has in each case to find an appropriate metre or stanza form— and sometimes *vers libre* may offer the only solution, provided it is not always used, for that would have the opposite effect to that which should be intended: it would substitute uniformity for Petronian variety and versatility. Reproducing the puns and the many (and frequently risqué) *doubles entendres* requires work, but provided a responsible freedom is exercised, all should yield to time and thought.

One important problem has been left to the last: the colloquial language of the *Cena Trimalchionis*. Because this is the most impressive and carefully conceived segment of the work extant it is also the *pons asinorum* of Petronian translators. A typical example of the freedmen's conversation at Trimalchio's table is Ganymedes' *convicium saeculi*:

> 'narratis quod nec ad caelum nec ad terram pertinet, cum interim nemo curat, quid annona mordet. non mehercules hodie buccam panis invenire potui. et quomodo siccitas perseverat. iam annum esur[it]io fuit. aediles male eveniat, qui cum pistoribus colludunt "serva me, servabo te". itaque populus minutus laborat; nam isti maiores maxillae semper Saturnalia agunt. o si haberemus illos leones, quos ego hic inveni, cum primum ex Asia veni. illud erat vivere . . . heu heu, quotidie peius. haec colonia retroversus crescit tamquam coda vituli . . . quid enim futurum est, si nec dii nec homines huius coloniae miserentur? ita meos fruniscar, ut puto omnia illa a diibus fieri. nemo enim caelum caelum putat, nemo ieiunium servat, nemo Iovem pili facit, sed omnes opertis oculis bona sua computant . . .'

The problem here is the delicate matter of translating this sort of conversation into an acceptable English form. There are on the one hand the demands of liveliness and modernity, which are a duty to the original and to the reader, and there is, on the other hand, the usual need for fidelity to the author's poise and irony. A prose which is too brusquely colloquial, too vehement, and indeed too obtrusively deploying the slang and vulgarisms of a quite different milieu, runs the risk of distorting the atmosphere of this episode and the character of the speakers. This has happened in the case of J. M. Mitchell's translation, which renders the above passage as follows:

> 'You fellows are talking of things which don't matter a scrap in heaven or earth, and no one seems to care about the ruinous rise in corn. I take my oath I couldn't find a bite of bread to-day. And look how the drought continues! We've been on short commons for a whole year now. Devil take the commissioners; they're hand in glove with the bakers. "You help me, and I'll help you"; the unhappy public is between the

upper and the nether millstone, while your lordly gluttons
have one long beanfeast. Ah, for a week of those sturdy
warriors whom I found here when I first arrived from Asia!
That was real life! . . . Alas, alas! It gets worse every day;
this place is growing downwards like a calf's tail . . . What will
become of the wretched place forsaken by God and man? I
bet my bottom dollar that this is the hand of Providence. Not
a soul says his prayers; nobody fasts; nobody cares a jot for
Jove. We con our ledgers with our eyes glued to the
figures . . .'

This idiom of course makes the characters sound like English
schoolboys, and rather pretentious schoolboys at that. They are
strident and manly, but for all their liveliness, they are utterly unlike Petronius' carefully observed freedmen. Certainly they would
carry no conviction for the modern reader. For a more authentic
and convincing idiom one would have to turn to William Arrowsmith's translation, which renders the above passage as follows:

'Stuff like that doesn't matter a bit to man or beast. But nobody mentions the real thing, the way the price of bread is
pinching. God knows, I couldn't buy a mouthful of bread
today. And this damn drought goes on and on. Nobody's
had a bellyful for years now. It's those rotten officials, you
take my word for it. They're in cahoots with the bakers: you
scratch me and I'll scratch you. So the little people get it in
the neck, but in the rich man's jaws it's jubilee all year. By
god, if we only had the kind of men we used to have, the
sort I found here when I arrived from Asia. Then life was
something like living . . . But that's what I mean, things are
just getting worse and worse. Why, this place is running
downhill like a heifer's ass . . . Mark my words, we're in for
bad times if some man or god doesn't have a heart and take
pity on this place. I'll stake my luck on it, the gods have got
a finger in what's been happening here. And you know why?
Because no one believes in the gods, that's why. Who observes the fast days any more, who cares a rap for Jupiter?
One and all, bold as brass, they sit there pretending to pray,
but cocking their eyes on the chances and counting up their
cash . . .'

The freedom requisite for such liveliness is defended by Arrowsmith on these grounds:

> The *Satyricon* requires the context and vigor of a *particular* language, a language at once vividly colloquial and vigorously literary, and no contemporary idiom of English seems to me to supply that particularity in such full ripeness as American English . . . Further, since translation to be complete usually involves a transference of culture as well as language, I have tried to create a recognizably contemporary version of the *Satyricon*, without, however, wholly modernizing it . . .[17]

And there is much in this argument. Nevertheless, it might be felt that Arrowsmith's solution makes Trimalchio and his circle almost *too* modern, and this American modernity may jar with the unassimilated Latin elements which are kept for the sake of fidelity to the original text. Arrowsmith fortunately did not carry this too far: he realized that 'a ruthless realism, the precise realism of a particular place and an unmistakable time, [is] jarring and destructive'.[18] And it may be that his language strikes only an English ear as too modern and too American for the tone of the original. (This prompts the thought that the *Satyricon* would have to be translated into each dialect of English to have its proper effect—which would be too much to expect!) Trimalchio's circle, however, is neither English nor American, and some account must be taken of the alien nature of that circle, as well as of its surprising timelessness.

This timelessness of course is easily paralleled in contemporary literature dealing with a similar ambience. The conversation of Mrs Bolton with Sir Clifford in D. H. Lawrence's *Lady Chatterley's Lover* presents some striking coincidences with the manner and substance of the conversations in the *Cena*. These snatches, for example, almost seem to echo Ganymedes' remarks:

> 'But there you are, grown-ups are worse than the children: and the old ones beat the band. Talk about morality! Nobody cares a thing. Folks does as they like, and much better off they are for it, I must say. But they're having to draw their horns in nowadays, now th' pits are working so bad, and they haven't got the money . . . But the women, oh, they do carry on! . . . And boys the same . . . Why, it's another world. And they fear nothing, and they respect nothing, the young

don't . . . the lads aren't like their dads. They're sacrificing nothing, they aren't: they're all for self . . . Oh, they're rough an' selfish, if you like. Everything falls on the older men, an' it's a bad outlook all round.'

It would seem that the *populus minutus* talks in the same way all the world over and all through the centuries: about money, about morality, about the degeneracy of the present compared to the past. But there are differences in the idiom (and in the particulars harped upon) that should not be smothered. With the *Cena*, if we use a modern dialect too tied to its particular place and time, the reader will feel that Roman freedmen simply did not talk like this, and he will refuse to suspend his belief to the proper extent.

My own solution to this problem, as against Arrowsmith's, was to adopt an even less localized language than his conventional American—a language based upon English vulgar language which would give the impression of a dialect, but not the dialect of any particular modern period or place in England. By it I hoped to express something of the vividness of the original but also the artificial quality of Petronius' literary construction—the real Mrs Boltons of Nottinghamshire do not talk like Lawrence's Mrs Bolton either. My version of Ganymedes' conversation therefore ran as follows:

'You're all talking about things that don't concern heaven or earth. Meanwhile, no one gives a damn the way we're hit by the corn situation. Honest to god, I couldn't get hold of a mouthful of bread today. And look how there's still no rain. It's been absolute starvation for a whole year now. To hell with the food officers! They're in with the bakers—"you be nice to me and I'll be nice to you." So the little man suffers, while those grinders of the poor never stop celebrating. Oh, if only we still had the sort of men I found here when I first arrived from Asia. Like lions they were. That was the life! . . . Ah me! It's getting worse every day. This place is going down like a calf's tail . . . What's going to happen to this place if neither god nor man will help us? As I hope to go home tonight, I'm sure all this is heaven's doing. Nobody believes in heaven, see, nobody fasts, nobody gives a damn for the Almighty. No, people only bow their heads to count their money . . .'

As ever, *traduttore traditore*: to represent the alienness, the elegance, and the economy of Petronius' artistic pastiche of plebeian dialogue means sacrificing the native immediacy, the natural impact, that it would have had even on the sophisticated ears of the Neronian circle. Yet the members of that circle would be as interested in the artistry of the imitation as in its truth to life. Even on the lower planes of literary endeavour—and the Alexandrian critical debates about the proper modes of writing still echoed in the Neronian age—style rather than matter was the prime consideration. Accordingly, to transpose the language freely into convincing modern idiom and strenuously local colloquialisms, to depart at will from the actual text in the interest of an up-to-date vividness and a supposedly perfect naturalness, may result in a subtle injustice to Petronius' refined art, for he is *not* trying to write in the style of the Pompeian *graffiti*. The translator, and the reader, have to decide where the proper compromise is to be made; and the decision is analogous to the decisions that have to be made about metres, when verse translation is in question. Freedom and fidelity are mistresses whose claims conflict, yet neither of them can be discarded.

Although this problem, the language of the conversation in the *Cena*, is the hardest that faces the translator of Petronius, it is similar to those that confront the translator of any Latin work in what one may call the 'Italian' tradition, the tradition that uses an artistic version of down-to-earth, ordinary idiom: Plautus, parts of Catullus, and any of the satirists or epigrammatists are obvious examples. It is this tradition, perhaps even more than the loftier genres such as epic, that makes one reflect that the classics have to be retranslated almost every generation. And their translatability in each age will be the measure of their vitality and relevance or their moribundity and unimportance.

Notes

1 One might mention *Petronius Arbiter, The Satyricon* by 'Sebastian Melmoth', which was attributed, wrongly, to Oscar Wilde, whose pen name this was (Paris, 1902); *The Satyricon of Petronius Arbiter* by W. C. Firebaugh (New York, 1922); *The Complete Works of Gaius Petronius* by Jack Lindsay (1927); the Loeb version by Michael Heseltine (London, 1913); *Petronius: The Satyricon* by J. M. Mitchell; *The Satyricon of Petronius* by Paul Dinnage (1953); *Petronius: The Satyricon* by William Arrowsmith (Ann Arbor,

1959); and my own *Petronius: The Satyricon and the Fragments* (Penguin, 1965). There are a number of undistinguished versions of the *Cena Trimalchionis* and several successful translations of a few of the fragments which need not concern us here.

2 *The Satyr of Titus Petronius Arbiter. A Roman Knight. With its Fragments recovered at Belgrade. Made English by Mr Burnaby of the Middle-Temple, and another Hand* (1694).

3 *Nation and Athenaeum* 33 (1923), 331.

4 See C. Cichorius, *Römische Studien*, Leipzig, 1922, 438ff, and cf. *Priap.*, 26, 32, 46, 73 etc.

5 It is not impossible that these last two episodes are misplaced and that they really belong to Book xiv, as is suggested by the interpolator of Fulgentius (*Myth.*, 3.8.73). The opening chapters (1–11) would then belong to Book xv. This surgery, however, would be too radical to adopt in a translation.

6 Compare in general Seneca's portraits of Calvisius Sabinus and Maecenas (*Ep.*, 27.5–8 and 114.6, 9, 26f); and for Trimalchio's views on the common humanity of slaves (*Sat.*, 71.1), cf. Seneca, *Ep.*, 47; for his mock funeral, cf. Seneca, *Ep.*, 12.8, where a similar anecdote is told about Pacuvius. This does not exhaust the resemblances. The whole question of Senecan parody is discussed below (pp. 165f).

7 By Sir Richard Fanshawe. It was printed in the preface to his translation of the *Lusiads* of Camoëns and has been reprinted most recently in *Arion* 5 (1966), 369ff.

8 See e.g. R. Browning, *CR* 6 (1956), 46ff, K. F. C. Rose, *Latomus* 20 (1961), 821ff, and G. Pugliese Carratelli, *PP* 3 (1946), 381.

9 Compare with the Petronian passage Seneca, *Nat. Quaest.*, 4 praef. 8; 2.59.3–4; *Consolatio ad Polybium*, 9.6–7; *Consolatio ad Marciam*, 10.6; 11.3–5; *De brevitate vitae*, 20.5; *De remediis fortunae*, 5.2,4,5; *Ep.*, 92.34–5; 99.8–9; 101.4,6. For other parodies of Senecan moralizing, compare *Sat.*, 88 with *Ep.*, 115.10–12 and *Nat. Quaest.*, 7.31.1ff; *Sat.*, 110.1 with *Ep.*, 73.6–8 and 88.12; and *Sat.*, 125.4 with *Ep.*, 105.7–8 etc. On the whole question, see J. Gottschlich, 'De parodiis Senecae apud Petronium' in *Misc. Phil. lib. zu Frid. Haase Jubiläum* (Breslau, 1863), P. Faider, *Études sur Sénèque* (Ghent, 1921), 15ff, and J. P. Sullivan, *The Satyricon of Petronius, A Literary Study* (London, 1968), 193ff.

10 The whole letter is worth consulting, as are letters 123 and 124, which contain further attacks on high society and Epicureanism. The abuse of the latter contrasts strikingly with the sympathetic use of Epicurean doctrine in the early books of the *Epistulae Morales*.

11 W. Arrowsmith, *Petronius: The Satyricon* (Ann Arbor, 1959), xiv.

12 Not merely writers. Encolpius' horror at Trimalchio's use of unguents for the guests' feet (*Sat.*, 70.8) seems a satiric glance at the future emperor Otho's introduction of this eastern custom to Nero's court (Pliny, *Natural History*, 13.20).

13 Cf. e.g. Persius, *Sat.*, 1 *passim*; Martial, x.4; Juvenal, Satire., 1.1ff.

14 See C. Jensen, *Philodemus über die Gedichte, fünftes Buch* (Berlin, 1923), 7f, 110ff.

15 For similar programmes, see Martial, III.85, VIII.3, XI.15, and for a general discussion of the poem, H. Stubbe, *Die Verseinlagen im Petron, Philologus Supplbd.* 25 (Leipzig, 1933), 150ff. On the more significant points of the interpretation: for Cato's symbolic function in Roman literature, see e.g. Cicero, *Ad Atticum*, 16.1.16; Seneca, *Ep.*, 97.8, 10; Martial, 1. *Epistula ad lectorem*; Juvenal, Satire 2.40; Valerius Maximus, 2.10.8; on *simplicitas*, see Martial, 1. *Epistula ad lectorem* and 11.20.10, and I. Borszák, 'Die *Simplicitas* und die römische Puritanismus', *EPhK* 70 (1947), 1ff, and for its stylistic implications, see Juvenal, Satire 1.151–3, E. T. Sage, 'Atticism in Petronius', *TAPA* 46 (1915), 47ff, and G. M. A. Grube, *The Greek and Roman Critics* (Methuen, 1965), 202; for Epicurean teachings on the subject of sex, see H. Usener, *Epicurea* (Leipzig, 1887), fr. 68—the quotation is in fact from the περὶ τέλους.

16 Cf. e.g. *De brevitate vitae*, 12.8; *Nat. Quaest.*, 1.16.3; *Ep.*, 88.37; *Consolatio ad Polybium*, 1.2; *De beneficiis*, 6.35.5. It is noteworthy that Juvenal is fond of it and Horace and Persius are not.

17 Op. cit., xix, xx.

18 Op. cit., xxi.

VII

Statius

A. J. Gossage

The self-conscious artistry of Silver Latin reaches one of its peaks in the poetry of P. Papinius Statius, who flourished under the Flavian emperors. The main literary figures of the Flavian period (A.D. 70–96) whose works have survived—Valerius Flaccus, Silius Italicus, Statius, Martial and Quintilian—were men of a different stamp from the writers of the previous age and their works are different in character.

After the bitter political and military struggles of A.D. 69–70 it was necessary for the Flavian emperors to establish their political power on a firm basis, and the rule of Domitian in particular was characterized by strong autocratic tendencies. Autocracy produces adulation or protest in the literature of any age. If the protests are obscured by allegory or innuendo they may escape detection and pass on to mystify posterity, but if they are expressed openly they are systematically suppressed and their authors banished or put to death. It is known that influential Stoic writers courageously protested under Domitian, but neither they nor their writings survived.[1] Statius and Martial preferred adulation and the survival that it guaranteed; in any case, their position in society was such that neither of them had any prospect of a political career, and consequently neither needed to protest on behalf of a class whose political aspirations were frustrated. The disappointed Vitellian Silius Italicus recalled past glories of the Roman Republic in his nostalgic epic, the *Punica*, written in the obscurity of retirement, while Pliny and Tacitus, two men of great literary potentiality, preferred not to damage their political careers by ill-timed criticism of the emperor and maintained a non-committal silence, storing up their resentment until Domitian had been murdered and it became safe to 'think what one wished and say what one thought'.[2] Consequently, much of the extant literary work of the Flavian period was produced by men of no political standing and with no passionate resentments to satisfy. Nevertheless, it presents a picture of a society with serious and often noble aims, as well as multifarious faults, and it deserves serious consideration. It is less powerful than the sensationalism and the nervous rhetoric of Seneca and Lucan or the deliberate strictures on society penned by Tacitus and Juvenal, but it has its own sensible appeal.

A consciousness of the stifling effects of imperial autocracy impelled educated men to analyse the causes for the decline of oratory. In the *Dialogus de Oratoribus*, a work purporting to reproduce a discussion that took place in Rome during the reign of Vespasian (A.D. 70–79) among leading literary figures of the day, it is pointed out that the limited scope of oratory in imperial times made it impossible for another Cicero to arise.[3] Nevertheless, it is assumed by one of the speakers that oratory was more profitable and more gratifying than composing poetry. No attempt is made to seek analogous causes for the decline of poetry, but it might have been said, for example, that under the Flavians the sense of national solidarity was not felt so deeply as it was under Augustus, or that the emperors themselves, despite their tangible achievements and the general security of the Roman world, were unable to arouse a similar sense of achievement in their subjects. The personalities of the Flavian emperors and their chief ministers, and the patronage with which they fostered literature and rhetoric (while the practice of philosophy was severely restricted), produced a somewhat artificial literary atmosphere, with the result that works prompted by a desire for imperial favour were stereotyped and lacking in grandeur or conviction and those inspired by genuine feeling eschewed to a greater or lesser degree the realities of the political scene and became introspective or antiquarian. Just as in oratory the necessary conditions for a Cicero to develop were lacking, so too in poetry not only would the restrictions on freedom of expression have prevented a Catullus or a Lucretius from giving spontaneous utterance to their thoughts and feelings as they did in the middle of the first century B.C. but not even another Virgil or another Horace would have been inspired to glorify the Flavians in the spirit in which they glorified Rome under Augustus.

The literary achievements of the Flavian era were limited in range and effect. There is no contemporary account of poetical ideals, but these were no doubt very similar to the avowed ideals of oratory as stated in the *Dialogus*.[4] Literary tastes had changed radically since republican days and it was now important for an orator to affect the ears of his audience with *uoluptas*; for this reason a speech had to be concise and its characteristics of style were *nitor*, *cultus*, *laetitia*, *pulchritudo* and *poeticus decor*. The poets whose works were the main quarry for an orator seeking this *decor* were Horace, Virgil, and Lucan. Thus the taste of the Flavian period favoured brilliance and splendour above all, and the *Dialogus* makes an illuminating reference to the splendour of contemporary architecture for comparison.[5]

Statius was in many ways a typical product of his age, accepting the political establishment without question and conforming generally to the prevalent literary fashions. He ostensibly supported the imperial family and their ministers and favourites,[6] occasionally composing to order and satisfying his social and political superiors with poems that flattered but sometimes lacked spontaneity and exhibited the required graces without profundity of thought or feeling. Fortunately, this represents a comparatively small part of his extant work, and there remain other poems that reveal a spirit earnestly seeking a better world and examining and exposing the depths of the human personality in that search.

Most of what is known about Statius and his family is derived from his own works. Details related by Dante in the *Purgatorio* are a mixture of intelligent but often distorted inferences from the *Thebaid* and legends that had accumulated during the Middle Ages. Only a few biographical facts can be learnt from the *Thebaid*; the main information is to be found in the *Silvae*.

Statius' exact dates are not known. He was born at Naples, probably about A.D. 45, and since there is no reference in his poems to the death of Domitian or any later event it is generally agreed that he died in or very soon after A.D. 96. His father's family came from Velia, a Greek colony on the Lucanian coast south of Paestum, which had originally been settled by Phocaean refugees in 540/39 B.C. and had subsequently become a Roman *municipium*, but they moved to Naples when he was a boy. As a boy, the elder Papinius was evidently a local prodigy, who competed in the musical events at Neapolitan festivals and amazed everyone by his success. Later he became a teacher of some repute and counted men of high political standing among his pupils. All that is known of his poetical works is that he composed a poem on the fighting between Vitellian troops and the supporters of Vespasian on the Capitol in A.D. 69, for which he earned approval. A poem on the great eruption of Vesuvius ten years later had been planned but not composed when he died in A.D. 79 or 80. The man's character and teaching had an important influence on his son's poetical career, as Statius himself makes clear.[7]

Statius spent his early years in Naples, but at some point he moved with his parents to Rome. Under his father's care he developed his poetical gifts and proved an apt pupil. He recited his compositions in Rome with apparent success. From his own words it can be seen that he conformed to contemporary taste and strove to provide the *uoluptas* demanded by a Flavian audience:

> Latios quotiens ego carmine patres
> mulcerem . . .

(Silvae, v.3.215–16)

(whenever I charmed the Latin fathers with my song)

and Juvenal gives further proof of his popularity and his ability to satisfy the popular taste:[8]

> curritur ad uocem iucundam et carmen amicae
> Thebaidos, laetam cum fecit Statius urbem
> promisitque diem; tanta dulcedine captos
> adficit ille animos tantaque libidine uolgi
> auditur.   (VII.82–6)

(Men flock to hear the pleasing voice of Statius and his recital of the *Thebaid* that they adore, when he has made the city happy by announcing the day; so great is the delight with which he captivates their spirits, so great the pleasure the crowd takes in hearing him.)

This evidence taken in conjunction with what is said by other authors about public recitals leads to an interesting conclusion. In the *Dialogus de Oratoribus*, for example, it is said by Aper that poets achieve less fame (which is their only object) than orators, 'since indifferent poets remain unknown and few people know the good ones. Their recitals are few and far between, and when does news of them spread through the whole city?' And elsewhere a general lack of interest in such recitals is reported.[9] Statius was apparently an exception to this general tendency, and he must therefore have been regarded as an outstanding poet in his own day. He competed in several contests for poets at religious festivals: he was victorious in the *Augustalia* at Naples and in the contest at Alba instituted by Domitian but was greatly disappointed in not winning the prize at the Capitoline festival in Rome.[10] This failure, however, cannot be interpreted as a withdrawal of favour on the part of Domitian, who had awarded Statius the wreath of victory at Alba. The emperor commissioned a number of occasional poems and knew and approved of the *Thebaid*, which had brought the poet considerable fame in his lifetime and made him the object of jealousy in some quarters.[11]

In view of the difficulties experienced by poets, Statius was perhaps fortunate to win recognition among his contemporaries; but in any case repute did not guarantee a poet his living in the Flavian period.[12] There is no evidence to suggest that Statius received financial assistance from the emperor as Saleius Bassus did from Vespasian,[13] but he possessed a small estate at Alba, which he or his father may have received as a gift from Vespasian or Domitian; a supply of running water for this estate was provided by Domitian, who himself owned a residence in the neighbourhood.[14] Even when he was attracting large audiences to his public recitals, in the years when the *Thebaid* was being composed, Statius was forced to sell a dramatic work entitled *Agave* to the famous actor Paris, a favourite of the emperor Domitian, to relieve his poverty.[15] In his later years he enjoyed the patronage of a number of men influential in the imperial administration or in the literary world, as well as the favour of Domitian himself. Their names are commemorated, and in some cases their personalities are pleasantly revealed, in the poems of the *Silvae*, and Statius acknowledges his debt to their generosity. Most of the *Silvae* poems were composed either at their suggestion or as tokens of good-will on the part of a grateful client.

Besides the *Thebaid*, an epic poem in twelve books, the *Silvae*, five books of shorter miscellaneous poems, the *Achilleid*, one book and part of a second book of an unfinished epic, and the *Agave*, of which only the name survives,[16] it is known that Statius composed a poem on Domitian's war in Germany, four lines of which are quoted by a later commentator. He mentions a projected poem to celebrate other exploits of Domitian, but he says that he has not yet sufficient confidence in his own ability to do them full justice.[17] He also writes that he will give Plotius Grypus a poem more worthy of him than the hendecasyllables that are addressed to him in the fourth book of the *Silvae*.[18] This poem, if it was ever composed, has not survived. Again, it is possible to see a reference to other poems no longer extant in the lament for his foster-son, where he speaks of himself in the following lines:

> ille ego qui—quotiens!—blande matrumque patrumque
> uulnera, qui uiduos potui mulcere dolores,
> ille ego lugentum mitis solator, acerbis
> auditus tumulis et descendentibus umbris . . .
>
> *(Silvae, v.5.38–41)*

(Yet I am he who—so often!—was able to charm and soothe the pains of mothers and fathers and their sorrows of bereavement; I, the gentle consoler of those who mourn, whose voice was heard at their untimely tombs by spirits as they left the earth . . .)

In this passage *quotiens* suggests a number of such poems, which must have resembled in form and sentiment the consolation-pieces addressed to Atedius Melior and Flavius Ursus in the second book of the *Silvae*.[19]

The *Thebaid* was begun in about A.D. 78, when Statius' father was still alive and able to advise him on practical details, and finally published in about A.D. 90; its composition and revision was a labour of twelve years' duration, and Statius probably completed one book each year and recited parts or even whole books at the recitals mentioned by Juvenal.[20] Most of the *Silvae* poems can be dated to the last six or seven years of the poet's life, although some of them may have been written much earlier and revised for publication in the books as they now stand.[21] The composition of the *Achilleid* seems to have been planned in much the same way as that of the *Thebaid*, with recitals of completed parts from time to time. It was probably begun early in A.D. 95 or not long before.[22]

The Thebaid

The Theban legend was a rich quarry for poets in antiquity. Besides the poems on Thebes in the early epic cycle and the famous works of the three great Attic tragedians, there was an epic *The-baid* in twenty-four books by the fourth-century poet Antimachus of Colophon. The early literature of Rome includes many adaptations of Greek works on legendary themes, but the majority of these were taken from Homer and the Trojan cycle, and the stories about Thebes appear to have figured hardly at all. As the Romans gained in literary experience, however, and became more familiar with Greek culture as a whole, many more Greek themes became acceptable to them. The neoteric poets of the first century B.C. persisted with their treatment of Greek legends; Calvus wrote an *Io*, for example, and Cinna a *Zmyrna*. In Augustan times Ponticus, a friend of Propertius, composed an epic on the Theban legend,[23] and in the next generation Seneca found material for two of his tragedies, the *Phoenissae* and the *Oedipus*, in the same source. Consequently, there was no lack of precedent for Statius when he sought an epic theme in the Theban legend.[24]

The part of the legend that Statius chose was the story of Eteocles and Polynices, the sons of Oedipus, who disputed the Theban kingdom and eventually killed each other in single combat during the war fought by the Argive allies of Polynices against Thebes. At first sight this story, despite the excellent dramatic potentialities in its main conflict and in its various episodes, might appear to be less promising as material for an epic poem than a group of legends woven around the career of a central hero, as in the *Iliad*, the *Odyssey*, the *Aeneid* and even the *Argonautica*; but Statius must have chosen it for a special purpose, after careful thought, and probably after consultation with his father. It offered plentiful opportunities for vivid description and he must have felt that it suited his poetical outlook. A brief attempt will be made in the present chapter to analyse this outlook and to suggest what his purpose might have been.

After a formal introduction, the narrative begins in Book I with Oedipus calling upon the Fury Tisiphone to sow dissension between his sons. His prayer is answered and the brothers agree to share the Theban kingdom and rule in alternate years. Eteocles holds power immediately and Polynices departs from Thebes. At a meeting of the gods, Jupiter states his purpose of causing a deep conflict between the brothers to punish mankind for past wickedness. The rest of the book tells of Polynices' journey to Argos, his meeting with another exile, Tydeus, their fight and reconciliation, their reception by Adrastus the king of Argos, and the story of Coroebus, related by Adrastus to explain a local festival in honour of Apollo. The second book comprises three main sections. In the first of these the ghost of Laius, at Jupiter's command, rises out of Hades and appears to Eteocles in Thebes to warn him of Polynices' ambition to seize the throne for himself; thus active hostility between the brothers is aroused. The second section describes the marriages of Polynices and Tydeus to the daughters of Adrastus. The third section opens with Polynices brooding on the kingdom of Thebes; Tydeus goes to Thebes on his behalf and angrily claims the royal power for him. Eteocles refuses to concede his right, and after Tydeus has left the palace he sends fifty chosen men to lie in ambush for him; Tydeus kills forty-nine of them and allows the one survivor to return to Thebes with the news of their death. The survivor returns in the first section of Book III; he recounts his story, and there follows a description of the grief of the Theban people as they collect the dead from the battle-field. The rest of Book III is taken up with the reactions of Polynices, Adrastus and others to what Tydeus relates about his recent experiences, the taking of the auspices in Argos, and the growth of hostile feelings against Thebes. There are three main sections again in Book IV. In the first of these the Argives arm themselves and gather their forces for war. The scene changes to Thebes in the second section, which is devoted mainly to a *nekyia* in which the ghosts of the dead are called up to prophesy on the issue of the war; the third section returns to the Argives and tells how Bacchus, in an attempt to save Thebes, causes a drought to delay their army. The Argives are led to a stream of running water by Hypsipyle, who is now the nurse of Opheltes, the infant son of Lycurgus, king of Nemea.

Books V and VI form an interlude and digression from the main story. At the request of the Argives Hypsipyle tells of the massacre of the Lemnians by their wives and the arrival of the Argonauts at Lemnos. While she is speaking, the child Opheltes, whom she has left on the ground a little distance away, is killed by a monstrous serpent. The last section of Book V describes the reactions of the Argives and of Hypsipyle and Lycurgus to this event. Book VI is devoted entirely to the funeral of Opheltes and the funeral games held in his honour.

After this delay, the action starts afresh in Book VII with Jupiter

sending Mercury to command Gradivus (Mars) to rouse the
Argives to war once more. Preparations for war are made in
Thebes and the Theban forces are described. The Argives approach Thebes and the first battles begin. At the end of this book
Statius narrates the deeds of Amphiaraus and his marvellous death
when the earth opens and swallows him up in his chariot. Book
VIII begins with a scene in Hades, followed by the consternation
in the Argive camp at Amphiaraus' disappearance; Thiodamas is
appointed to replace him as seer. The rest of the book describes
further miscellaneous battles and especially the exploits and death
of Tydeus. Book IX contains the exploits and death of two more
Argive heroes, Hippomedon and Parthenopaeus. There are three
main sections in Book X: in the first of these there is an account
of a night venture by Hopleus and Dymas, two Argives, to recover the corpses of their leaders, Tydeus and Parthenopaeus; the
second turns to the beleaguering of Thebes and the *deuotio* and
death of Menoeceus on behalf of the city; in the third the deeds
and death of Capaneus, the fifth and most violent of the Argive
leaders, is described. The climax of the whole poem, which has
been gradually built up and postponed from time to time through
various delaying devices, occurs in the central section of Book XI.
Here the brothers fight their duel and are both killed. The scene is
prepared in the first part of the book, with further delays and
attempts to prevent the fatal combat. The last section of Book XI
describes events in Thebes after the deaths of Eteocles and Polynices. Creon, now king of Thebes, forbids the burial of the Argive
dead and sends Oedipus into exile.

The last book of the poem is an epilogue, in which the widows
of the Argive dead procure burial for their husbands' bodies.
Argia, the wife of Polynices, and Antigone do this in defiance of
Creon's ban, while the other women make their appeal in Athens
to Theseus, who leads a brief expedition against Creon and slays
him in single combat.

Some severe criticisms have been made against the *Thebaid* from
time to time. Besides occasional obscurities of detail and lapses
from good taste which mar certain passages, it is held that the
poem is episodic and lacks unity, that some of the episodes,
especially Adrastus' narration in Book I and the whole of Books
v, vi, and xii, are unnecessary excrescences, irrelevant to the main
story, that the double motivation of the action obscures the poet's

main purpose, and that there is no central hero. These are the most general criticisms. By examining them briefly, it may be possible to suggest an approach towards an appreciation of the work as a whole.[25]

First of all, it is important to understand what the main theme of the poem really is. It is stated by the poet clearly enough in the opening lines of the introductory section:

> fraternas acies alternaque regna profanis
> decertata odiis sontesque euoluere Thebas,
> Pierius menti calor incidit.

(1.1–3)

(Pieria fires my spirit to recount the strife of brothers, and their battle for alternate reign fought to the end with impious hatred, and the guilt of Thebes.)

These lines refer to the struggle between Eteocles and Polynices (*fraternas acies*), the latter assisted by his Argive allies, for the Theban kingdom after their agreement to rule in alternate years has broken down (*alternaque regna . . . decertata*); they also mention the spirit of hatred (*profanis . . . odiis*) in which the struggle was carried on to the end, and the more general guilt of the Theban royal family (*sontesque . . . Thebas*). Thus from the outset Statius gives a clear indication that in addition to a narrative account of the story of the Seven against Thebes he is going to study the motives of the main participants and the spirit in which they acted, and to pass moral judgment on their actions.

The first episode of Book 1, after the introduction, shows Oedipus calling upon the Fury to destroy the natural bond between his two sons, and it begins with the significant word *impia* (46). This episode contains the poet's first analysis of human motives and the spirit in which men act, and *impia* sets the tone immediately. The Fury Tisiphone here is a personification of the evil passions in the human soul. In answer to Oedipus' prayer she visits Thebes and fills the brothers with *furor*,[26] so that each is impatient of the other's presence, and they agree reluctantly to share the kingdom by ruling for a year each in turn. Statius ironically comments:

> haec inter fratres pietas erat . . . (1.142)

(Such was the bond of affection that united the two brothers . . .)

The relationship between brothers, which should be one of *pietas*, has been perverted by Tisiphone into *discordia* (130, 137). The poet emphasizes their perverted spirit by pointing out that Thebes in any case was a poor kingdom, hardly worth quarrelling over, and he ends this episode with an effective climax:[27]

> loca dira arcesque nefandae
> suffecere odio, furiisque immanibus emptum
> Oedipodae sedisse loco. (1.162–4)

(An accursed land and a city of abomination were enough to cause their hatred; they spent their mad fury to claim their place on the throne of Oedipus.)

In these early episodes Statius is already amplifying the allusion to the 'profane hatred' of the brothers that he makes in the first two lines of the poem. As a result of Oedipus' prayer, fulfilled by Tisiphone, the spirit in which Eteocles and Polynices act towards each other is one of *furor*, and their sole motive for action is *nuda potestas* (150). But although they are in this frame of mind, they are not yet in open conflict, since there is still a *mora* (142) restraining them, namely their agreement to share the kingdom. Statius carefully distinguishes between their mutual hatred and the occasion for their open hostility. He can see that something further is required to set in motion the main conflict that he is going to relate. Already he has anticipated the issue—as he frequently does —in the words

> periit ius fasque bonumque
> et uitae mortisque pudor. (1.154–5)

(The laws of God and man, all righteousness, and honour both in life and death passed away.)

There follows a transitional passage in which Polynices is now in exile for a year while Eteocles rules in Thebes. An unnamed Theban citizen complains of the lot that the Thebans have to bear, calling upon the ruler of the gods and asking whether the ancient fate of Cadmus and the warring of brothers must still continue in the present generation (178ff). In this speech two important themes are mentioned: one is the divine purpose in the war between brothers and between Thebes, where Eteocles is ruling at present, and Argos, where Polynices finds his military and moral support, and the other is the involvement of innocent people in the crimes and misfortunes of their rulers:

> nos uilis in omnis
> prompta manus casus, domino cuicumque parati.
>
> (1.191–2)

(We are a worthless crowd, ready for every chance and ready to perform the will of any lord, whoever he may be.)

This undoubtedly reflects the poet's own feelings and those of many of his contemporaries in the insecurity of the political situation after the fall of the Julio-Claudian line of emperors.

Statius next introduces a council of the gods. This was a typical feature of ancient epic poetry, and although it may be condemned as an artificial and unrealistic device, it served the important function of giving the poet a legitimate occasion for expressing his views on the divine purpose in the world, which might be equally applicable to the events in his poem and to those that occurred in the world in his own lifetime. Lucan had been able to dispense with the whole divine machinery of epic, though as a Stoic he still needed to explain by various means the causes and purpose that he could find in historical events. How right he was not to attempt to combine historical personages with Olympian gods in his poem can be seen by considering the *Punica* of Silius Italicus, where the presence of the gods in a well-known historical situation gives a most bizarre effect. In the mythological setting of the *Thebaid*, however, there can be no such objection to the appearance of the traditional gods. Within the accepted scheme Statius finds sufficient scope for variation. Bacchus and Diana, for example, are tutelary deities, one of Thebes and the other of the hero Parthenopaeus, whereas others, in particular Mars, are functional. In addition, important functional abstractions, such as Pietas and Virtus, are elevated to a divine or semi-divine status.

Jupiter is clearly and unequivocally the ruler of heaven in the *Thebaid*. His power is autocratic, like that of Domitian on earth, but he possesses characteristics that Statius and other writers of his age attributed to their ideal rulers.[28] He is essentially a kind deity—*bonus ille deum genitor* (III.556)—but inexorable in his most momentous decisions, however harsh these may be. The issue with which he is now concerned is the wickedness of mankind:

'terrarum delicta nec exsaturabile Diris
ingenium mortale queror.' (1.214-15)

(I complain of Earth's transgressions, and Man's mind that
not even the Avenging Furies can sufficiently punish.)

and he has decided to punish the royal houses of Thebes and
Argos. Thus Statius answers the doubts of the Theban who asked
what Jupiter's purpose was, and at the same time passes moral
judgment on Thebes and finds a divine purpose in the human
sufferings that are to follow. Given the perverted state of mind of
the two brothers as an existing condition, the divine purpose has
the material for its operation and fulfilment. All that is needed in
addition to this is some impetus to set the actual war between the
brothers in motion. Jupiter provides the impetus by commanding
the ghost of Laius to appear to his grandson Eteocles and urge
him to refuse to give up the throne to Polynices at the end of his
year of rule:[29]

'germanum . . .
. . . procul impius aula
arceat, alternum regni infitiatus honorem.
hinc causa irarum, certo reliqua ordine ducam.'
(1.299-302)

('Let him blot out natural affection and keep his brother far
from his court and deny him the honour of ruling in his turn.
Hence angry deeds will arise, and the rest I will bring to pass
in due order.')

What has often been condemned as the dual motivation of the
Thebaid would thus appear rather to be a deliberate attempt by
Statius to explain the unhappiness of the human race by reference
to human psychology and the divine purpose for mankind. The
analysis given in Book I is kept in view throughout the poem, and
from time to time further reference is made to the spiritual corruption and perversion of the main characters, while the divine purpose is re-examined or reinforced at intervals.[30] Seen in this light,
the appearance of Laius' ghost to Eteocles in Thebes in Book II
is not an idle repetition of Tisiphone's visitation in Book I. Their
functions are different, even though they tend to the same ultimate event, the destruction of the brothers.[31]

In the course of the council of the gods Statius introduces almost casually as a side-issue a matter which interests him and which belongs to his explanation of the divine purpose. Juno, protesting at Jupiter's plans, asks:

'quod si prisca luunt auctorum crimina gentes
subuenitque tuis sera haec sententia curis,
percensere aeui senium, quo tempore tandem
terrarum furias abolere et saecula retro
emendare sat est?'   (1.266–70)

('But if the nations are now atoning for evil deeds committed by men in the past, and this resolution to look back over times gone by has come so tardily to serve your concerns, how far back in time must you look in destroying earth's madness and exacting punishment for ages that have already passed away?')

Jupiter makes no immediate reply to this, but in Book III, when he is rousing Mars to war, he speaks of *ueterum poenas . . . malorum* and *diros . . . punire nepotes* (244–5), and in Book VII, when he explains his purpose to Bacchus, who is anxious on behalf of Thebes, he refers again to *ueteres seraeque in proelia causae* (198). He says that his anger is quickly allayed and that he is sparing of human blood and always reluctant to punish even the most guilty:

'Labdacios uero Pelopisque a stirpe nepotes
tardum abolere mihi;'   (VII.207–8)

('But I am slow to destroy the seed of Labdacus and the sons of Pelops' line.')

The cumulative guilt of Thebes over a period of several generations has gone unpunished, but now Jupiter can tolerate no more; the latest representatives of the royal house have gone too far:

'ast ego non proprio diros impendo dolori
Oedipodionidas: rogat hoc tellusque polusque
et pietas et laesa fides naturaque, et ipsi
Eumenidum mores.'   (VII.215–18)

('But it is not to satisfy a private resentment that I sacrifice the sons of Oedipus: earth and heaven demand it, and family affection and injured trust and Nature and the ways of the Avenging Furies themselves.')

In explaining the ways of Jupiter to man, Statius is keenly aware of the old and difficult problem: if Jupiter is a good deity and considerate of mankind, why is there so much suffering on earth, even among the innocent? His answer is that men, and especially their rulers, become depraved in spirit and commit monstrous crimes, and that Jupiter even so delays their punishment until there is no hope of redemption, and then he incites them to destroy each other, even if this involves many innocent people as well.[32]

The *Thebaid* is thus in the first place an attempt to probe by poetical means the mainsprings of human action, and in particular of human wickedness, and to relate them to the divine purpose for mankind. The general structure of the poem and, to a considerable extent, its 'episodic' nature reflect this underlying theme in its various ramifications. When *furor* takes possession of the human spirit and shatters the natural ties between members of a family or nation, conflict follows; when a family set at variance by *furor* holds political power, many innocent people become involved in the issue and suffer for the crimes of their rulers. Statius repeatedly emphasizes the profound guilt of the Theban royal family and its various members, from Cadmus to Oedipus and his two sons.[33] In Book II the digression in which he gives an account of Harmonia's necklace is a good example of how apparently irrelevant details are skilfully related to the main theme. What at first sight seems to be a typical *ekphrasis*, a set piece of description on a mythological subject, is in fact an illustration of the power of evil working through the necklace on the Theban family. Among the women who had worn it were Harmonia, the wife of Cadmus, Semele and Jocasta. On the present occasion it has been given by Polynices to Argia, the daughter of Adrastus, but already it is coveted by Eriphyle:

> quos optat gemitus, quantas cupit impia clades!
> digna quidem, sed quid miseri decepta mariti
> arma, quid insontes nati meruere furores?   (II.303–5)

(What groans she desires! What disasters she impiously covets! Worthy is she, indeed, but what has her unfortunate husband deserved, and his deluded weapons, and the guiltless frenzy of her son?)

The guilt of Thebes will spread to Eriphyle when she possesses the necklace, and she in turn is *impia*.

Statius regards *furor* as a perversion of human nature. From
time to time he sets against it and against the wickedness of man
other forces that struggle to restore reason and a natural spirit of
affection. Although much of the poem is taken up with the fulfilment of Oedipus' prayer, consideration is given to *uirtus* and to
pietas, *fides*, and *natura*,[34] which had been outraged by the enmity
between Eteocles and Polynices. Of these *pietas* is the most important concept, and various aspects of it are portrayed in striking
examples. The natural opposition between *pietas* and the insane
passions of the human soul, personified by Tisiphone, forms a
perspective for many episodes throughout the poem. In Book xi,
where the struggle between supra-human forces is depicted most
clearly, Tisiphone and Megaera, embodying the spirits of unnatural hatred and insane fury, stir up the brothers to combat.
Jocasta tries to mollify Eteocles, and Antigone to mollify Polynices, but the Furies intervene and drive the brothers on to the
plain to fight. Adrastus makes an appeal but is powerless to alter
their mood. Finally, Pietas appears and actually succeeds in calming the spirits of the opposing armies and even makes an impression on the brothers themselves; but she is put to flight by
Tisiphone, and the mood of hatred returns. In these scenes the
conflicting *furor* and *pietas* in the minds of the combatants are projected into the confrontation between Tisiphone and Pietas on
the battle-field.[35]

In view of Statius' interest in these deep-seated motivating
forces it is not difficult to understand his purpose in narrating the
Lemnian story in Book v, which is only remotely connected with
the story of the Theban expedition. What at first appears to be an
irrelevant digression is nevertheless pertinent to the basic theme
of the *Thebaid*, as the poet himself makes clear in Hypsipyle's
opening words:[36]

> 'immania uulnera, rector,
> integrare iubes, Furias et Lemnon et artis
> arma inserta toris debellatosque pudendo
> ense mares: redit ecce nefas et frigida cordi
> Eumenis. o miserae, quibus hic furor additus!'
>
> (v.30–4)

('Great are the wounds, O king, that you bid me open afresh,
the story of Lemnos and its Furies and of weapons brought

even to the embrace of the marriage-bed, and of menfolk
slain by the shameful sword; see! the wickedness comes back
to me, the chill Fury grips my heart! Alas! wretched were
the women to whom this frenzy came!')

The diction, as often in the *Thebaid*, is concentrated on motifs
suggestive of human depravity: *Furias, nefas, Eumenis, furor* are
words habitually employed in the poem in descriptions of the
Theban family and their wickedness and of the rage of the warring
armies, and they are equally applicable to the wickedness of Lemnos.[37] As a whole, the Lemnian story is an illustration of the
effects of *furor* within human families, and Hypsipyle's action in
saving her father is a shining example of *pietas*. But the Argives
who hear her story, and in particular Polynices whom they support, are unable to appreciate the warning and the example as it
applies to themselves.[38]

In the course of the battles round Thebes, with their attendant
violence and savagery, a fine example of *uirtus* and *pietas* is the
self-sacrifice of Menoeceus as a ritual act to preserve his city.
Virtus, personified as a deity, inspires him to this—he becomes
multo possessus numine pectus (x.676)—and at the moment of his
death he is *pius Menoeceus* (x.756). The significance of this act for
Statius is unmistakable:[39]

> ast illum amplexae Pietas Virtusque ferebant
> leniter ad terras corpus; nam spiritus olim
> ante Iouem et summis apicem sibi poscit in astris.
>
> (x.780–2)

(But Piety and Virtue clasped his body and bore it lightly to
the earth; for his spirit long since is before the throne of
Jupiter, and demands a crown for itself among the highest
stars.)

There are few rays of hope in the poem as a whole, but this is a
clear instance, and despite the lurid tones of Book xi the promise
is fulfilled in Book xii, where the mood finally changes. There is
another, less powerful ray, but of a similar kind, in Book i, where
Adrastus tells the story of Coroebus, who incurred Apollo's anger
by leading a band of young men to kill a monstrous serpent that
the god had sent to scourge the country. Coroebus offered himself
alone to Apollo for vengeance, in the hope of saving Argos:

'non missus, Thymbraee, tuos supplexue penates
aduenio: mea me pietas et conscia uirtus
has egere uias.'   (1.643–5)

('Not sent by any man, nor as a suppliant, O Thymbraean,
do I approach your shrine: my conscience and my sacred
duty have led me on this path.')

The man's courage and nobility of character shine out and show
Apollo by contrast in a very poor light.[40]

One of the details of the Theban story announced by the poet
in his introduction is *tumulis . . . carentia regum funera* (1.36–7). This
becomes an important theme later in the poem, but its importance
is already foreshadowed in Book III, when Creon orders the corpse
of Maeon, the only survivor of the fifty warriors sent out to ambush Tydeus, to lie without funeral rites:[41]

sed ducis infandi rabidae non hactenus irae
stare queunt; uetat igne rapi, pacemque sepulcri
impius ignaris nequiquam manibus arcet.   (III.96–8)

(But in the madness of his rage the evil ruler cannot stay at
this; he forbids them to consume the corpse with fire, and in
defiance of human rights he vainly denies the peace of the
tomb to the unwitting ghost.)

In Book VIII there is a passage in which the lord of the underworld
gives Tisiphone her hideous commands. These reinforce the
furor in the action of the poem. Among the commands occurs this
typical provision:

'sit qui . . .
                        . . . igne supremo
arceat exanimes et manibus aethera nudis
commaculet . . .'   (VIII.71–4)

('Let there be one who . . . shall bar the dead from their
funeral fire and pollute the air with unburied corpses.')

After the death of the brothers, Creon assumes the royal power
and gives effect to this command:

primum adeo saeuis imbutum moribus aulae
indicium specimenque sui iubet igne supremo
arceri Danaos, nudoque sub axe relinqui
infelix bellum et tristis sine sedibus umbras.

(XI.661–4)

(First, as an example and proof that he was deep-dyed in the savage customs of the palace, he gave orders for the Danai to be barred from their funeral fire, and the unhappy host to be left unburied and exposed to heaven and their gloomy shades without a resting-place.)

Against these examples of unnatural behaviour inspired by immoderate and perverted passions the poet sets the grief of men and women searching for the bodies of their kinsmen and honouring them with proper funeral rites and sincere lamentation. This, for Statius, is another important aspect of *pietas*.[42] Already in Book III, in anticipation of scenes in the actual war around Thebes, he devotes a passage of a hundred lines (114–217) to the grief and lamentation of the Thebans seeking the bodies of the men whom Tydeus had killed and the ensuing funeral ceremonies. The dead are nameless, and individually they and their kinsmen are insignificant, but the length of this passage is proof of the importance that Statius attached to such matters, even in the composition of an epic poem. Amid the battles before Thebes particular attention is given to the deaths of young men such as Atys (VIII.544ff, 636ff), Crenaeus (IX.315ff), and the youngest of the Argive leaders, Parthenopaeus (IX.683ff), and the grief caused to their womenfolk. In Book X Hopleus and Dymas, two Argives, make a sortie into the enemy's lines by night to search for the corpses of their two leaders, Tydeus and Parthenopaeus, and die nobly in the attempt. Statius, in fact, gives them a much worthier motive than the heroes of other such night sorties in earlier epics, and with Virgil's Nisus and Euryalus in mind commends them in the following apostrophe:

> uos quoque sacrati, quamuis mea carmina surgant
> inferiore lyra, memores superabitis annos.
> forsitan et comites non aspernabitur umbras
> Euryalus Phrygiique admittet gloria Nisi.   (x.445–8)

(You too are given sacred honours, although my songs rise up from a lyre less powerful [than Virgil's], and will be remembered in ages to come. Perhaps even Euryalus and Phrygian Nisus in their glory will condescend to accept your shades as companions.)

But the main concentration on lamentation and funeral rites

occurs in Books VI and XII,[43] which critics have often censured. Book VI is devoted entirely to the funeral of Opheltes, the infant son of Lycurgus, king of Nemea, and the funeral games held in his honour, while Book XII begins with the funerals of Menoeceus and other Thebans who have fallen in the war and continues with the mission of Argia and the Argive women seeking proper funeral honours for the Argive dead. Most of Book XII is taken up with the fulfilment of this mission and with Argia's courageous journey to find the corpse of Polynices. In the course of their procession, the Argive women turn aside to Athens and approach the altar of Clementia as suppliants. Theseus takes up their cause, marches on Thebes and overcomes Creon, so that the Argive dead are finally given their proper dues.

The description of the altar of Clementia (XII.481ff) is unique in Latin literature. Whether such an altar existed or not in Athens hardly matters for Statius: its importance for him, and for the *Thebaid*, is that it symbolizes a change of spirit from the turmoil and evil in human life. There is no image of the deity, who dwells rather in the human mind and spirit:

> nulla autem effigies, nulli commissa metallo
> forma dei, mentes habitare et pectora gaudet.
>
> (XII.493–4)

(There is no image, and the divine form has not been entrusted to marble, but the deity is glad to dwell in men's minds and hearts.)

The altar is a refuge for those who suffer (XII.503ff). Here the Furies of Oedipus were overcome (XII.509–10), and here the Argive women find rest from their sorrows:

> . . . sedatis requierunt pectora curis.   (XII.514)

(. . . their troubles were allayed and their hearts took rest.)

Thus it may be said that the story of the *Thebaid* is enacted on two levels. The expedition against Thebes, arising from the quarrel of the brothers, ends in their death in Book XI, which is the dramatic end of the story. Critics have often felt that the poem should have ended at this point, but Statius was not concerned solely with dramatic effect; for him it was necessary to complete the other aspect of the theme and describe the final supremacy of calmer and better feelings over *furor*. Already he has suggested in various episodes, especially in Books v and vi, which delay the dramatic action of the poem, lessons from which the value of *pietas* might be learnt. The importance of the *mora* in this part of the poem is made clear by Amphiaraus (*pius Oeclides*, v.731) after the death of Opheltes, when he interprets the will of the gods and suggests the course of action to be taken:

> 'det pulchra suis libamina uirtus
> manibus: atque utinam pluris innectere pergas,
> Phoebe, moras, semperque nouis bellare uetemur
> casibus, et semper Thebe funesta recedas!'   (v.742–5)

('Let virtue give noble drink-offerings to a virtuous shade, and let Phoebus continue to devise more delays! Would that new chances might always keep us from making wars! And you, O deadly Thebes, always withdraw from our approach!')

At that stage *furor* was still the reigning passion in men's spirits, despite the delay at Nemea, and Amphiaraus' hope was vain. In Book xii, after the conflict, burial of the dead as an act of *pietas* is necessary to restore the balance, as it were; and the altar of Clementia, at which the human spirit regains its peace, finally puts an end to the *furor* aroused by Oedipus' prayer and the work of Tisiphone in Book i. Even Oedipus himself has now found peace (xii.509–10).[44] Book xii, therefore, like Books v and vi and the story of Coroebus in Book i, is relevant to Statius' purpose, and, even more than they, essential for the completion of his theme. The whole structure of the poem, instead of following a simple dramatic plan, reflects this inner purpose.

Finally, the major characters of the *Thebaid*, like the diction, the imagery, and the digressions, contribute to the sombre mood of the poem and illustrate the power of *furor* or, in a few cases, *pietas*. Some of them, possessed by demonic influences, are broadly sketched with little variation of detail. Oedipus appears only at the beginning of the action, when he utters his tremendous prayer to Tisiphone, at the end of the main action in Book xi, and in Book viii, when he takes a strange joy in the impending fate of his sons. After the duel in Book xi the tension breaks and he weeps at last:

> 'tarda meam, pietas, longo post tempore mentem

percutis? estne sub hoc hominis clementia corde?
uincis io miserum, uincis, Natura, parentem!'

(XI.605–7)

('Does affection tardily, after so long time, thrill my heart?
Does mercy dwell in this mortal breast? Ah! You conquer,
Nature, you conquer an unhappy father!')

At this point he begins to feel that he is a human being once more;
hitherto he has been in what in modern times would be called a
pathological condition, and his character is delineated hardly at
all. For his past he claims no responsibility:

'furor illa et mouit Erinys
et pater et genetrix et regna oculique cadentes;
nil ego.' (XI.619–21)

('Madness caused those evils, and the Fury, and my father
and mother, and my kingdom, and my blinding—not I!')

Eteocles is painted quite consistently in dark hues. He is under the
spell of Tisiphone and affected by *furor*; he is *impius, iniquus, ferus,
durus, perfidus, trux, saeuus, dirus, nefandus*,[45] and his actions are in
keeping with these epithets. Polynices is similarly described, but
in his case there is more variety of characterization, since he is
seen in Argos as the husband of Argia, whose love lightens the
gloom of his career for a brief interval. Both she and Antigone are
faithful to him and after his death risk their own lives to give his
body the fitting honours. In addition, he is portrayed rather more
sympathetically than Eteocles, since he is an exile unjustly deprived of his share of the kingdom; and his friendship with
Tydeus, after their initial quarrel, shows that despite his *furor* he
is capable of generous feelings towards others.

Of the other seven Argive leaders three are brutal and violent in
thought and action. These are Tydeus, Capaneus, and Hippomedon. As a character the last-named is of no particular interest.
Capaneus is *superum contemptor et aequi impatiens* (III.602–3), like an
exaggerated Mezentius[46]; he finally attempts to set fire to Thebes
and challenges the gods to battle but is destroyed by a thunderbolt
from Jupiter.[47] Tydeus is quick-tempered and no less violent. He
too is an exile in Argos, and like Polynices he marries a daughter
of Adrastus. For a time he appears in a fair light as Polynices'
friend, on whose behalf he undertakes the embassy to Thebes,

and Polynices is deeply grieved at his death; but his violence does not desert him even in his last moments, and as he dies he savagely gnaws the head of the enemy who has dealt him his death blow.[48] Parthenopaeus, on the other hand, is depicted as a boy-hero, too young to understand fully the meaning of war. He shows prowess but is rash, and his strength soon wanes, and his end is described with much pathos.[49]

The remaining two Argive leaders are conspicuous for a different type of character. Adrastus, the commander-in-chief, is an old man and a reluctant warrior. He is typified by the epithet *mitis*;[50] he is a just king and a calming influence on the passions of younger men, but he is overruled and hastened to war against his better judgment—*uix sponte* (IV.440). When his final attempt to prevent Polynices from meeting Eteocles in single combat has failed, he flees from the battle-field and appears no more. Similarly, Amphiaraus the seer, beloved of Apollo, is *pius*[51] and tries in vain to prevent the Argives from rushing to war in their blind folly. It is perhaps difficult to know why a man depicted in this way should join the expedition, and Statius mentions his reasons briefly and without elaboration: despite his hesitation and his foreknowledge of the outcome, Amphiaraus yields to the necessity of what he knew was fated for him and succumbs to treachery on the part of his wife (IV.187ff). After his remarkable disappearance into the depths of the earth near Thebes his loss is mourned by the Argives, who now feel that the gods have forsaken them (VIII. 169ff).

As a dramatic poem the *Thebaid* suffers to some extent by having no central hero. Its whole conception, however, is far different from that of the *Iliad* or *Odyssey* and the nature of the theme makes it impossible for any of the characters to be cast as its hero. From the prayer of Oedipus in Book I until the double flame appears on the funeral pyre of Eteocles and Polynices in Book XII the emphasis is on discord and division, just as the moral and spiritual atmosphere is pervaded by the antipathy between Tisiphone and Pietas. It is not the actions of a hero but the sufferings of a family divided against itself that Statius portrays. This was a theme close to the thoughts of his own contemporaries, whose political experience was of suffering caused by discord at the heart of the nation. Statius fully exploits the potentialities of his theme; the question for doubt is whether it was suitable for an epic poem.[52]

The theme of the *Thebaid* in its broad outline represents an eventual triumph of right over wrong and of spiritual reintegration over the forces of disintegration that Statius himself probably longed for in human society. Such poetical visions may be flights from reality into a world of fancy where everything comes right in the end, but their tangible expression serves as a hope, if not as an objective, for the poet's own generation and for posterity. Statius' hope is unmistakable in the verses that follow the duel and deaths of Eteocles and Polynices:

> ite truces animae funestaque Tartara leto
> polluite et cunctas Erebi consumite poenas!
> uosque malis hominum, Stygiae, iam parcite, diuae.
> omnibus in terris scleus hoc omnique sub aeuo
> uiderit una dies, monstrumque infame futuris
> excidat, et soli memorent haec proelia reges.

(XI.574–9)

(Go, savage souls, and pollute deathly Tartarus by your own deaths, and exhaust all the punishments of Erebus! And you, O Stygian goddesses, now have mercy on man's afflictions. Let this crime, seen on one day alone, suffice for all ages and every land, and let posterity forget the report of its horror and no one but kings recall this combat.)

The Silvae

The title *Silvae* was fancifully applied to a collection of miscellaneous poems,[53] which Statius had composed on various occasions, often at the request of one of his patrons, and collected for publication in books dedicated to particular patrons or friends. Four of these books were published by Statius himself in their present form; the fifth, unlike the first four, is prefaced not by a general letter of dedication containing a short description of the contents but by a letter to the recipient of the first poem. The last poem in Book v is incomplete. It appears that this book is a collection of pieces that Statius had not yet included in other published collections, although the first two, like many of the poems in Books i to iv, had already been presented separately to the persons who occasioned or commissioned them. The last three poems in Book v are purely personal; Statius probably composed them for no other purpose than his own satisfaction and may not in fact have intended them for general publication, although they were possibly circulated among his closest friends.

The *Silvae* poems are quite unlike the *Thebaid* in many respects, and this is not surprising in view of their purpose and the manner of their composition. Whereas his work on the *Thebaid* occupied Statius for twelve years, he spent no longer than two days over any of the poems in Book I of the *Silvae*, and some of them took only a few hours to compose.[54] The same facility and speed of composition must be assumed for the majority of the poems in the other books, even though some of them may have been revised before they were published in their present form. As Statius himself says more than once, if he had not produced a poem quickly on certain topics the occasion for it would have passed. He fears that the poems themselves bear the marks of haste and speaks of *quam solam habuerunt gratiam celeritatis*.[55]

There is no space in the present chapter for a detailed account of all the *Silvae* poems, but some indication of their scope and subject-matter must be given.[56] Of the total of thirty-two pieces, including the unfinished fifth poem of Book v, the majority exceed one hundred lines in length; the longest (v.3) contains 293 lines, the shortest only 19.[57] All except six are in hexameters; of these six two are lyrics and the rest hendecasyllabics.[58]

One of the most conspicuous features of the *Silvae* as a whole, difficult for modern readers to appreciate and repulsive to modern taste, is their adulation of the Emperor Domitian, similar to that which is found in Martial's epigrams. Domitian exercised an autocratic rule over his subjects and expected their deference. For a poet under his patronage there was no alternative but to observe the fashion of the court and address the emperor in the tones that he expected. Even in the reign of Trajan, the younger Pliny observed that *omnes enim, qui placendi causa scribunt, qualia placere uiderint, scribent*.[59] Statius, as a client and dependant of a number of influential Romans in his own day, and owing much to imperial patronage, wrote to please and knew what was expected of him: addressing Abascantus, an imperial freedman who held an important office under Domitian, he says, *latus omne diuinae domus semper demereri pro mea mediocritate conitor*.[60] But the poems directly addressed to Domitian, and others in which he is mentioned, contain more than merely empty expressions of flattery.

The poem on Domitian's equestrian statue (i.i) was commissioned by the emperor himself.[61] An event such as the dedication of a statue needed to be given publicity, and the most natural way for this to be done was to request a famous poet to produce a piece for the occasion. Statius had a good sense of occasion for events of this sort. He was able to catch the mood of celebration and the feeling of almost naive wonder with which many Romans must have witnessed the statue and its dedication; and there is a sense of magnificence in the poem, typical of Domitian himself, and a vivid power of description. There is also a wealth of mythological allusion, as so often in these poems, and the poet employs one of his favourite devices of pretending that a neighbouring deity or spirit appears in visible shape to express his admiration at what is happening. Here the hero Curtius appears:[62]

> ipse loci custos, cuius sacrata uorago
> famosique lacus nomen memorabile seruant,
> innumeros aeris sonitus et uerbere crudo
> ut sensit mugire forum, mouet horrida sancto
> ora situ meritaque caput uenerabile quercu.
>
> (i.i.66–70)

(When the guardian of the place himself (whose memorable name is preserved by the sacred chasm and the famous pool) heard the countless hammerings of bronze and the Forum bellowing with boisterous blows, he raised his countenance, stiff with decay but well revered, and his head respected for the oak-wreath that he had richly deserved.)

The same mood of celebration and rejoicing appears in the poem on Domitian's seventeenth consulship (iv.i) together with a pride in Rome's greatness and achievements, and in the poem of thanksgiving (iv.2) composed after attending a banquet given by Domitian, in which Statius expresses the magnificence of the imperial palace:

> tectum augustum, ingens, non centum insigne columnis,
> sed quantae superos caelumque Atlante remisso
> sustentare queant. stupet hoc uicina Tonantis
> regia, teque pari laetantur sede locatum
> numina.   (iv.2.18–22)

(An august edifice, vast, conspicuous with its columns—not a hundred columns, but as many as could support heaven and the gods when Atlas had been relieved of his burden. The neighbouring palace of the Thunderer stands in amazement, and the divine powers rejoice that you are housed in a dwelling no less magnificent.)

the splendour of the banquet:

> hic cum Romuleos proceres trabeataque Caesar
> agmina mille simul iussit discumbere mensis,
> ipsa sinus accincta Ceres Bacchusque laborat
> sufficere. (IV.2.32–5)

(Here when Caesar has bidden the Roman chiefs and the knights in their robes of state recline together at a thousand tables, Ceres herself with gown upgirt and Bacchus toil to satisfy them.)

and above all the radiance of the emperor himself:

> sed mihi non epulas Indisque innixa columnis
> robora Maurorum famulasque ex ordine turmas,
> ipsum, ipsum cupido tantum spectare uacauit
> tranquillum uultus et maiestate serena
> mulcentem radios summittentemque modeste
> fortunae uexilla suae (IV.2.38–43)

(But I had no time to look at the banquet or the tables of Moorish wood supported by columns of Indian ivory, or the slaves in their ordered companies, so eager was I to look upon the peaceful countenance and serene majesty of the Emperor himself as he tempered his radiance and modestly played down the blazoning of his good fortune.)

The language of adulation is excessive, but it appears nevertheless that Statius was deeply gratified to feel that as a poet he was able to participate, however humbly, in the glory of the emperor and the Roman world:

> qua mihi felices epulas mensaeque dedisti
> sacra tuae, talis longo post tempore uenit
> lux mihi, Troianae qualis sub collibus Albae,
> cum modo Germanas acies modo Daca sonantem
> proelia Palladio tua me manus induit auro.
> (IV.2.63–7)

(After long waiting, the day on which you granted me a place at your table and the sacred blessings of your feast dawned for me as bright as that on which, beneath the hills of Trojan Alba, I sang first of German wars and then of Dacian battles and your hand set the golden crown of Pallas upon my head.)

If passages such as these in poems offered to Domitian are too fulsome, there is abundant evidence elsewhere of Statius' approval of the emperor, and perhaps he expresses more in a quiet reference occurring incidentally in a poem addressed to a friend than in the deliberate flourishes written to satisfy the emperor's ears. To quote only one instance, he describes Domitian as the ruler

> quo Pietas auctore redit terrasque reuisit,
> quem timet omne nefas. (v.2.92–3)

(. . . under whose influence Loyalty has come back and revisited the earth, and of whom every misdeed is afraid.)

Many of the *Silvae* poems are what might be called genre pieces, dealing with topics traditionally recognized by rhetorical and poetical theory. For example, there is the joyful *epithalamium* addressed to L. Arruntius Stella (1.2), the *soteria* for Rutilius Gallicus after his recovery from illness (1.4), the *propempticon* wishing Maecius Celer a safe journey (iii.2), and the descriptions of villas and baths (1.3 and 5; ii.2 and cf. iii.1). These are all well suited to the occasions for which they were written. They naturally follow the traditions of the several genres and contain a good many commonplaces and the usual mythological allusions. The poem on the baths of Claudius Etruscus (1.5), for example, is full of clever artifice, with its invocation of the Nymphs, its description of the marble columns, and its references to Venus and Narcissus; but there is little poetical worth in a piece of this kind, hastily written as a *tour de force*,[63] and it is positively marred by the insipid hyperboles in the account of the fire that heats the water and the sunlight that illuminates the baths:[64]

> stupet ipse beatas
> circumplexus opes et parcius imperat ignis.
> multus ubique dies, radiis ubi culmina totis
> perforat atque alio sol improbus uritur aestu.
>
> (1.5.43–6)

(The very fire stands amazed as it encompasses these riches, and controls the ardour of its power. Everywhere light abounds, where the fierce sun, piercing the roof with all its rays, is nevertheless scorched by another kind of heat.)

Perhaps the most attractive of these genre pieces is the account of the villa of Pollius Felix at Surrentum (II.2). Much of it is light-hearted and fanciful without becoming absurd, and it contains some good descriptions of the coast, the cliffs, and the views from various windows and conveys the peaceful atmosphere of the place quite successfully:

> mira quies pelagi: ponunt hic lassa furorem
> aequora, et insani spirant clementius austri;
> hic praeceps minus audet hiems, nulloque tumultu
> stagna modesta iacent dominique imitantia mores.
>
> (II.2.26–9)

(The peace of the sea is wonderful; here the weary waves lay aside their fury, and the raging south winds blow more mildly; here dashing storms are less bold, and the pools lie unruffled and undisturbed, taking on the same character as their master.)

Although Statius is capable of skilful objective description, he knows also how to impart a human feeling to much of his poetry as in this passage. The poem ends with a charming appraisal of Pollius himself and his wife, Polla; in lines reminiscent of Lucretius, Statius refers to the Epicurean tranquillity of Pollius' life:[65]

> nos, uilis turba, caducis
> deseruire bonis semperque optare parati,
> spargimur in casus: celsa tu mentis ab arce
> despicis errantes humanaque gaudia rides.
>
> (II.2.129–32)

(We, the crowd of little worth, slaves to ephemeral wealth and always ready to form new desires, are tossed from one chance to another; but you, from the high citadel of your mind, look down upon us as we stray, and laugh at the joys of mankind.)

Six of the poems belong to a quite different genre. These are

addressed to bereaved persons after the death of some near kinsman or favourite slave, offering them condolence and consolation.
Statius evidently regarded himself as being particularly well
qualified for this role:

> ille ego qui (quotiens!) blande matrumque patrumque
> uulnera, qui uiduos potui mulcere dolores;
> ille ego lugentum mitis solator, acerbis
> auditus tumulis et descendentibus umbris . . .   (v.5.38–41)

(Yet I am he who—so often!—was able to charm and soothe
the pains of mothers and fathers and their sorrows of bereavement; I, the gentle consoler of those who mourn, whose voice
was heard at their untimely tombs by spirits as they left the
earth . . .)

His own grief at the death of his father had given him an understanding of what others felt:

> neque enim mihi flere parentem
> ignotum; similis gemui proiectus ad ignem.
> ille mihi tua damna dies compescere cantu
> suadet: et ipse tuli quos nunc tibi confero questus.
>
> (III.3.39–42)

(For I too know what it is to lament for a father; like you, I
have groaned prostrate before the funeral pyre. That day
urges me to soften the effects of your loss by song; I myself
have experienced the laments that I now offer you.)

There is considerable depth of feeling in most of these poems,
especially in v.3, on the death of the poet's own father. Moreover,
as in the *Thebaid*, proper funeral honours for the dead and sincere
lamentation are regarded as marks of true *pietas*. The consolation
for Claudius Etruscus (III.3) begins with this invocation:

> summa deum, Pietas, cuius gratissima caelo
> rara profanatas inspectant numina terras,
> huc uittata comam niueoque insignis amictu,
> qualis adhuc praesens nullaque expulsa nocentum
> fraude rudis populos atque aurea regna colebas,
> mitibus exsequiis ades et lugentis Etrusci
> cerne pios fletus laudataque lumina terge.   (III.3.1–7)

(Pietas, most exalted of the gods, whose divinity so pleasing to heaven looks rarely upon the guilty earth, come to us wearing fillets on your hair and adorned with snow-white robe, as when you still lived among innocent peoples in the kingdoms of the golden age and had not yet been driven out by men's criminal deceit. Attend these gentle obsequies, and observe the tears of Etruscus as he mourns in heartfelt grief, and speaking words of praise dry his eyes.)

In thus going beyond the particular occasion, Statius is able to express his hope for the moral regeneration of mankind through *pietas*. The same hope is given further expression shortly afterwards:

                                adeste
dique hominesque sacris. procul hinc, procul ite nocentes,
si cui corde nefas   (III.3.12–14)

(Come, gods and men, to the sacred rites. Depart and keep your distance, all guilty ones, you in whose hearts there are thoughts of crime . . .)

and:

                    insontes castosque uoco   (III.3.17)

                (I call the guiltless and pure . . .)

Touches like these were hardly the outcome of instructions in rhetorical handbooks, although the consolatory poems contain many features showing the influence of such works: for example, descriptions of the deceased person, details of his career, references to the funeral and to the expensive incense offered at the pyre, and typical generalizations on the lot of mortal men. This does not imply, however, that the poems consist mainly of commonplaces. In addition to the considerable expressions of grief, they bear the unmistakable signs of Statius' own personality and poetical outlook.[66]

Of the two lyric odes, the first one, in Alcaic metre (IV.5), conveys the atmosphere of spring with a certain charm and shows Statius modestly content with his little Alban estate, but the second, in Sapphic metre (IV.7), with its pedestrian references to *orbitas*, is uninspired, and it almost contains its own condemnation in the words *torpor est nostris sine te Camenis* (IV.7.21). In any case, his lyric pieces inevitably invite comparison with Horace, and the comparison shows Statius a clever but inexperienced composer in this medium. The hendecasyllabic poems are more successful, although two of them, on Lucan's birthday (ii.7) and the Via Domitiana (iv.3) are longer than most Latin poems in this metre and their subject-matter might well have been suitable for hexameters. But in the former case the choice of hendecasyllabics was made deliberately as a mark of respect, to avoid the metre in which Lucan himself excelled.[67] This poem is serious in content and shows Statius as a sincere admirer of Lucan, whom he compares favourably to Ennius, Lucretius, Varro Atacinus, and even Virgil. It is perhaps significant that in a list of Lucan's poems he stops to mention one particular episode in the *De Bello Civili*—the funeral of Pompey and Lucan's lament for him:[68]

> 'tu Pelusiaci scelus Canopi
> deflebis pius et Pharo cruenta
> Pompeio dabis altius sepulcrum.' (ii.7.70–2)

('You will lament for the crime of Pelusian Canopus with pious tears and raise up to Pompey a memorial loftier than blood-stained Pharos.')

In Book ii there are two pieces which Statius describes in the preface as *leues libellos quasi epigrammatis loco scriptos*; one of these (ii.3), composed for the birthday of Atedius Melior, describes a tree with a remarkable shape on Melior's estate, and the other (ii.4) is a mock lament for Melior's dead parrot. A third piece immediately following these two (ii.5), on the death of a tame lion, was presented to Domitian while the lion's body was still lying in the amphitheatre and is marked by what Statius himself calls *eandem . . . stili facilitatem*. All three were impromptu poems and demonstrate both the poet's technical skill and the limitations of this type of writing, with its commonplaces, its mythological allusions and its rhetorical flourishes.[69] Statius acknowledges that the poem on Melior's tree is slight in substance—*quid Phoebum tam parua rogem?* (ii.3.6)—but it contains a delightful myth accounting for the shape of the tree and ends, like the poems on the villas of Vopiscus and Pollius Felix, with a benediction on the owner, who, like these other patrons of the poet, lives in tranquillity of spirit.[70]

A personal longing for peace is expressed in other poems, notably in the one which Statius addressed to his wife Claudia and in the short ode to Sleep. These two pieces are both autobiographical and show that Statius was ill during the last few years of his life. In the poem to his wife (III.5), which he describes in the preface to Book III as *sermo et quidem securus, ut cum uxore et qui persuadere malit quam placere*, and in which he expresses his feelings more freely than in most of his other works, the glamour of Rome and the empire gives way to something more precious. All that he wants now is to return to Naples, where men live peacefully:[71]

> pax secura locis et desidis otia uitae
> et numquam turbata quies somnique peracti.
> nulla foro rabies aut strictae in iurgia leges:
> morum iura uiris solum et sine fascibus aequum.
>
> (III.5.85-8)

(There is untroubled peace in those places, and you can enjoy a life of ease and leisure, undisturbed quiet and unbroken sleep. No angry litigants, no laws unsheathed for quarrels disturb the forum; the rights and duties of morality alone bind the citizens, and justice rules without the tokens of official power.)

The Achilleid

Little need be said here about the *Achilleid*. Only one book and part of a second were ever written, and Statius seems to have felt that his inspiration was flagging at the end of the first book.[72] In this book he depicts the boyhood of Achilles and the anxiety of his mother Thetis, who tries to conceal him from danger by dressing him as a girl and placing him among the maidens at the court of Lycomedes, king of Scyros. Here he is discovered by a ruse of Ulysses and he sails with the Achaeans to Troy.

In contrast to the *Thebaid*, what was written of the *Achilleid* depicts the joy of youth, and its tones are mainly bright and radiant. Among its chief attractions are the descriptions of Achilles, such as the following, where he has just returned from a lion-hunt:

> ille aderat multo sudore et puluere maior,
> et tamen arma inter festinatosque labores

> dulcis adhuc uisu: niueo natat ignis in ore
> purpureus fuluoque nitet coma gratior auro.
> necdum prima noua lanugine uertitur aetas,
> tranquillaeque faces oculis et plurima uultu
> mater inest: qualis Lycia uenator Apollo
> cum redit et saeuis permutat plectra pharetris.

(I.159–66)

(There he stood, covered with dust and sweat, and taller now, and yet despite his weapons and the toils through which he had hastened still sweet to look upon; his snow-white countenance was flushed with a red glow, and his hair shone more pleasing than tawny gold. No soft new beard had yet altered his boyish looks, his eyes were calm and bright, and there was much likeness to his mother in his features; such is Apollo when he returns from hunting in Lycia and puts aside his fierce quiver for the lyre.)

But besides the joy there is the deep anxiety of Thetis for her son; and no doubt the ultimate grief that she would experience at the death of the young hero would have been an important feature in the poem as Statius planned it. For this reason it was essential for him to devote a whole book in this way to Achilles' boyhood, as a preparation for the tragedy that would follow.

The poetical work of Statius is characterized by a conscious artistry. In the *Thebaid* he skilfully creates an atmosphere or evokes a mood as the setting for action or speech. Gloom, horror, violence or mystery are all portrayed by means of carefully chosen expressions, epithets, similes varied in detail, despite their conventional subject-matter, to suit the immediate context, and variations of tone, word-order, rhythm or sound-patterns. Taenarum, one of the entrances to the underworld (II.32–54), the site of the Theban ambush lying in wait for Tydeus (II.496–526), the wood where Tiresias conducts his interview with spirits of the dead (IV.419–42), the abodes of Mars (VII.41–63), and Somnus (X.84–117) are all described in set pieces for this purpose.[73]

Unfortunately, this artistry too often becomes artificiality, especially in the *Silvae*, where little time was spent over some of the individual pieces and the improvisor had recourse to a number of stereotyped themes and methods of treatment. Here Statius was certainly *doctus*, and was never at a loss for a mythological allusion to illustrate his theme. But the regular intrusion of mythological motifs fails to hide a poverty of true poetical invention in many places, and modern taste soon finds that such matter in the *Silvae* becomes tedious. Moreover, the striving for unusual effect in poetical conceits becomes grotesque at times. Statius is not alone among Silver Latin poets in this respect and evidently the taste of his age was not offended, but it is hard to find any positive merit in passages where exaggeration or mythological conceit results in absurdity. For example, the long central section of the *epithalamium* for Stella and Violentilla (*Silvae*, 1.2.46–193) contains an account of how Venus persuaded Violentilla to accept Stella's suit, and, careful to hide her own divine beauty, herself led forth the bride; similarly, Apollo and Aesculapius are represented as tending Rutilius Gallicus and curing him of his illness (1.4.58–114). Even if the conceits of these passages are accepted as appropriate to the poems in which they occur, when Venus conveys Earinus in her chariot to the palace of Domitian (III.4.21–59), when Aesculapius himself goes to perform the castration of the imperial favourite (III.4.65ff) and when Venus and Cupids cut locks of his hair (III.4.86ff) the conceit goes too far. Again there is absurdity in the description of the Amores tearing their hair and feathers and scattering them on Claudius Etruscus' funeral pyre (III.3.131–4). Similar absurdity in mythological conceits occurs in the *Thebaid*, when the river Inachos is in flood and 'swells with his son-in-law, Jupiter' (IV.120–1), or the river-god Ismenus, in order to flood his river, 'lifts his greedy countenance to the sky, sucks the moisture from the clouds and leaves the air dry' (IX.453–4).

The grotesque exaggeration that is so common in Lucan is common again in the *Thebaid*. In a battle-scene, for example, a cloud of missile weapons darkens the sky, the air has no room for all the javelins and there is no place for them to fall to earth (VIII.412–20); elsewhere a warrior's arm is shorn off, but as it lies on the ground it still grips his sword and shakes it (VIII. 441–3), or a trumpeter is struck on the head as he is about to give a signal, but the trumpet goes on sounding after his spirit has fled (XI.55–6). Similarly, in the *Achilleid* the ships of the fleet are so numerous that

> . . . ipsum iam puppibus aequor
> deficit et totos consumunt carbasa uentos.　　(1.445–6)

(The sea itself fails the ships, and their sails devour every breath of wind.)

The attribution of human feelings and emotions to beasts or inanimate objects is another device dear to Statius. When Thetis reaches the shore of Thessaly, for example,

> laetantur montes et conubialia pandunt
> antra sinus lateque deae Spercheios abundat
> obuius et dulci uestigia circuit unda.
>
> (*Achill.*, 1.101–3)

(The mountains are glad, the marriage-bowers open wide their recesses, and Spercheios with full, broad stream flows to meet the goddess and laps round her footsteps with his fresh water.)

and when Pollius Felix built a temple to Hercules at Surrentum,[74]

> stupet ipse labores
> annus et angusti bis seno limite menses
> longaeuum mirantur opus. (*Silvae*, III.1.17–19)

(The year itself stands in amazement at the toil, and the brief months as they pass on their twelvefold path wonder to see a work that will last through ages.)

Finally, there are passages where a striving for detailed realism results in absurdity, as when Tiresias, calling up the spirits of the dead, is inspired with prophecy and his grey hair thrills and stands erect, lifting up the fillets on his head (*Theb.*, IV.580–1); or the wind of a thunderbolt ripples the crest of a warrior's helmet as it passes him (*Theb.*, V.586–7); or mothers quench the ashes of a funeral pyre with milk as they beat their breasts (*Silvae*, V.5.15–17). Such details mar the passages in which they occur.

Apart from the references made by Juvenal, there is no mention of Statius by name in contemporary literature,[75] and the archaizing taste of the Antonine period is not likely to have favoured the Flavian poets. In the fifth century A.D., however, Statius was openly admired by Sidonius Apollinaris, poet and bishop of Auvergne, and in the works of Claudian and Ausonius there are unmistakable echoes of the *Thebaid* and *Achilleid*. It was for these two works that Statius was known in the Middle Ages, when he was read and respected by scholars and poets alike.

Sidonius knew the *Silvae*, but these seem to have been subsequently forgotten and remained more or less unknown for perhaps as long as eight hundred years, until a manuscript was discovered by Poggio in 1417.[76]

The York library possessed a work or works of Statius in the eighth century. From the ninth century onwards his name appears regularly in lists of Classical authors recommended for study,[77] and Dante, in the *De Vulgari Eloquentia* (ii.6.8off) mentions him as one of the main Classical models for 'construction', together with Ovid, Virgil, and Lucan. John of Salisbury quotes extensively from both the *Thebaid* and *Achilleid*, showing that these works had become an integral part of the educated man's heritage from Classical Latin, to be drawn upon when an apt illustration or phrase was required.

There is curious testimony to the influence of the *Thebaid* in the Middle Ages in a work of doubtful authorship entitled *super Thebaiden*.[78] This work assumes that poetry, like a nut, has an outer shell and a kernel, namely the literal meaning and the mystical meaning,[79] and the author chooses the *Thebaid*, which he says was composed by Papinius Surculus,[80] *mirae strenuitatis uir . . . Virgilianae Eneidis fidus emulator . . .*, to illustrate his point. The 'kernel' is extracted from the poem by interpreting the proper names according to imaginative but false etymologies. Thus Thebes is *anima humana*, Laius is *lux sancta* (*Lux ayos*; *ayos uero Grece sanctus Latine interpretatur*), Edippus is *lasciuia*, and so on. On this principle the final interpretation of the poem is given in the last sentence of the *super Thebaiden*: *tanto autem uitiorum conflictu Thebe, id est humana anima, quassata est quidem, sed diuinae benignitatis clementia subueniente liberatur.* This Christian interpretation of the *Thebaid* as a *psychomachia*, whatever intrinsic literary merit the poem may have been thought to have, assured its acceptance in the Middle Ages.[81]

Besides their great educational value, the Classical authors provided the Middle Ages with an incomparable store of legends and characters that poets could use when seeking suitable themes. To this store Statius had made his own peculiar contribution. The *Thebaid* was the ultimate source of at least the main plot of the French *Roman de Thèbes*, composed probably in the latter half of the twelfth century, and various prose romances were derived from this.[82] A number of details in the Theban story as related by

Boccaccio in his *De Genealogia Deorum*, for example the behaviour of Tydeus when he was mortally wounded and gnawed the head of Melanippus, may have been taken directly from another Medieval source, but again the ancient source from which they were drawn must have been Statius' *Thebaid*.[83]

Numerous adaptations and imitations, as well as detailed reminiscences of Statius are to be found in later Medieval authors. In England, Chaucer and Lydgate were familiar with the story of the *Thebaid* in some form or other and in various parts of their work they show his influence or express their admiration. In *The Hous of Fame* Chaucer relates how he saw:

> Upon an yren piler strong
> That peynted was, al endelong,
> With tigres blod in every place,
> The Tholosan that highte Stace,
> That bar of Thebes up the fame
> Upon his shuldres, and the name
> Also of cruel Achilles.[84]

In *Troilus and Criseyde* he puts into the mouth of Cassandra an account of the ancestry of Diomedes, in which the mention of Tydeus is sufficient pretext for relating briefly the story of the war against Thebes. The events mentioned and the order in which they occur make it clear that Statius was the ultimate source of the story.[85] Elsewhere in the same poem Pandarus visits his niece and finds her with a group of maidens reading 'the geste of the Sege of Thebes'. When she tells him that their book is the 'romance of Thebes' and briefly mentions the contents of what has been read so far, he replies:[86]

> 'al this knowe I myselve,
> And al th' assege of Thebes and the care;
> For herof been ther maked bookes twelve.'

The Knightes Tale begins with an account of Theseus' war against Creon on behalf of the suppliant Argive women, whom, on his return from Scythia, he finds in Athens 'in the temple of the goddesse Clemence'; and in the course of the same tale there is a description of 'the temple of mighty Mars' based on that of Statius in the *Thebaid*.[87] There is a briefer reference to the same 'grisly temple ful of drede' in the proem to *The Compleynt of faire Anelida*

and fals Arcite, and the story of this poem again begins with reference to the deaths of the Argive leaders and Theseus' expedition
against Creon. As Chaucer says in the proem: 'First folow I
Stace' (21).

In about 1420-1 Lydgate composed his *Siege of Thebes*, a poem
consisting of a prologue and three parts. The first part tells of the
foundation of Thebes, the accession of Layus to the Theban
throne, the story of Edippus' early career, his marriage to Jocasta
and his death, and the unfilial conduct of his two sons Ethiocles
and Polymyte; the second part deals with the compromise agreed
upon by the brothers to reign in Thebes alternately, the meeting
of Polymyte and Tydeus at the court of Adrastus, their quarrel
and reconciliation, their marriage to the daughters of Adrastus,
Tydeus' embassy to Thebes, the ambush of fifty warriors and the
return of Tydeus to Argos; the third part contains preparations
for war in Argos and Thebes, the episode of Hypsipyle (Isyphile),
the death of the child, the march to Thebes, the deaths of the
Argive leaders and of the two brothers, Creon's order forbidding
the burial of the Argive dead, and finally the mission of the Argive
women and Theseus' war against Creon. Whatever this poem
owes to earlier Medieval sources, it is clear that the *Thebaid* was
the ultimate source of the second and third parts,[88] which reproduce the main events of the story as told by Statius, and in the
same order. Despite many omissions and alterations of detail and
adaptations to the thought, outlook and customs of a different
age, the great influence of Statius is still recognizable in the *Siege
of Thebes*.[89]

The greatest testimony to the influence of Statius' work and the
esteem in which it was held in the Middle Ages occurs in Dante's
Divina Commedia. A number of details in the poem show Dante's
familiarity with the *Thebaid*: for example, the story and the character of Capaneus (*Inf.*, XIV.46-72; cf. XXV.13-15), Amphiaraus
(*Inf.*, XX.31-9), the double flame on the pyre of Eteocles and
Polynices (*Inf.*, XXVI.52-4), Tydeus gnawing the head of Melanippus (*Inf.*, XXXII.130-1), the mention of the two sons of Hypsipyle
and the grief of Lycurgus (*Purg.*, XXVI.94-5) and in general the
reference to *di Tebe furie* (*Inf.*, XXX.22). In *Purgatorio* (IX.34-9) the
simile of the sleeping Achilles being conveyed to Scyros in his
mother's arms and wondering where he is on waking is almost
certainly a reminiscence of the description that Statius gives in

Achilleid, 1.228–50. But above all, Dante's respect and admiration are expressed in those *canti* of the *Purgatorio* where Statius himself appears. Here Stazio is not only a native of Toulouse, according to the Medieval tradition,[90] but also a Christian who kept secret his religious conversion. Besides showing that he knew the *Thebaid* and the *Achilleid*, Dante regarded Statius as a worthy mouthpiece for explaining the causes of the earthquake that occurred on the Mountain and for expounding a doctrine of generation and the human soul.[91] Although Dante did not know the *Silvae* and followed mistaken traditions about the actual life of Statius, he was quick to perceive his Virgilian spirit and sympathy for human suffering; and there seems to be an echo of the poet of the *Silvae* in the line:[92]

> 'senza mio lagrimar non fur lor pianti'.
>
> (*Purg.*, XXII.84)

Notes

1 Pliny, *Ep.*, VII.19.5ff.
2 Tacitus, *Histories*, I.I.
3 *Dialogus de Oratoribus*, 36–7; cf. Pliny, *Ep.*, IX.2.2–3.
4 *Dialogus*, 20.2ff; 21.3.8–9; 23.6.
5 Ibid., 20.7. Plutarch (*Publicola* 15) has some interesting remarks on the luxury and costliness of public buildings at Rome under Domitian. He is critical of their inferior architectural taste.
6 In the *Dialogus* (11.4) Maternus, speaking on behalf of poetry, observes: *nam statum cuiusque ac securitatem melius innocentia tuetur quam eloquentia*. No doubt Statius would have supported this view, conformity being the best part of *innocentia*. See further below, p. 208 and n. 60.
7 All that is known about the elder Papinius is contained in *Silvae*, V.3.
8 F. Vollmer in *P. Papinii Statii Siluarum Libri* (Leipzig, 1898), 17, n. 2 asserts that 'Es ist kein Grund anzunehmen, dass diese Deklamationen in Rom, nicht in Neapel stattfanden', and adds that the *Latii patres* of *Silvae*, V.3.215 must be taken in a wider sense as equivalent to *Itali*. But *Latios patres*, like *Romuleam stirpem proceresque futuros* (ibid. 176) and *Latii proceres* (ibid. 203), must surely refer to influential men in Rome, and in any case the *urbs* mentioned by Juvenal (VII.83) cannot be any other city.
9 *Dialogus de Oratoribus* 10, 1–2. The words *fama, cui soli seruiunt et quod unum esse pretium omnis laboris sui fatentur* might almost be regarded as an inference from what Statius himself says (*Silvae*, V.3.213–14):

> primusque dedisti
> non uulgare loqui et famam sperare sepulcro.

(. . . and you first taught me lofty utterance, and to hope for fame even after death.)

Cf. also *Thebaid*, XII.810ff. On the lack of interest in *recitationes*, see *Dialogus*, 9.3–4; Pliny, *Ep.*, 1.13.

10 *Silvae*, III.5.28ff; IV.5.22–4; V.3.225ff.

11 *Thebaid*, XII.813. For Statius and Domitian, see below, n. 60.

12 *Dialogus*, 9.3ff. Juvenal's seventh *Satire*, esp. lines 79–97, is informative on this point, and it also brings out a contrast between the Flavian period, when Saleius Bassus and Statius were writing, and earlier times—e.g. the Neronian age, when men like Lucan could afford to write without patronage.

13 *Dialogus*, 9.5.

14 *Silvae*, III.1.61–3; IV.5.1; V.3.36ff.

15 Juvenal, VII.86–7.

16 Juvenal, loc. cit. The *Agave* must have been composed before A.D. 83, when Paris died.

17 *Silvae*, IV.4.95ff; *Achilleid*, 1.18–19.

18 *Silvae*, IV.9 and IV. praef.

19 Cf. II.1 and II.6.

20 *Thebaid*, XII.811–12.

21 For the dating of the *Silvae*, see esp. F. Vollmer, *P. Papinii Statii Silvarum Libri* (Leipzig, 1898), 3ff; L. Legras, 'Les Dernières Années de Stace I', *Rev. Ét. Anc.* ix (1907), 338–48; H. Frère, *Stace, Silves* (Budé), volume I (Paris, 1961), xxi–xxv.

22 In the poems of the *Silvae* there are four references to the *Achilleid*, which scholars tend to date indiscriminately to the summer of A.D. 95. But in IV.4.94 Statius says only that he is attempting the Achilles theme, whereas in IV.7.23–4 the poem has evidently made some progress (. . . *et primis meus ecce metis/haeret Achilles*—i.e. presumably, it is at a standstill at the end of the first book), and in V.2.162–3 a recital of some part of the poem, possibly the first book, was in the poet's mind as an event that would occur in the near future. The reference in V.5.36–7 (*nouumque Aeaciden*) adds very little, but it shows that Statius had not yet progressed very far.

23 Propertius, 1.7.1–2. The words *armaque fraternae tristia militiae* suggest that Ponticus in fact treated the same part of the Theban legend as Statius.

24 On Statius' use of the Theban legend, see esp. L. Legras, *Étude sur la Thébaide de Stace* (Paris, 1905), 15–141.

25 A fuller discussion of these and other, more detailed, criticisms would go far beyond the scope of the present chapter. The complaint of some critics that the *Thebaid* is boring hardly merits consideration, except in so far as to say that personal taste is bound to play some part in such judgments, and that those scholars, mainly historians of literature, who read the poem superficially, if at all, and repeat the strictures pronounced by previous generations without attempting to understand the poet's purpose, cannot be expected to speak with authority. It would be helpful to bear in mind the advice of Pliny (*Ep.*, V.6.42) when he says: *primum ego officium scriptoris existimo titulum suum legat atque identidem interroget se quid coeperit scribere, sciatque si materiae immoratur non esse longum, longissimum si aliquid accersit atque attrahit.* From this point of view, as this chapter will

try to show, Statius is not *longus*. For attempts to find profitable approaches to a study of the *Thebaid*, see esp. H. M. Mulder, P. *Papinii Statii Thebaidos liber secundus commentario exegetico aestheticoque instructus* (Groningen, 1954); B. Kytzler, 'Statius-Studien', unpublished thesis (Freie Univ., Berlin, 1955); W. Schetter, *Untersuchungen zur epischen Kunst des Statius* (Wiesbaden, 1960).

26 *Thebaid*, 1.123ff. In lines 126–7 *gentilis* is to be construed with *furor* and *inuidia* and *metus*, showing that these were characteristics of the Theban family.

27 The close repetition of a word in a different significance, as *loca . . . loco* here, is not untypical of Statius.

28 Jupiter's autocratic power is clear in 1.211–13; III.253ff, 304–10; and in his threat to deprive Mars of his warlike character and function in VII.27–32.

29 The use of *impius* is not simply predicative here. Jupiter acknowledges the prior spiritual corruption of Eteocles and sees in him a suitable agent for the fulfilment of his ultimate purpose. Mozley's translation (in the Loeb edition), 'in despite of kin', misses this point, although it appreciates the full connotation of *impius*.

30 For the divine purpose, cf. III.218–52, 304ff; VII.195–221; X.70–1.

31 In any case, these two journeys to Thebes, like the embassy of Tydeus in Book II, the march of the invading army, and the mission of the Argive women in Book XII, help to focus the listener's (or reader's) attention on Thebes as the main objective in the War of the Seven, and thus the main dramatic centre of the story, even when part of the action is taking place in Argos.

32 In Book I, when Polynices is ashamed to admit his parentage in the presence of the Argive court, Adrastus encourages him to forget the past:

> nostro quoque sanguine multum
> errauit pietas, nec culpa nepotibus obstat. (1.689–90)

(In our family also a lapse of due affection has caused many wrongs, but past guilt does not bind posterity.)

But Adrastus is depicted as a good king who is not tainted with the moral and spiritual corruption of other men, and therefore he is not beyond redemption. He alone of the Seven survives the war against Thebes and finally escapes from its horrors (XI.439ff; already foretold by omens, III.542–3; VI.924–46; see also below, p. 206). Further references to the delay of divine punishment occur in V.359–60 and 688–9 (showing how closely the underlying theme of the Lemnian story is related to that of the main Theban story—see below, n. 38) and in *Silvae*, V.2.84–7. Statius' interest in this evidently reflects contemporary philosophical thought. One of Plutarch's essays (*De sera numinis vindicta*) is devoted to the philosophical and theological implications of the same question. The sufferings and fears of innocent people are seen in 1.191–6; II.458–60, 479–81; III.114ff, 169–213, 578–9; IV.345–68; X.2–4 (reading *miserantis* in line 3), 563ff, 709–10.

33 E.g. 1.227–43, 684ff; 11.7–10, 462–5; 1v.483ff, 553ff, 604–44; x.584–7,
610–14, 796–801; x1.420–3, 619–20. For *furor*, see W. Schetter, *Untersuchungen zur epischen Kunst des Statius* (Wiesbaden, 1960), 5–21; P. Venini,
'*Furor* e psicologia nella Tebaide di Stazio', *Athenaeum* 42 (1964), 201–13.

34 See esp. v11.215–18 (quoted above, p. 197); x1.457–70, 605–7.

35 x1.57–112, 196–200, 315–406, 424–38, 457–96. The brothers are given
every chance to avoid the final conflict by these delays. The notion of
delay (*mora*) is suggested by the poet on various occasions (e.g. 111.718–19;
1v.667; v.744; v11.139; x1.109–11, 347, 447–8) to give the main characters
a breathing-space, as it were, and a chance to reflect on the folly of their
passions; but these intervals are allowed to slip away and the lessons that
might have restored good sense pass unheeded. The Fury is aware that
Adrastus would avail himself of any opportunity to prevent the combat
between the brothers, and she warns her sister to beware of delay:

> tibi pareat impius exsul,
> Argolicumque impelle nefas; neu mitis Adrastus
> praeualeat plebesque, caue, Lernaea moretur.   (x1.109–11)

(Keep the impious exile in obedience to yourself, incite the Argives
to their crime; do not let the placating spirit of Adrastus prevail or
the host of Lerna delay you.)

In this passage and elsewhere *impius* is used typically of the characters who
are under the influence of Tisiphone. Adrastus is *mitis* because he seeks
to lessen the tension of the brothers' furious passions.

Dramatically, the *morae* in the *Thebaid*, whether brief, as in Book x1, or
protracted, as elsewhere, serve to relax the immediate tension before or
after a climax in the action and to create suspense. This cannot be appreciated if episodes are read in isolation. On *mora*, see also below, p. 204.

36 The echoes of Virgil, *Aeneid*, 11, are unmistakable. Formally, the Lemnian
story, as narrated here, resembles Aeneas' narrative of the sack of Troy,
with the central figure rescuing a beloved parent from the slaughter. For
Statius' debt to Virgil, see 'Virgil and the Flavian Epic' in *Virgil*, Studies
in Latin Literature & its Influence, ed. D. R. Dudley (Routledge & Kegan
Paul, 1969), 67ff.

37 Examples of *furor*, *furiae*, *discordia* are common in Book v, e.g. 74, 91, 148,
155ff, 202–3, 298, 302.

38 The Lemnian massacre, like the war between the Theban brothers, is
interpreted as divine punishment for human guilt:

> dis uisum turbare domos, nec pectora culpa
> nostra uacant . . .   (v.57–8; cf.492)

(It was the will of the gods to wreck our families, but our own
hearts are not free from guilt.)

As in the main story, so here too divine punishment is delayed:

> mouet et caelestia quondam
> corda dolor lentoque inrepunt agmine Poenae.   (v.59–60)

(Even celestial hearts are touched at last by resentment, and the
avenging deities move slowly on.)

Other events in the story of Hypsipyle are similarly interpreted, e.g. v.359–60, and by implication v.620–8, where the death of Opheltes through Hypsipyle's neglect is seen as an extension of the divine purpose for Lemnos, still valid after many years and far from the scene of the massacre. And similarly, the Lemnian women are maddened and perverted (by Venus and the infernal powers) and thus slay their menfolk: v.64ff, 73–4, 90ff, 155ff, 202–3, 302–3. Structurally, Book v is part of the long central *mora* in the poem. See below, p. 204.

39 For a sympathetic discussion of this passage, see esp. C. S. Lewis, 'Dante's Statius', *Medium Aevum* 25 (1957), 138. Statius is sparing in his application of *pius* as a direct epithet to characters in the poem. When it occurs in this way it is deliberate and effective.

40 The Apollo of this episode is a cruel, insensitive god. For a similar view of Apollo, see R. S. Conway, *Ancient Italy and Modern Religion* (Cambridge, 1933), 69–70. The episode of Coroebus (which scholars have regarded as an irrelevant digression, introduced only because Virgil in *Aeneid* VIII introduced the story of Cacus when Evander, like Adrastus in the *Thebaid*, was entertaining guests and explaining a local religious festival) shows how Statius relates even digressions from the main story to the underlying theme of human wickedness and the *uirtus* and *pietas* by which that wickedness might be overcome. Coroebus' reference to his own *pietas* and *uirtus* should not be regarded as mere priggishness. When a man found himself in a difficult situation which he could not understand, in facing a deity he examined his own conduct and his own motives to see in what respect he had been at fault. Coroebus pleads that his motives were honourable. Similarly, Aeneas, in bewilderment at the way in which he is treated by Juno, excuses himself to Venus in the words *sum pius Aeneas* (*Aeneid*, 1.378). The Coroebus episode is sympathetically discussed by C. S. Lewis, art. cit., 136–7.

41 Cf. Servius on *Aeneid*, XI.107: *mortuorum pax sepultura est*. The *impius* . . . *arcet* of line 98 recalls Jupiter's command in 1.300–1: *procul impius aula arceat* . . . See above, p. 196.

42 If proper funeral honours are necessary for the *pax mortuorum*, then lamentation is a necessary part of those honours; cf. Servius on *Aeneid*, VI.325: *nam sine fletu sepultura non est*. For other specific examples, see Catullus, 101.7–10; Virgil, *Aeneid*, XI.96–7; Ovid, *Fasti*, IV.849–50.

43 Statius appears deliberately to have placed a book in which funeral rites are the main subject at the end of each half of the poem to stress the importance of this aspect of *pietas*. The words of Pliny (*Ep.*, v.6.44), *non enim excursus hic eius, sed opus ipsum est*, used of digressions in Aratus, could well be applied to Books VI and XII (and v) of the *Thebaid*.

44 For want of space, this account leaves out of consideration such details as Oedipus' reaction to the death of his sons in XI.605ff, and the strife of the two brothers even in the flame of the funeral pyre (XII.429ff), which a fuller account would necessarily discuss.

45 *Thebaid*, 1.300; II.384, 386, 485; III.1.78, 82, 98; IV.361, 606; XI.335, 341, 346, 393, 552, 569; XII.57, 421, etc.

46 For this aspect, see 'Virgil and the Flavian Epic' in *Virgil*, Studies in Latin Literature & its Influence, ed. D. R. Dudley, 87.

47 *Thebaid*, x.827ff. The end of Capaneus is vividly described in x.927ff.

48 Ibid., VIII.716–66.

49 Statius seems to have had a special affection for Parthenopaeus, perhaps partly because the name reminded him of his own boyhood in Naples (Parthenope); cf. also *Silvae*, II.6.41–3. This picture of the *Heldenknabe* is developed from those of Pallas, Lausus, Camilla, Nisus and Euryalus in the *Aeneid*. Cf. R. Heinze, *Virgils epische Technik* (Stuttgart, 1957), 213ff; Schetter, op. cit., 43ff.

50 *Thebaid*, 1.448, 467; VII.537; XI.110.

51 Ibid., V.731.

52 The *Thebaid* was a new kind of poem in this way. Although in other ways it looked back to its precedents and traditional models, its emphasis on the moral and spiritual condition of mankind made it capable of being interpreted in later times as a *psychomachia* (see below, p. 220 and n. 81) and hence it looks forward to the *Divina Commedia* of Dante and Milton's *Paradise Lost*.

53 This is what the title is intended to convey; cf. Aulus Gellius, *Noctes Atticae, praef.* 5ff: *quia uariam et miscellam et quasi confusaneam doctrinam conquisiuerant, eo titulos quoque ad eam sententiam exquisitissimos indiderunt. namque alii Musarum scripserunt, alii siluarum . . .'* The *Garland* of Meleager was another such title, and the word 'anthology' expresses a similar notion. The fact that Statius' poems were often composed rapidly and at short notice does not prove that *siluae* was used in the sense mentioned by Quintilian (x.3.17): *diuersum est huic eorum uitium, qui primo decurrere per materiam stilo quam uelocissimo uolunt et sequentes calorem atque impetum extempore scribunt: hanc siluam uocant.*

54 See especially the dedicatory epistles to Books I and II.

55 In the dedicatory epistles Statius is apologetic for many of these poems. The quotation in the text is taken from the epistle prefaced to Book I.

56 Book by book they are as follows:

Book I. Dedicated to L. Arruntius Stella
  1 The equestrian statue of the emperor
  2 Epithalamium for Stella and Violantilla
  3 The villa of Manilius Vopiscus
  4 Thanksgiving for the recovery of Rutilius Gallicus from illness
  5 The baths of Claudius Etruscus
  6 The Kalends of December

Book II. Dedicated to Atedius Melior
  1 A poem of consolation for Melior on the death of a favourite slave
  2 The villa of Pollius Felix
  3 The tree of Atedius Melior
  4 Melior's parrot
  5 The tame lion
  6 A poem of consolation for Flavius Ursus on the death of a favourite slave
  7 To Polla, commemorating the birthday of Lucan

Book III. Dedicated to Pollius Felix
1 The temple of Hercules built by Pollius Felix at Surrentum
2 A *propempticon* (valedictory poem) for Maecius Celer
3 A poem for Claudius Etruscus on the death of his father
4 The dedication of the hair of Flavius Earinus
5 To his wife, Claudia, asking her to return with him to Naples
Book IV. Dedicated to Vitorius Marcellus
1 The seventeenth consulship of the emperor Domitian
2 A poem of thanksgiving offered to Domitian after a banquet in the imperial palace
3 On the new Via Domitiana
4 To Vitorius Marcellus, a letter in verse
5 An Ode to Septimius Severus
6 On a bronze statuette of Hercules owned by Novius Vindex
7 An Ode to Vibius Maximus
8 A poem of congratulation to Julius Menecrates on the birth of his third child
9 A poem written in jest to Plotius Grypus
Book V.
1 A poem of consolation for Abascantus on the death of his wife, Priscilla
2 Praises of Crispinus, son of Vettius Bolanus
3 The poet's lament for the death of his father
4 To Sleep
5 The poet's lament for the death of his foster-son.

57 The fact that the shortest immediately follows the longest in the present order may reflect Statius' own sense of balance and contrast. For his arrangement of pieces in the several books, cf. H. Cancik, *Untersuchungen zur lyrischen Kunst des P. Papinius Statius Silvae* (Hildesheim, 1965), 16–23.
58 *Silvae*, 1.6; II.7; IV.3 and 9 (hendecasyllabics); IV.5 and 7 (lyric metres).
59 Pliny, *Ep.*, III.18.10.
60 The words occur in the letter to Abascantus which serves as preface to Book v of the *Silvae*. Statius' relations with the emperor are discussed by J. J. Hartman, 'De Domitiano Imperatore et de poeta Statio', *Mnemosyne* 44 (1916), 338–72, and with the emperor and influential men at Rome by G. Ruediger, 'Quibuscum uiris fuerit Statio poetae usus consuetudo familiaritas', unpublished thesis (Marburg, 1887), 2–20. See also K. Scott, 'Statius' adulation of Domitian', *AJPhil.* 54 (1933), 247.
61 *Centum hos uersus, quos in equum maximum feci, indulgentissimo imperatori postero die, quam dedicauerat opus, tradere iussus sum* (*Silvae*, I, praef.).
62 Similarly, at the building of the *Via Domitiana*, in a poem less expressive of magnificence and in a somewhat lighter vein, the god of the river Vulturnus rises and thanks the emperor for cleaning his channel and building a splendid bridge (IV.3.67ff). Cf. also 1.2.158ff; 3.70ff; III.1.144ff; IV.1.11ff.
63 *Balneolum a me suum intra moram cenae recepit* (I, praef.).
64 In the descriptions of baths and other buildings lists of the imported marbles used in their construction are prominent (*Silvae*, 1.2.148ff;

5.34ff; II.2.85–93; IV.2.26–9). For an analysis of I.5 and its technique, see H. Cancik, op. cit., 24–5. For *stupet*, see below, n. 74.

65 Some of the finest touches in the descriptions in Statius' poetry occur when the language subtly suggests a reference to human psychology and thus brings about a poetic harmonization between the outer and the inner world. In the passage quoted earlier in this paragraph *furorem* and *clementius* not only express the calming of the sea and the winds but also suggest the tranquillity of mind achieved by Pollius Felix after 'life's storms'. For such descriptions in the *Thebaid*, cf. E. M. W. Tillyard, *The English Epic and its Background* (London, 1954), 102–3. The villa of Manilius Vopiscus is less successful in this respect, although it is cast in the same mould. In addition, its rhetorical effects are overdone, e.g. *quid primum . . . canam . . .?* (line 34—this figure was known as *addubitatio*, cf. Lactantius on *Thebaid*, I.4); *mirer . . . ?* (line 37); *huc oculis, huc mente trahor* and *dicam . . . ?* (line 38); *quid . . . mirer?* (line 57); *quid referam . . . ?* (line 64); repetition of *cedant* (lines 83, 85, 88). Even the poem on Pollius' villa is not free from these devices.

66 In II.1.209ff Statius' poetical skill succeeds in turning what might have been threadbare commonplaces into poetry of considerable merit, with subtly varied rhythms and sounds and a solemn grandeur worthy of the theme that it expresses and of the poet of the *Thebaid*. On the other hand, the lament for the slave of Flavius Ursus (II.6) is uninspired and unconvincing.

67 *ego non potui maiorem tanti auctoris habere reuerentiam quam quod laudes eius dicturus hexametros meos timui* (II, praef.).

(I could not show a greater respect for so great a poet than by losing confidence in my own hexameters when I was going to sing his praises.)

68 Here, as so often in the *Silvae* and the *Thebaid*, *pietas* in connection with funeral rites and lamentation for the dead is again emphasized.

69 There is a clever twist at the end of II.4 when Statius speaks of the parrot's funeral pyre and combines the *locus* of the funeral incense with a reference to the phoenix rising from its ashes (lines 34–7).

70 Melior's character and personality are praised in terms recalling the description of the poet's father in V.3. Compare II.3.64ff with V.3.246ff. On II.3 cf. Cancik, op. cit., 48ff.

71 Naples in the first century A.D. was quite different in character from the modern city. Cf. Silius Italicus, *Punica*, XII.31–2:

> nunc molles urbi ritus atque hospita Musis
> otia et exemptum curis grauioribus aeuum.

(Now the city's ways are pleasant and there is leisure to entertain the Muses and life is free from graver cares.)

72
> tardius sueto uenit ipse Thymbrae
> rector et primis meus ecce metis
> haeret Achilles. (IV.7.22–4)

(Even the lord of Thymbra comes more slowly than his wont, and see!—my Achilles stays at the first turning-point of his course.)

But this may have been a stereotyped exaggeration, suggesting to Vibius Maximus that Statius was inspired by his presence.

73 Another good example of Statius' deliberate artistry is his description of the storm breaking on a peaceful night in the Peloponnese, in *Thebaid*, 1.336–54. The tranquillity described in the first nine verses of this passage is skilfully suggested by the rhythm. The verses are arranged in three groups of three, with a strong pause at the end of each group, and each third line is a 'golden line' with nouns and adjectives arranged symmetrically around a central verb or participle. In the second line of each group there is a strong pause, but this does not interrupt the smooth rhythm of the passage. Then the storm approaches and the rhythm becomes agitated, with breaks in the lines and frequent enjambment. This change is accompanied by subtle changes in the sound-pattern. The storm itself is a fitting prelude to the stormy events that follow.

74 The verb *stupere* is applied by Statius to various other inanimate objects as well as to flocks and herds: e.g. *ualles* (*Theb.*, IV.448); *nubila* (VI.309–10); *Cithaeron* (VIII.346); *unda* (IX.228–9); *cruor* (IX.529); *ratis* (X.185); *ignis* (*Silvae*, 1.5.43–4); *populus et . . . pinus* (II.3.52); *regia* (IV.2.20); cf. *nemus adstupet* (*Theb.*, II.13). In certain instances the verb is perhaps not altogether metaphorical, and the clouds, the water, the blood, the ship, the fire and the flocks and herds 'stop in their tracks' or 'come to a standstill' rather than 'are astonished'. The other examples, however, can hardly be explained in this way and are perhaps rather to be seen as a heritage of the Roman tendency to animism.

75 See above, p. 187.

76 The *Silvae* being more or less unknown, no authentic details of the poet's life were available and some strange legends and confusions arose. Dante regarded him as a native of Toulouse who had embraced the Christian religion (*Purg.*, XXI.88–90; XXII.88–90): this was a confusion with L. Statius Ursulus, a rhetorician from Toulouse of the first century A.D. Statius was even known to the Middle Ages as Sursulus, by a corruption of the rhetorician's name. On the other hand, *Silvae*, 1.2 greatly influenced the development of the Latin epithalamium in later ages: see Z. Pavlovskis, 'Statius and the late Latin epithalamia', *CPhil.* 60 (1965), 164–77. On the history of the *Silvae*, see Vollmer, op. cit., 32ff. C. C. Coulter, writing on the possible influence of *Silvae*, v.4 on Fiametta's prayer to Sleep, suggests (*AJPhil.* 80 (1959), 394–5) that some of the poems of the *Silvae* may have circulated separately.

77 Statius is mentioned in the late ninth century in Mico's *Exempla diuersorum auctorum*, in the late tenth or eleventh century in Aimeric's *Ars lectoria*, where he is placed according to merit in the highest of three classes, in Wipo's *Tetralogus*, as one of the main poets of antiquity inspired by the muses, in Walther of Speier's list of classical poets, in a letter written by Froumund of Tegernsee, who tries to procure a copy of Statius' text, in a work by Ekkehart of St Gallen, in a reading-list of classical models recommended by Gerbert of Reims, and at various times in the twelfth century in lists of classical texts made by Conrad of Hirschau, Eberhard and the Englishman Alexander Neckham.

Occasionally Statius is rejected with other Latin authors as a pagan. Thus Wolfere of Hildesheim, for example, writes:

reicitur gnarus scelerum sacer Amphioraus,
Spinges et Edippi sit rhetor Sursulus ipsi;

Warner of Basel includes Statius with Virgil and Horace in the denunciatory line,

stupra deos fatum fert horum pagina uatum;

and Franco of Lüttich observes: *'quid est enim, obsecro, Thebais uel Eneis? illa Papinii Statii Sursuli idest sursum canentis, illa Virgilii Maronis doctissimi poetarum. quid igitur nisi leue quoddam et inane poetice fictionis inuentum?'* For the sources, see M. Manitius, *Geschichte der lateinischen Literatur des Mittelalters*, Volume 2 (Munich, 1923), 314, 316, 326, 505, 524–5, 567, 580, 731, 783, 785; R. R. Bolgar, *The Classical Heritage and its Beneficiaries* (Cambridge, 1954), 125–6, 197, 221, 423.

78 This work appears in R. Helm's edition of Fulgentius in the Teubner series, under the name of S. Fulgentius Episcopus. A plausible explanation of the composition of the *super Thebaiden* is that it was a late imitation of the allegorizing *Expositio Vergilianae continentiae* of Fabius Planciades Fulgentius and was erroneously attributed to an author called Fulgentius.

79 Fulgentius, ed. R. Helm (Teubner), 180: *'in nuce enim duo sunt, testa et nucleus, sic in carminibus poeticis duo, sensus litteralis et misticus: latet nucleus sub testa: latet sub sensu litterali mistica intelligentia.'*

80 This name, like Sursulus, is a corruption of Ursulus. See above, n. 76. For a medieval attempt to explain the name, see the quotation from Franco of Lüttich in n. 77.

81 On the *psychomachia* in the *Thebaid*, irrespective of Fulgentius' explanation and its bearing on 'the favourite theme of the Middle Ages', see C. S. Lewis, *The Allegory of Love* (Oxford, 1936), 44ff and esp. pp. 54–5.

It is likely that the Christian interpretation of the *Thebaid* contributed more than anything else to the medieval tradition that Statius himself was a Christian. Verrall's ingenious examination of passages in the *Thebaid* that could be said to have a 'Christian' flavour is hardly necessary (A. W. Verrall, *Collected Literary Essays* (Cambridge, 1913), 153–203).

A curious feature of the outline of the story of the *Thebaid* as it is given in the *super Thebaiden* is that it begins with Laius reigning in Thebes with Jocasta as his wife and Edippus his son. The mention of this and of Laius' murder and Oedipus' incestuous marriage, events which are not narrated by Statius in his main story, may have been intended partly as an introduction and partly because the author particularly wanted to include his interpretation of Laius' name as *lux sancta* and of Jocasta's as *iocunditas casta*, and show how corruption enters into the human soul. However this may be, the French *Roman de Thèbes* and Lydgate's *Siege of Thebes* both begin with Laius in the same way (see below, n. 82 and p. 222) although the plot and arrangement of Statius' *Thebaid* were still known (see below, n. 85). Again, the spellings Edippus, Ethiocles, Ipsiphile (or Isiphile) show the corruption of proper names that is seen further in the French epic, in Chaucer and in Lydgate. The *super Thebaiden* may thus have been an important intermediate source in the transmission of the story of the *Thebaid* to later medieval works on the same theme. On the other hand, other works mention Statius by name, even though their acquaintance with the *Thebaid* may often be slight, and there are sometimes references to the poem and even quotations (e.g. the *super Thebaiden*, Helm, 184, quotes *Theb.*, 11.429), which suggests that the Latin text still had a direct influence.

82 The *Roman de Thèbes* begins, like the brief synopsis given by the author of the *super Thebaiden* (see above, n. 81), with Laius and the early history of Oedipus and then moves on to the story of the *Thebaid*, which it follows in its general outline. The main additions are the episodes of Montflor and Daire le Roux, and perhaps the most important variation is that Capaneus is not killed as in the *Thebaid* but survives the war of the Argives against Thebes (this version was followed also by Lydgate; see below, n. 89). A significant omission is the scene in which Tydeus gnaws the skull of Melanippus. The author refers more than once to Statius (whose name now becomes 'Estace', 'Estaisce', 'Huitasse', 'Wistasse' and other variations), but whether he had direct knowledge of the *Thebaid* is a difficult and complicated question. He does not reproduce the 'double motivation' of the poem (see above, pp. 192–6), but Oedipus' prayer calls on both Jupiter and Tisiphone:

> Puissenz reis des cieus, Jupiter,
> Tesiphoné, fure d'enfer,
> Les orgoillos me destruisiez
> Qui mes ueuz mistrent soz lor piez. (509–12)

The presence of Tisiphone is an authentic detail, and the last line quoted recalls *Thebaid*, 1.238–9. For the relation of the poem to the *Thebaid*, see further the introduction to the edition by L. Constans, volume 2 (Paris, 1890), cxixff; E. Faral, 'Recherches sur les sources latines des Contes et Romans courtois du moyen âge' (Paris, 1913); G. R. Sarolli, 'Il Roman de Thèbes, Fonti e Datazione', *Rendiconti dell' Istituto Lombardi* 87 (1954), 283–320, and especially 286–307, where detailed comparisons are made between the text of the *Thebaid* and the *Roman de Thèbes*.

83 Many other details of the *Thebaid*, such as the fight with the gigantic serpent, the abode of Mars, the awesome wood where Tiresias consulted the spirits of the dead, the double flame on the brothers' funeral pyre and the terrifying, hellish figure of Tisiphone, must have held a considerable fascination for the medieval mind. But no less must heroic and virtuous figures like Amphiaraus (whom Chaucer calls 'the bisshop Amphiorax'), Argia, Antigone and Menoeceus have made their appeal. The mission of Theseus as a champion of the oppressed Argive women was another favourite theme. Statius' use of allegory contributed further to the medieval acceptance of his poetry. Cf. Lewis, op. cit., 48–56.

84 *The Hous of Fame*, 1457ff (III.367ff). The other ancient authors on pillars that Chaucer mentions—Statius is the second in order—are Josephus, Homer, Virgil, Ovid, Lucan and Claudian.

85 *Troilus and Criseyde*, v.1485–1510. The mention of 'gestes olde' (1511)

233

shows that certain versions of the Theban story, derived ultimately from the *Thebaid*, had a firmly established place in the medieval stock of legends. This story of Cassandra is preceded in the text by twelve verses of Latin outlining the argument of the twelve books of Statius' *Thebaid*:

> associat profugum Tideo primus Polimitem;
> Tidea legatum docet insidiasque secundus;
> tercius Hemoniden canit et uates latitantes;
> quartus habet reges ineuntes proelia septem;
> mox furiae Lenne quinto narratur et anguis;
> Archimori bustum sexto ludique leguntur;
> dat Graios Thebes et uatem septimus umbris;
> octauo cecidit Tideus, spes, uita Pelasgis;
> Ypomedon nono moritur cum Parthenopeo;
> fulmine percussus decimo Capaneus superatur;
> undecimus sese perimunt per uulnera fratres;
> Argiuam flentem narrat duodenus et ignem.

86 *Troilus and Criseyde*, II.78–108. The 'bokes twelve' again shows the original influence of Statius, although the contents of the 'Sege of Thebes' almost certainly included matter that is not related in the *Thebaid*. See above, n. 82. The reading, when interrupted by Pandarus, had reached the point in the story where it is told

> How the bisshop, as the book can telle,
> Amphiorax, fil thurgh the ground to helle.

The *envoie* to *Troilus and Criseyde* (v.1786ff) runs:

> Go, litel book, go, litel myn tregedye,
> Ther god thi makere yet, er that he dye,
> So sende myght to make in some comedye!
> But litel book, no makyng thou n' envie,
> But subgit be to alle poesye;
> And kis the steppes, where-as thou seest pace
> Virgile, Oveyde, Omer, Lucan, and Stace.

87 The 'temple of the goddesse Clemence' is obviously a reference to *Thebaid*, XII.481ff; and the abode of Mars in VII.40ff is Chaucer's model for 'the temple of mighty Mars' (*The Canterbury Tales*, A 1967ff). Other passages in *The Canterbury Tales* recall the *Thebaid* in an uncertain way: e.g. the double flame on the pyre is given a new context in A 2292–4 and is curiously referred to Statius:

> Two fyres on the auter gan she beete,
> And dide hir thynges, as men may biholde
> In Stace of Thebes, and thise bookes olde.

This suggests that there was at least one intermediate source and that details of Statius' poem were often drastically altered in transmission. Similarly, in *The Wife of Bath's Prologue* (D 740–6) the story of Eriphyle and the deceit that she practised on 'Amphiorax' has gathered new details, and the reference to 'Theodamas' in *The Marchantes Tale* is puzzling.

In general, see B. A. Wise, *The Influence of Statius upon Chaucer* (Baltimore, 1911).

88 Cf. above, n. 82, and see esp. E. Koeppel, *Lydgate's Story of Thebes* (Munich, 1884), 16–65.

89 The most notable changes in the order of events are that Edippus dies in the first part of the *Siege of Thebes*, whereas in the *Thebaid* Oedipus lives through the war and is exiled by Creon, and that Capaneus, who dies in an attempt to scale the walls of Thebes in the *Thebaid* (Book x), survives the deaths of the other Argive leaders but dies in a later assault on the walls during Theseus' war. A notable omission is Hypsipyle's story, for which Lydgate refers the reader to 'the book that John Bochas made whilom of wommen' (i.e. Boccaccio's *De Claris Mulieribus*). A notable addition is Tydeus' sojourn in the castle of Lycurgus on his return from the embassy to Thebes. Here his wounds are tended by the king's daughter. But Lydgate adheres on the whole more closely than the author of the *Roman de Thèbes* to the main story of Statius' *Thebaid*.

90 See above, n. 76.

91 *Purgatorio*, XXI–XXII; XXV.28ff.

92 No attempt is made here to trace the influence of Statius beyond the fifteenth century. Already before this time, while the direct influence of the *Thebaid* is still discernible in some quarters, other echoes are faint and irregular and sometimes confused (see above, n. 87). When the influence is indirect it becomes fragmented in such a way as to be recognizable separately in plots, situations, character-types, imagery and detailed expressions that were used by authors probably unaware of their origins in classical antiquity. Thus, for example, Chaucer is acknowledged in the prologue to the *Two Noble Kinsmen* as the source of the plot of the drama, but when, in Act I, Sc. i, one of the three Queens kneels before Theseus and speaks as follows:

> We are 3 Queenes, whose Soveraignes fel before
> The wrath of cruell Creon; who endured
> The Beakes of Ravens, Tallents of the Kights,
> And pecks of Crowes, in the fowle feilds of Thebe;
> He will not suffer us to burne their bones,
> To urne their ashes, nor to take th' offence
> Of mortall loathsomeness from the blest eye
> Of holy Phoebus, but infects the windes
> With stench of our slaine Lords . . .

the basic situation, despite its many changes of detail, can be seen to have been derived ultimately from the twelfth book of the *Thebaid*. In *Gorboduc*, with its rivalry between the brothers Porrex and Ferrex for their father's throne, any resemblance to the *Thebaid* is limited to the main plot, and this resemblance itself may well have been unintentional. Little would be gained by examining any examples such as these in greater detail. In the eighteenth century Pope translated the first book of the *Thebaid*, but this does not seem to have led to a revival of direct influence. The dramatic work of Metastasio, *Achille in Sciro*, also composed in the eighteenth century, was inspired by the *Achilleid*.

VIII

Martial

A. G. Carrington

The short reign of the second Flavian Emperor, Titus (79–81), was marked by two great events, for neither of which Titus could claim the credit. One was the destruction of Pompeii and Herculaneum by Vesuvius, the other the construction of the great Flavian amphitheatre. The latter had been planned and almost completed in the reign of Vespasian; Titus merely added the final touches and celebrated its inauguration with lavish spectacles in its arena. The amphitheatre, afterwards known as the Colosseum, from the huge Colossus of the Sun that stood nearby, was so impressive that later generations said of it:[1]

> While stands the Colosseum, Rome shall stand;
> When falls the Colosseum, Rome shall fall;
> And when Rome falls, the world.

Its grandeur had another consequence. A young Spaniard, resident in Rome, was inspired to 'burst out into sudden blaze' of poetry.

Martial's poems on the spectacles in the arena, marking the inauguration of the Colosseum, are not, of course, 'vintage Martial', but some of their new wine is not beneath the notice of the connoisseur. A noble exordium numbers the Colosseum among the wonders of the world. The next poem touches on the history of its site—for the building rested on the ground where formerly rose Nero's sumptuous Golden House. *Reddita Roma sibi est* ('Rome has been restored to herself'), wrote Martial thankfully.

The poem in this group, however, to which I shall here particularly draw the reader's attention is one in which Martial's wit was the cause of wit in another famous poet. Martial's poem

(*Spect.* 21) describes how a condemned criminal acted in the arena the part of Orpheus; he was made to play the harp before a group of wild beasts, by one of which he was afterwards torn to pieces thus making (if one may smile that he may not weep about such cruelty) like Antigonus in *The Winter's Tale*, an 'exit, pursued by a bear'.

The last line of the poem, according to the received text, runs *haec tamen tum res est facta ita pictoria*, of which even the great Friedlaender could make nothing. It was reserved for Housman, a poet himself and a scholar given to publishing editions of Latin authors '*in usum editorum*', to display himself as the first commentator on Martial who remembered that the poet was 'doctus utriusque linguae'. Housman deciphered the line as *haec tantum res est facta παρ' ἱστορίαν*, implying that only in the matter of Orpheus' death did the 'producer' of the 'spectacle' depart from the 'book of the film'.

Although the poems about the arena—*Liber Spectaculorum*—were not great poetry, they seem to have made Martial famous (Epigrams, I.I) throughout the Roman world.[2] He had now found his métier as a writer of epigram, and proceeded for the next two decades to write epigrammatic poetry of varying quality. Epigram as a genre had started with the Greeks, and originally denoted an inscription in verse on a tomb, or a poem intended as such. Epigrams of this type are the famous poems by Simonides on the Spartan dead at Thermopylae, and the Athenian dead at Plataea. Well-known, too, is the one by Plato, used by Shelley as an introduction to his 'Adonais', on the death of Keats:

> Thou wert the Morning-star among the living
> Ere thy fair light had fled.
> Now, having died, thou art as Hesperus, giving
> New splendour to the dead.

Cory's translation of an epigram of Callimachus on the dead Heraclitus is also admired, though less economical of words than the original. Epigram, however, was later widened to include dedicatory inscription, poems about works of art, lampoons and the like. But Martial gave the epigram its modern flavour. It may be said, facetiously, that, before Martial, epigram had a beginning; after Martial, it had a beginning and an end, and the end was pointed. The sepulchral column had become a Cleopatra's

Needle. The conclusion, to which the rest of the epigram was carefully contrived to lead, *rem*, so to speak, *acu tetigit*.

Martial, then, is the father of epigram as we know it. If we may use the lesser genre to illustrate the greater, the difference between epigram before and after Martial is comparable to the difference between the limerick as Edward Lear left it and the later limerick. Lear was content to let the last line merely repeat the first, but as the genre of limerick developed, the last line was used to bring the theme to its desired—if often undesirable—conclusion. (The undesirability of the limerick, as well as its structure, can claim some kinship with Martial's epigrams.)

All witty little poems furnished with a 'sting in the tail' are therefore the descendants of Martial's epigram. When John Byrom wrote:

> God bless the King, I mean the faith's defender;
> God bless—no harm in blessing—the Pretender;
> But who Pretender is, or who is King,
> God bless us all—that's quite another thing.

he was writing in the style of Martial. When Ogden Nash wrote:

> I give you now Professor Twist,
> A conscientious scientist.
> Trustees exclaimed: 'He never bungles'
> And sent him out to distant jungles.
> Camped by a tropic riverside,
> One day he missed his loving bride.
> She had, the guide informed him later,
> Been eaten by an alligator.
> Professor Twist could not but smile.
> 'You mean' he said 'a crocodile!'

he also was writing in the style of Martial. But when Matthew Prior wrote:

> To John I owed great obligation,
> But John unhappily thought fit
> To publish it to all the nation,
> So John and I are more than quit.

he was imitating an epigram of Martial (v.52).

The emperor Lucius Verus stupidly referred to Martial as his

'Virgil', instead of taking Martial's own modest word on that subject; for Martial himself said that even at his best he could not be a Virgil, but only a Marsus (VIII.56). He could not write great epic, but merely epigram. Yet the works of a certain great writer of epic are not without reminiscences of Martial. Milton in his 'Ode on the Morning of Christ's Nativity' describes the awe-stricken stars as lingering in the sky, in spite of 'Lucifer, that often warned them thence'. Martial, in a poem on the eve of the emperor's return to Rome, not only bids the morning star to bring back the day, but suggests that the stars and moon are deliberately waiting in the sky to see 'Ausonia's Chief' arrive (VIII.21).

Two of Milton's sonnets, moreover—'To Mr Lawrence' and 'To Cyriack Skinner'—are much like Martial's epigram to Silius Italicus (IV.14), which also consists of fourteen lines. All three poems urge relaxation in season, and the season seems to be the festive part of winter. The Cyriack sonnet contains more echoes of Martial than does the Lawrence. 'To drench deep thoughts in mirth' is found more tersely expressed in *madidis iocis*. The Swede and the French counterbalance—in their outlandish way— Hannibal and the Carthaginians. 'What the Swede intends' is manifestly akin to *astus Hannibalis*. 'British Themis' and 'barbaric frenzy' do not, even when Milton is reproving the former, have much in common, but each is used in the second line of its poem to denote the field of research or mental exertion which has given the poet's recipient cause for pride.

Tennyson, in writing 'such a tide as moving seems asleep' appears to echo *viva quies ponti* (X.30). Pope, in his beautiful poem beginning:

> Happy the man whose wish and care
> A few paternal acres bound

is building his lofty rhyme after a plan used by Martial in his *vitam quae faciunt beatiorem* (X.47) of which the Earl of Surrey had made a famous translation two centuries earlier.

Milton, Tennyson, Pope: *terribiles visu formae* they appear beside the puny figure of a mere writer of epigram; yet, to have antici-pated such distinguished mountaineers in climbing spurs of Parnassus or to have acted as their Sherpa was no small achieve-ment for Martial.

To return once more to poets who not only wrote in Martial's style but imitated him, we may mention Fletcher's

> He called thee vicious, did he? lying elf!
> Thou art not vicious; thou art vice itself.

This is Martial, xi.92. There is also the anonymous poem which reads:

> Trapped by my neighbour in his clover
> Three pigs I fee'd you to recover.
> Before the court you gravely stand
> And stroke your wig and smooth your band.
> Then, taking up the Kingdom's story
> You ope your case with Alfred's glory;
> Of Norman William's curfew bell
> And Coeur de Lion's prowess tell,
> How through the ravaged fields of France
> Edward and Henries shook the lance;
> How great Eliza o'er the main
> Pursued the shattered pride of Spain
> And Orange broke a tyrant's claim.
> All this, good Sir, is mighty fine,
> But now, an please you, to my swine!

The author of this was merely bringing up to date—as Johnson did with two of Juvenal's satires—an epigram of Juvenal's friend Martial (vi.19), to which we shall return.

One feature of the English poem quoted above is a certain carelessness of finish. It is in rhyme, but displays such unsatisfactory rhymes as 'clover' and 'recover', 'claim' and 'Spain'. Though not in the original of this poem, Martial was guilty of carelessness in others, as his *da veniam subitis* (*Spect.*, 31) and his reference to *libellos non exactos* (ix.81) prove. It is perhaps because of this light-hearted carelessness that the text of his epigrams seems to hover between three versions, each of which Martial himself could have written—and probably did. Perhaps, on occasion, when asked for a version of some popular earlier epigram, he failed to remember it all, and replaced some forgotten phrase with another that served his purpose. For instance, in xiii.26, any of the three participles *tendentia*, *durantia* and *ditantia* could be used to make sense in the passage. There are also three readings of xiii.65.2: *in piscina ludere, in lautorum condere* and *in lautorum mandere*; and xiv.29.2 wavers between *mandatus* and *nam ventus*.

Again, the author of an anonymous couplet:

Thou swearest thou'll drink no more; kind Heaven send
Me such a cook or coachman, but no friend.

had obviously read Martial, xii.30.

Traces of Martial's influence appear in English prose also. Addison used a line from Martial, xii.92 ('Were you a lion, how would you behave?') as the text for his witty *Spectator* homily on 'Nicolini and the Lions'. Fourteen other passages from Martial head essays of both Addison and Steele in the *Spectator*.

Sir Charles Sedley, the Restoration poet, wrote adaptations of a series of Martial's epigrams under the title 'Court Characters'. Sedley, by the way, deserves well of classical scholars, for T. E. Page considered his rendering of Horace's ode to Barine (ii.8) as 'the only adequate English rendering of any ode of Horace'; and Prior declared that 'Sir Charles could write, but translate better'. More names could be added to this tedious list from English and other European literatures. The list leaves visible merely the top of the iceberg, whose submerged nine-tenths the reader will have no insuperable difficulty in finding for himself; his search will not be titanic.[3]

Not in epigram, though, is Martial's greatest influence visible. He influenced also the genre of satire. If any apologist of epigram would deny that epigram is inferior to satire, the evidence of the master-epigrammatist himself can be brought against him, for Martial says:

audemus saturas: Lucilius esse laboras.
ludo leves elegos: tu quoque ludis idem.
quid minus esse potest? epigrammata fingere coepi.

xii.94

(I venture Satire but to see
You strain Lucilius to be.
I sport in couplets light; you do the same.
What lesser art is there to do?
I turn to epigram.)

The other point of view, however, can be defended by reference

to a great authority—*victrix causa deis placuit, sed victa Catoni*—no
other than the home of lost causes itself; for the *Oxford Book of
Latin Verse* includes many of Martial's epigrams, but deliberately
excludes Juvenal, as being less of a poet than a rhetorician.

Martial's friend Juvenal was induced by the satirical content of
Martial's epigrams to write satire. To 'amicitia' quite as much as
'indignatio' are his verses due. A look at four of Martial's poems
will show us the germ of Juvenalian satire at its best, that is, in
Juvenal's first, third and sixth satires:

> quae te causa trahit aut quae fiducia Romam,
>   Sexte? quid aut speras aut petis inde? refer.
> 'causas' inquis 'agam Cicerone disertior ipso
>   atque erit in triplici par mihi nemo foro.'
> egit Atestinus causas et Civis (utrumque
>   noras); sed neutri pensio tota fuit.
> 'si nihil hinc veniet pangentur carmina nobis;
>   audieris, dices esse Maronis opus.'
> insanis: omnes gelidis quicumque lacernis
>   sunt ibi Nasones Vergiliosque vides.
> 'atria magna colam.' vix tres aut quattuor ista
>   res aluit, pallet cetera turba fame.
> 'quid faciam? suade, nam certum est vivere Romae.'
>   si bonus es, casu vivere, Sexte, potes.
>
> (III.38)

> (What cause or confidence to Rome attracts you?
>   What hope you, Sextus, thence or seek? Declare.
> 'I'll plead' you say 'more eloquent than Tully.
>   The Forums three will never see my peer.'
> Take Civis and that other noted pleader;
>   You knew them both. His rent could either pay?
> 'If pleading bring no gain, I'll live by verses,
>   And hearing them "It's Virgil's self!" you'll say.'
> You're mad. The folk you meet in threadbare garments
>   With Virgil's, Ovid's genius were blest.
> 'I'll court great patrons.' Three or four that business
>   Supports. They're pale with hunger, all the rest.
> 'Advise me what to do. On Rome I'm struck.'
>   If honest, Sextus, you can live by luck.)

vir bonus et pauper linguaque et pectore verus,
  quid tibi vis urbem qui, Fabiane, petis?
qui nec leno potes nec comissator haberi
  nec pavidos tristi voce citare reos
nec potes uxorem cari corrumpere amici
  nec potes algentes arrigere ad vetulas,
vendere nec vanos circum Palatia fumos,
  plaudere nec Cano plaudere nec Glaphyro:
unde miser vives? 'homo certus, fidus amicus ———'
  hoc nihil est: numquam sic Philomelus eris.

                                                    (IV.5)

(Good man and poor and true in tongue and heart,
  Say, what's your aim in coming to the city?
In Sot-and-Pandar's Stakes you fail to start.
  You don't denounce the fearful without pity.
Your best friend's wife you'd shudder to seduce,
  Or play the lecher to some withered hag,
Or sell vain boast 'Your influence to use';
  In praise of vile pop-singer's scream you lag.
'A man of trust, a loyal friend ———' That all?
Your chance of being Somebody is small.)

In these two poems are met the complaisant husband, the sly go-
between, the hungry client, the gigolos who prosper through the
infatuation of rich old women, and Juvenal's Umbricius, who has
to leave Rome because honesty is a hindrance there. We also meet
the rich freedman.

Two epigrams are worked by Juvenal into his sixth satire, that
remarkable tirade against women:

  unus de toto peccaverat orbe comarum
    anulus, incerta non bene fixus acu.
  hoc facinus Lalage speculo, quo viderat, ulta est,
    et cecidit saevis icta Plecusa comis.
  desine iam, Lalage, tristes ornare capillos,
    tangat et insanum nulla puella caput.
  hoc salamandra notet vel saeva novacula nudet,
    ut digna speculo fiat imago tua.

                                                    (II.66)

(One curl from full round 'heaven of hair' was straying
   Fixed insecurely with a careless pin;
The very looking-glass, this crime betraying,
   Was used to strike the chambermaid for sin.
O cease to have your hair adorned for gazers;
   Don't let your maid touch that distempered head.
May salamander mark it! Scrape it, razors!
   Reflected locks no longer blood will shed.)

cum tibi non Ephesos nec sit Rhodos aut Mitylene
   sed domus in vico, Laelia, patricio,
deque coloratis numquam lita mater Etruscis,
   durus Aricina de regione pater,
κύριέ μου, μέλι μου, φυχή μου congeris usque,
   pro pudor! Hersiliae civis et Egeriae.
lectulus has voces, nec lectulus audiat omnis,
   sed quem lascivo stravit amica viro.

(x.68.1–8)

(You hardly hail from Ephesus
   Or Rhodes or Mitylene town;
Your house is sited on Patrician Street.
   Your mother, too, was one of us.
   Our Tuscan summers tanned her brown.
Aricia was your dad's ancestral seat.
   And yet in Greek you prattle thus:
   'My lord, my life, my honey!' Down!
Remember you're Italian, my sweet.
   A bed should hear this kind of fuss;
   Not every bed, but one that's found
Where courtesan for lecher spreads the sheet.)

These two epigrams supply Juvenal with matter for nearly fifty
lines of satire. This is not all. Who knows whether Martial's 'sit
non doctissima coniunx' did not 'father forth' the twenty-two
lines in the sixth satire on that 'more intolerable woman', the
blue-stocking, erudite enough to have, like Browning's gram-
marian,

        settled Hoti's business,
        Properly based Oun.

Other little touches from his friend's epigrams are reproduced by Juvenal. The profitable fires in Rome (Martial, III.52: Juvenal, 3.220), the Porta Capena dripping because of the aqueduct passing over it (Martial, IV.18: Juvenal, 3.11), the importance of sharing a guilty secret with the great (Martial, VI.50: Juvenal, 3.49), the fig tree whose roots demolish a tomb—an idea that Martial took from Persius, whom he admired (Martial, X.2: Juvenal, 10.145).

The imaginative scholiast commenting on Juvenal's line: *argentum vetus et stantem extra pocula caprum* waxed eloquent in explaining that Caper was an abstemious philosopher who 'stood away from the wine-cup'. Assuming, however, that Juvenal was referring to a silver cup embossed with the figure of a goat, we notice that Martial had already mentioned this before him (III.35; III.41).

In the region where Irony rules (assuming that region to be less extensive than was claimed for her by the anonymous author of

> Irony, on land and ocean
> All are victims of your sway:
> Yet the Greek for your devotion
> Failed a temple-stone to lay.)

Juvenal was Martial's guide. He taught Juvenal to regard the notorious gambling-bouts in Rome as a kind of warfare (Martial, XIII.1.5; Juvenal, 1.88–91), to call the barnyard cock 'the hen's husband' (Martial, XIII.64; Juvenal, 3.91), and to compare puny necks to that of Hercules wrestling with the giant Antaeus (Martial, XIV.48; Juvenal, 3.89).

Satire was claimed by the Romans as their own; Lucilian satire, as exemplified in the works of Horace, Persius and Juvenal, was the greatest type of Roman satire; and of Lucilian satire the greatest exponent was Juvenal, who owed much to, and was greatly influenced by, Martial.

It is a far cry from Juvenal's verse to Orwell's prose, but of Juvenalian satire which sent the decrees of its power through Dryden, Pope and Johnson, it may be said that Orwell's satire *ultima pars aulae deficientis erat* (Martial, *Spect.*, 2); for is not Orwell's famous *mot* 'All animals are equal, but some animals are more equal than others' expressing in another form, and about another species, Juvenal's *dat veniam corvis, vexat censura columbas?*

Although he resided in Rome for thirty-four years, Martial

never tires of telling the reader that he is a Spaniard. One of his countrymen he terms *nostraeque laus Hispaniae* in a long poem (1.49) describing the delights of the Celtiberian district. The 'hungry Tuccius' emigrating from Spain to Rome wisely turns back to Spain on hearing about life in Rome (III.14). Another long poem to a Spaniard (IV.55) recounts the glories of Spanish scenery and says 'let us, sprung from Celts and Iberians, not be ashamed to recall in grateful verse the harsher names of our native land', and concludes that those harsh-sounding names are yet more euphonic than some Italian place-names, for example 'Bututi'. Writing of a plane-tree planted at Cordoba by Julius Caesar, Martial shows himself to be as home-sick for his native district as was Rupert Brooke for Grantchester. For distance has lent enchantment to Martial's view of home, and he tells of fauns sporting there, of Pan, of the rustic dryad lurking (IX.61). Even so Brooke records that in Grantchester

> clever modern men have seen
> A faun a-peeping through the green,
> And felt the Classics were not dead
> To glimpse a Naiad's reedy head.[4]

In another epigram Martial writes wistfully of the Salo drawing him to gold-bearing shores, and that he would fain see the hillside rocks of his native-land (X.20). Bidding Maternus farewell, he tells of the superior blessings of a life in Spain (X.37) and offers to carry out for Maternus 'any commission to the Spanish ocean'. Some poems later (X.104), 'fair stood the wind for Spain' to waft his little book by sea thither, with instructions to buy 'at a wholesome price some retreat, pleasant and not hard to keep up' for the poet.

Martial did not share his friend Juvenal's dislike of Greeks, yet he did snub one of them: 'Seeing that you call yourself a countryman of the Corinthians—and no one denies it—why am I called brother by you, I, who was born of the Iberians and Celts, and am a native of Tagus, You stroll about with curled hair. My locks are stiff and Spanish' (X.65). Martial, however, was not slaying this Greek with his Spanish birth because of national prejudice, but because he objected to this particular Greek's effeminacy.

'What act', writes Browning, 'proved all its thought had been?' Martial's life on his return to Spain was not entirely happy. He missed certain amenities of life in Rome, 'the libraries, theatres, meeting-places, where pleasure is a student without knowing it' (preface to Book xii). Yet the bounty of his Spanish patroness Marcella allayed, as he writes (xii.21), his longing for the Queen City, and made a Rome in Spain for him.

There is one more passage where Martial's love of and pride in Spain seems visible. It is the opening of the famous poem addressed to Quintilian, the great Spanish rhetorician and author:

> Quintiliane, vagae moderator summe iuventae,
> gloria Romanae, Quintiliane, togae.   (ii.90)

Here each half of both hexameter and pentameter ends in the syllable 'ae'. The repeated 'ae-ae' sound seems to convey a sigh of regret—the Greek 'ai ai'—at the fact that Spain's greatest son could only claim the distinction of being the glory of the *Roman* gown.[5]

Before leaving the subject of Spain, another point may be mentioned; Martial arrived in Rome during the reign of Nero, and was at first a client of the famous Spanish family of the Senecas. The downfall of that family he deplored (xii.36; iv.40), and he remained loyal to its survivors. There are epigrams written to Polla Argentaria, Lucan's widow, on the anniversary of Lucan's birthday (vii.21,22). How much Martial was influenced by Nero's tutor, Seneca, it is hard to say. Perhaps he received from him the impulse to write epigrams, for some epigrams by Seneca have survived. It is true that a ponderous couplet like

> omnia mors poscit. lex est, non poena, perire.
> hic aliquo mundus tempore nullus erit.

is unlike Martial's sprightly style. However, the fact that epigram was practised in Senecan circles (Martial quotes a line from Lucan's bawdier efforts in x.64) must have encouraged the young client to try his hand. Another interesting point is that the great Seneca was a Stoic philosopher who wore his Stoicism with a difference. Contrary to the tenets of his school, he amassed a great fortune, and though he was finally executed, like other Stoics, it was not for Stoicism, but because of his un-Stoical wealth. Was it from Seneca that Martial learned to despise 'dyed-in-the-wool' Stoics, and to admire those with a more practical outlook, like the Spaniard Decianus (i.8)?

Another mark of Martial's poetry is its preoccupation with 'life', as the following instances will show:

hoc lege, quod possit dicere vita 'Meum est'. (x.4)

quodque cinis paucis, hoc mihi vita dedit. (v.13)

rebus in angustis facile est contemnere vitam. (xi.56)

agnoscat mores vita legatque suos. (viii.3)

lasciva est nobis pagina, vita proba. (1.4)

and, of course, *viva quies ponti* (x.30). But Martial is chiefly preoccupied with 'life' in a more positive sense, that of 'enjoyable life':

quisquam vivere cum sciat moratur? (v.20)

cras vives? hodie iam vivere, Postume, serum est;
ille sapit quisquis, Postume, vixit heri. (v.58)

Titulle, moneo, vive: semper hoc serum est; (viii.44)

vivere quod propero pauper nec inutilis annis
da veniam; properat vivere nemo satis. (11.90)

This zest for life makes Martial—though far from Victorian in outlook—remind the reader of the Victorian poet Browning, with his

How good is man's life, the mere living,
how fit to employ
All the heart and the soul and the senses
for ever in joy!

Martial says to a stingy millionaire: 'either *live* or return to the gods their million' (1.103) and reminds a thrifty father that 'even fathers can enjoy life, believe me!' (vi.27). To a man happily married for fifteen years he states: *vixisti tribus, O Calene, lustris* (x.38). If more examples are needed, we can take: *tam vicina iubent nos vivere Mausolea* (v.64), in which may be noticed the juxtaposition of life and death, the quick dactylic movement of *vivere* and the slow spondaic *Mausolea*; and *non est vivere sed valere vita est* (vi.70).

His love of life, as well, perhaps, as the above-mentioned influence of Seneca, may have induced Martial to despise those Stoics who 'buy with their blood an easy fame' (1.8); and to consider as insane the man who commits suicide to escape capture by a deadly foe. Yet at times he can approve of suicide, if it ends a 'death in life' (1.78) or saves the lives of many (IV.8). He also welcomes death for a little girl stricken with illness: *non licet hic de brevitate queri* (XI.91).

It would not be out of place to present a few of Martial's poems and show how much care he expended on them. *Da veniam subitis* is his own criticism of his writing, and indeed such lines as *inque suo nullum limine limen erat* (VII.61) appear to have been written in haste. However, some of his works *sunt bona* (1.16), are at any rate carefully constructed. The second epigram in the first book runs:

> qui tecum cupis esse meos ubicumque libellos
>   et comites longae quaeris habere viae,
> hos eme, quos artat brevibus membrana tabellis;
>   scrinia da magnis, me manus una capit.
> ne tamen ignores ubi sim venalis et erres
>   urbe vagus tota, me duce certus eris:
> libertum docti Lucensis quaere Secundum
>   limina post Pacis Palladiumque forum.

> (If you my little books desire
>   Beside you constantly:
> If you their cheerful company
>   For weary road require,
>
> Buy these, in parchment skilfully
>   And tiny pages pressed.
> Put larger volumes in a chest—
>   One hand will carry me.
>
> And lest with knowledge ill-supplied
>   Of where I'm sold you stray
> All over town, and lose your way,
>   Go straight, with me to guide:
>
> Learned Lucensis' freedman trace—
>   Secundus; him to find,
> Leave temple-door of Peace behind,
>   And Pallas' market-place.)

The second line in the Latin with its internal rhyme emphasizes the syllable '-ae' and suggests '-ai ai' or 'alas!'—a fitting cry of distress for the 'weary wayworn traveller'.[6] In the first half of the fourth line three long syllables (*da magnis*) show us the porter struggling on painfully beneath his load, whereas the bearer of Martial's little books runs along trippingly in the dactyls of *me manus una capit.*

The third couplet (*ne . . . eris*) displays in its first line a confused jumble of words of varying numbers of syllables; the tidy pentameter has the monosyllable *me* flanked on either side by three dissyllables, as if to signify that when Martial takes over the duties of a guide, confusion is ended and order restored. In the last couplet, as in the English proverbs 'look before you leap' and 'he who laughs last laughs longest', the alliteration helps the hearer to remember the instruction more easily.

Traces of the poet's care are visible also in the next epigram (1.3):

> Argiletanas mavis habitare tabernas,
>> cum tibi, parve liber, scrinia nostra vacent?
> nescis, heu, nescis dominae fastidia Romae;
>> crede mihi, nimium Martia turba sapit.
> maiores nusquam rhonchi: iuvenesque senesque
>> et pueri nasum rhinocerotis habent.
> audieris cum grande sophos, dum basia iactas,
>> ibis ab excusso missus in astra sago.
> sed tu ne totiens domini patiare lituras
>> neve notet lusus tristis harundo tuos,
> aetherias, lascive, cupis volitare per auras.
>> i, fuge! sed poteras tutior esse domi.

> (In the shops of Argiletum you've a preference to
>> dwell?
> My book-shelf, little book, has room for you.
> You know not, ah, you know not Rome, the
>> queenly scorner, well.
> Too smart, believe me, are the Martian crew.
> Nowhere do greater sneers abound; on young and
>> elder set
> Are noses the rhinoceros could grow.
> Your master's many alterations kindle much your ire.
>> His pen-strokes through your wit too roughly roam.
> To flutter through the breezes far you wantonly
>> desire?
> Go! Fly! You might have safer been at home.)

Martial was an admirer of Persius, whom he praises in another epigram (iv.29). Persius in his first satire (which, by a strange coincidence, also contains a warning about the reception awaiting the author's works) refers to the *canina littera*, by which he means the letter 'r', which sounds like the growl of a dog. Such a growl would greet the satirist if he should annoy the great. Whether out of compliment to Persius and to show that his epigrams were also satire, or by coincidence, Martial has filled the epigram quoted above with 'canine letters'. Not only does the syllable 'ar' (a true growl) appear some eight times in twelve lines, but the epigram contains several other usages of the letter 'r'.

The 'o' sound, accented by forming the internal rhyme of the eighth line, seems to be calling attention to the distressful cries of the victim tossed in the blanket; *harundo*, which his writings fear so much, looms terribly as the largest word in its line; and *Martia turba* aptly signifies the hostility and disorderly conduct of a lynch-mob.

A brief glance at the next epigram (1.4) shows that it is carefully suited in its style to the majesty of the emperor. Of the poems here considered, it contains proportionally the largest number of polysyllables and the fewest monosyllables. Its imagery brings to mind 'a brow like Jove's to threaten and command', a commander leading his troops in triumph, and a 'command performance' in the theatre. Thus is 'art concealed by art' in the beginnings of the series of epigrams that marked the maturity of Martial's powers.

Lancelot Gobbo in *The Merchant of Venice* tells Bassanio: 'The old proverb is well parted between my master Shylock and you, sir. You have the grace of God and he has enough.' Two epigrams, close to each other in the fifth book (v.8 and v.14) similarly part between them a Shakespearean line. They are on a theme that fascinated Martial—the social-climbing interloper being forcibly removed from sitting among the Knights at public shows. The Shakespearean line parted between the poems is 'the pomp and circumstance of glorious war'. One epigram is marked by 'pomp and circumstance' and the other by not very 'glorious war'. Here is the first epigram (v.8):

> Edictum domini deique nostri,
> quo subsellia certiora fiunt

et puros eques ordines recepit,
dum laudat modo Phasis in theatro,
Phasis purpureis ruber lacernis,
et iactat tumido superbus ore:
'Tandem commodius licet sedere,
nunc est reddita dignitas equestris;
turba non premimur, nec inquinamur.'
haec et talia dum refert supinus,
illas purpureas et adrogantes
iussit surgere Leitus lacernas.

(By edict of our god and lord
   Are seats in stricter order rated;
The Knights have now their rights restored,
   And now sit uncontaminated.
This edict lately Phasis praised—
   In purple mantle Phasis glowing—
While in the theatre he raised
   Proud boast in haughty utterance flowing:
'At last we Knights can sit at ease.
   These seats our dignity restore.
The mob can't jolt us as they please
   Or soil our garments any more.'
While lolling back he said his say,
   Came someone in official guise
And made that purple mantle rise
   And shooed that arrogance away.)

The poem begins pompously, quoting one of the emperor Domitian's official titles. Its hero has the distinguished name of Phasis, bringing to mind 'Colchis' strand' and the renown of the Argonauts. Phasis equals in his swelling phrases the flow of the noble river that is his namesake. He talks of *dignitas equestris* and is *superbus* in his disdain of the mob. He wears a purple mantle which is evidently such a part of him that Martial allows it to represent Phasis in the last line of the epigram. Contrast the other epigram, v.14:

Sedere primo solitus in gradu semper
tunc cum liceret occupare Nanneius
bis excitatus terque transtulit castra,

252

et inter ipsas paene tertius sellas
post Gaiumque Luciumque consedit.
illinc cucullo prospicit caput tectus
oculoque ludos spectat indecens uno.
et hinc miser deiectus in viam transit,
subsellioque semifultus extremo
et male receptus altero genu iactat
equiti sedere Leitoque se stare.

(In days when none regarded where
   One sat, Nanneius used to go
   And settle in the foremost row.
Now other rule is rampant here.
Twice, thrice they roused him up. At that
   He shifted camp and made a kind
   Of third between two seats, behind
Where Lucius and Gaius sat.
He thence with head now hooded close
   With one eye viewed ungracefully
   The games; but bidden thence to flee,
He sought the space between the rows.
Half-propped by bench, with either knee,
   Though cramped, he varied view supplied:
   'He's seated' thought the Knight beside;
'He's standing' mused Authority.)

This epigram contains no mention of equestrian dignity. Indeed, the Knights mentioned in it are called bluntly by their *praenomina*. The poem seems to be reminding us that a Knight is, strictly speaking, a soldier. It contains military terms like *occupare*, *transtulit castra, deiectus*. Its hero, 'a soldier for the working day', wears no eye-catching purple. He tries to be inconspicuous; his movements are like those of a raiding-party in war. Instead of 'lolling back' proudly, he crouches. His name, too, lacks impressiveness: 'Nanneius' resembles somewhat 'Nanus', the word for 'dwarf'. Furthermore, the metre, as though in sympathy with the woes of this suffering campaigner, has become the limping iambic.[7]

Another poem which was carefully constructed by Martial is the second epigram in Book II:

Creta dedit magnum, maius dedit Africa nomen,
  Scipio quod victor quodque Metellus habet:
nobilius domito tribuit Germania Rheno;
  et puer hoc dignus nomine, Caesar, eras.
frater Idumaeos meruit cum patre triumphos;
  quae datur ex Chattis laurea, tota tua est.

> (By Crete was yielded mighty name.
> From Africa a greater came.
>   Metellus' victories
>   And Scipio's won these.
>
> But did not Germany resign
> A nobler on the conquered Rhine?
>   Your boyhood too had claim,
>   O Caesar, to the name.
>
> Your brother with your father won
> His triumph o'er the Jews; but none
>   Claims part of *your* renown—
>   Your German laurel-crown.)

This is an adulatory poem in honour of Domitian's assumption of
the name *Germanicus* after his triumph over the Chatti. The first,
second and fourth lines present an interesting appearance:

(1) Creta						Africa
	dedit				dedit	
			magnum	maius		
(2) Scipio						Metellus
		quod			quodque	
			victor			
(4) puer						Caesar
		hoc			nomine	
			dignus			

There is a proper noun at or near either extremity of each line
except the fourth, where the common status of *puer* is counter-
balanced by its importance in the sentence and its apposition with
Caesar. Each line thus forms a 'V for victory' that precedes
Churchill, and even Beethoven, by centuries.[8]
  The second poem in which word-order plays a part is x.50:

frangat Idumaeas tristis Victoria palmas,
    plange, Favor, saeva pectora nuda manu,
mutet Honor cultus, et iniquis munera flammas
    mitte coronatas, Gloria maesta, comas.
heu facinus! prima fraudatus, Scorpe, iuventa
    occidis et nigros tam cito iungis equos.
curribus illa tuis semper properata brevisque
    cur fuit et vitae tam prope meta tuae?

(Let Victory in sadness break her Idumaean palms.
    Beat, Favour, with your cruel hand upon your
    naked breast.
Let Honour change to mourning garb, and on the
    spiteful flames
    Cast, Glory, as an offering the locks your crown
    once pressed.
Alas! defrauded of your youth, when first its bloom
    outbroke,
    You fell, great horseman! Death's dark steeds so
    quickly now you yoke.
That goal brought ever nearer by your chariot's
    career,
    Ah! To the limit of your life why was it brought
    so near?)

The ease with which Scorpus controlled his horses is symbolized
by the facility with which Martial yokes four pairs of lines in this
epigram. The first and third lines form one pair, the second and
third another, the fifth and seventh are the third yoke, and the
sixth and eighth the last. The first two pairs can be seen to have
these points of similarity:

(1) frangat (jussive subjunctive) . . . Victoria (personification)
    . . . palmas (external decoration)
(3) mutet (jussive subjunctive) . . . Honor (personification)
    . . . cultus (external decoration)
(2) plange (imperative) . . . Favor (personification) . . . pec-
    tora (part of body)
(4) mitte (imperative) . . . Gloria (personification) . . . comas
    (part of body)

The third pair, (5) and (7), have each a perfect participle as their largest word, and the last pair are noticeable for these points of similarity:

(6) occidis (indicative) . . . et . . . tam cito
(8) cur fuit (indicative) . . . et . . . tam prope

It is an ironical touch that 'Victory' is followed immediately by 'popular favour'. One wonders whether this couplet gave Juvenal the idea which he amplified into:

> sed quid
> turba Remi? sequitur fortunam, ut semper, et odit
> damnatos. (x.72)

One of the traditions of epigrammatic poetry, upheld by Martial, was the use of broad expressions and sexual themes, a characteristic which epigram shared with satire. One of Martial's milder efforts in this direction discusses the number and catholicity of Caelia's lovers (VII.30). In this epigram the poet is content with shocking the respectable with only three 'seven-letter' words; but there is more to the poem.

Juvenal in his tenth satire speaks of the many paramours of a lady called Oppia. Was it merely coincidence that Martial had already called a woman of similar type Caelia? For each of these names is derived from that of one of the seven hills of Rome, and neither is that of the Aventine, the hill of chaste Diana (XII.18). Was Juvenal, even in this unimportant instance—for what's in a name?—influenced by Martial?

The names of the nations which provide Caelia with lovers are neatly arranged. The first line contains foreign nations on the frontiers of Rome's empire—Parthians, Germans and Dacians. In the second line are placed representatives of the conquered provincial peoples—Cilicians and Cappadocians. The next couplet provides spacious accommodation for the Egyptian and the Indian. These are obviously meant to represent two wealthy peoples. The Egyptians are pointedly given the epithets 'Pharian' and 'Memphian'—Pharos and Memphis being sites of wonders of the ancient world. The 'Indian' (an elegantly vague term) is associated with the Red Sea, which Martial in another epigram (v.37) linked with the pearl industry. The third couplet is reserved for 'peculiar peoples'—the circumcized Jews and the Alani; the spacious couplet does not, like its predecessor, symbolize the 'wide house' of rich people, but the fact that the Jews were widely dispersed and the Alani were nomadic.

The verbs or predicates in this poem are significant. *Das*: the Romans could not exist as a nation if they yielded to the demands of frontier peoples. *Navigat tibi*: Egyptian and Indian sail to Rome for Caelia's advantage—she makes financial gain from them. *Fugis*: the Romans had an aversion for Jews, whom they regarded as superstitious in worshipping no visible gods. *Transit*: the restless Sarmatian was always on the move, unlike civilized peoples. Yet for Caelia *omnia naturae praepostera legibus ibunt*. When she is present, there is a complete reversal of the usual state of affairs. Frontier peoples have their demands granted. Subject peoples are not despised. The presence of Eastern peoples is an advantage to Caelia though Romans like Juvenal deplored the flow of the Orontes into the Tiber (III.62); and Caelia causes restless Sarmatian peoples to adopt for a time a more settled type of existence.

In short, Caelia's world is a topsy-turvy one. The British troops marching out after their surrender at Yorktown are said to have played a tune called 'The world turned up-side-down'. Such or similar was Caelia's world—a fact symbolized no doubt by two catalogues of peoples listed strictly in reverse alphabetical order (Parthians, Germans, Dacians, Cilicians, Cappadocians: and Pharians, Memphians, Indians). Caelia is a very sophisticated Alice in a 'looking-glass world' all her own.

The same careful and orderly arrangement is seen in the epigram (v.58) describing the vain search performed by 'those that after a tomorrow stare':

> cras te victurum, cras dicis, Postume, semper.
>   dic mihi, cras istud, Postume, quando venit?
> quam longe cras istud, ubi est? aut unde petendum?
>   numquid apud Parthos Armeniosque latet?
> iam cras istud habet Priami vel Nestoris annos.
>   cras istud quanti, dic mihi, possit emi?
> cras vives? hodie iam vivere, Postume, serum est:
>   ille sapit quisquis, Postume, vixit heri.

> (You'll live tomorrow, Postumus,
> Tomorrow—still you prattle thus.

When, Postumus, comes that tomorrow, pray?
How far tomorrow's residence?
We have to bring it hither—Whence?
In Parthia or Armenia lurks it? Nay.
Already that tomorrow years
Of Priam or of Nestor bears.
For that tomorrow tell me what to pay?
You'll live tomorrow, Postumus?
To live *today*'s too late for us;
The wise man, Postumus, lived yesterday.)

The searchers for tomorrow are brought gradually westward and homeward from Parthia, through Armenia, Asia Minor (Priam), Greece (Nestor), to (in the words of Kipling) 'the shop next door' —*cras istud quanti, dic mihi, possit emi*. They are brought back from the 'Rising Sun' to find that the sun they seek has already set: 'he is wise, whoever he be, who lived yesterday.'

The aptness of the imaginary name Postumus in the poem above is manifest. Martial had in mind that greater and more famous poem regretting the passage of time—the fourteenth ode in Horace's second book. The reader's mind is taken back to the wistful sweetness of *eheu fugaces, Postume, Postume, labuntur anni*.

The names which Martial used in his poems were usually fictitious, as is to be expected from a client-poet who found it expedient *parcere personis, dicere de vitiis*. He often showed much aptness in their choice. For instance, in one epigram (II.44) he tells of the behaviour of his 'old comrade' Sextus the money-lender, whenever Martial has made an expensive purchase. Sextus, being fearful 'lest I should ask a loan, murmurs to himself, but so that I may hear: seven thousand I owe to Secundus, to Phoebus four, eleven to Philetus, and there is not a farthing in my chest!' Martial comments that it is harsh to refuse when one is asked—harsher to refuse before one is asked. The names Sextus and Secundus are in a noble tradition of money-lenders' names. Horace, in his *Beatus ille* epode, mentions the money-lender Alfius. Written as 'Alphius', this is allied to the Latin 'Primus'— as in Martial IX.95. Thus, two of Martial's money-lenders have, like Horace's, ordinal numerals for names (and Sextus is talkative, like Alfius). The richest of the others—the one who evidently has the most to lend—is Philetus. This name means 'the beloved one'. Did Martial choose the name because of Horace's line *et bene nummatum decorat suadela Venusque*? As for Phoebus—evidently the money-lender with the least to lend—is his name traceable to an earlier epigram (1.76) decrying the small wages of poetry?

Quid petis a Phoebo? nummos habet arca Minervae.
haec sapit, haec omnes faenerat una deos.

Moreover, the money-lender who has lent the second largest sum of the three is, strangely enough, Secundus.

Martial, like all Latin and Greek writers, indulged in the rhetorical practice of μίμησις or *imitatio*. A poet would incorporate into his own writing phrases or idioms from those of earlier writers. One of the most remarkable instances is in the sixth book of the *Aeneid*, where Virgil makes his hero say *Invitus, regina, tuo de litore cessi*. This is an imitation of Catullus, who in one of his translations from Callimachus has a lock of hair saying *Invita, regina, tuo de vertice cessi*.

Two instances of Martial's imitating Greek epigrammatists seem of interest. The first is a poem already mentioned (VI.19), which is an adaptation of an epigram of Lucilius:

> Χοιρίδιον καὶ βοῦν ἀπολώλεκα, καὶ μίαν αἶγα,
> ὧν χάριν εἴληφας μισθάριον, Μενέκλεις·
> οὔτε δέ μοι κοινόν τι πρὸς Ὀθρυάδαν γεγένηται,
> οὔτ' ἀπάγω κλέπτας τοὺς ἀπὸ Θερμοπυλῶν·
> ἀλλὰ πρὸς Εὐτυχίδην ἔχομεν κρίσιν· ὥστε τι ποιεῖ
> ἐνθάδε μοι Ξέρξης καὶ Λακεδαιμόνιοι;
> πλὴν κἀμοῦ μνήσθητι νόμου χάριν, ἢ μέγα κράξω
> '"Αλλα λέγει Μενεκλῆς, ἄλλα τὸ χοιρίδιον.'

> G.A., XI.141

Where Lucilius mentions the theft of a pig, a cow and one goat, Martial, with the wand of a Circe, transforms the animals into three goats. Lucilius' barrister mentions only one historical incident; Martial amplifies the garrulity of his barrister by mentioning six—three in the realm of foreign wars, three in civil war. The only unhistorical name mentioned is that of the lawyer Postumus (and again the name 'upbraids him with the loss of time'); Lucilius clutters his epigram with the name of his lawyer as well as that of his neighbour. Martial (perhaps as a reminder about the three goats) seems to have made 'three' the keynote of his epigram (three wars, three heroic figures, three possible crimes, *vi, caede, veneno*; and there are thrice three lines in the poem).

For another instance of *imitatio* we must return to the *Liber Spectaculorum*. The opening poem has already been mentioned as numbering the Colosseum among the wonders of the world:

> Barbara pyramidum sileat miracula Memphis,
>   Assyrius iactet nec Babylona labor;
> nec Triviae templo molles laudentur Iones,
>   dissimulet Delon cornibus ara frequens;
> aere nec vacuo pendentia Mausolea
>   laudibus immodicis Cares in astra ferant.
> omnia Caesareo cedit labor Amphitheatro;
>   unum pro cunctis fama loquetur opus.

> (Barbaric Memphis, silently
> The Pyramids, your wonders, see.
> Assyrian toil, in Babylon lose pride.
> Diana's fane, no more bring down
> On soft Ionians renown.
> Her altar many-horned let Delos hide.
> The Mausoleum, poised in air,
> Why, Carian, to stars uprear
> With praises which within no limits fall?
> All labours find their vanquisher
> In Caesar's Amphitheatre.
> One work shall Fame exalt in place of all.)

This is imitated from Antipater's epigram, G.A., ix.58, which extols the temple of Artemis at Ephesus.[9] Martial has made, in his imitations, a few improvements on the plan of the Greek original. His poem from the beginning seems to be leading up to a grand climax. This is skilfully done by the use of subjunctive verbs. Antipater, on the other hand, uses only one verb to govern the first six wonders. Martial's wonders are also homogeneous— all architectural, which makes it easier to judge their relative grandeur in comparison with the Colosseum. Martial's verbs all give a certain liveliness to the poem; behind the wonders of the world we see the peoples that built them boasting, praising, extolling, or hiding themselves in shame at being surpassed. Martial economizes in words by combining Babylon's two wonders, the wall and the gardens, into the one word *Babylona*, in the sentence 'Let not Assyrian toil boast of its Babylon.' In its arrangement of the wonders his poem starts off with those built by 'barbarians', rises to those built by Greeks, and culminates in the Roman achievement that outweighs them all.

In another poem Martial has anticipated what a critic considers to be a characteristic of Alexander Pope's wit. Norman Callant in his chapter on Pope in the *Penguin Guide to English Literature*, vol. 4, writes: 'Take a couplet from Pope's *Epistle to Augustus*:

> Authors like coins grow dear as they grow old.
> It is the rust we value, not the gold.

The "image" has been given to the thoughts without any perceptible interval. We do not dwell on the nature of coins and writers, because Pope does not require us to do so. He has made his point with economy and restraint; with the result that he leaves us meditating the thought itself rather than the image which has driven it home.' These words, with Martial's name replacing Pope's, are perhaps the best comment on Martial's famous epigram in reply to critics of his poetry:

> Lector et auditor nostros probat, Aule, libellos,
>   sed quidam exactos esse poeta negat.
> non nimium curo; nam cenae fercula nostrae
>   malim convivis quam placuisse cocis.   (IX.81)

> (Although the man that reads or hears
>   My verse declares it good,
> Have these my lines—a poet sneers—
>   The polish which they should?

> I cannot say I care a lot.
>   My banquet I intend
> To give delight to diners, not
>   To make the cooks commend.)

Imagery is similarly used for making his point with economy and restraint in the epigram rebuking one who urged Martial to publish his poems, yet yawned interminably while they were read: 'A weary traveller, do you give in so soon, and although you have to drive to Bovillae, want to change horses at the Camenae?' (II.6). The same identification at sight is achieved in the couplet:

Septima iam, Phileros, tibi conditur uxor in agro,
plus nulli, Phileros, quam tibi reddit ager.   (x.43)

(Already, Phileros, your seventh wife is being buried on
your land. Better return than yours, Phileros, land makes to
no man.)

Here the ideas of burial, planting, seed, harvest, and a rich be-
quest are all neatly blended. The unexpectedness of Martial's wit
is achieved in many ways. He may use a famous quotation from
an epic to make his point as Housman did in the couplet:

Malt does more than Milton can
To justify God's ways to man.

Martial, explaining why he wrote so many epigrams on the same
theme, says:

edita ne brevibus pereat mihi cura libellis,
dicatur potius τὸν δ' ἀπαμειβόμενος.)   (1.45)

(That my labour be not lost because published in tiny
volumes, rather let there be added τὸν δ' ἀπαμειβόμενος.)
(That is, I must stuff it with repetitions; the Greek words
occur often in Homer.)

Martial may turn the well-known syllables of a famous verse into
names as in:

si tibi Mistyllos cocus, Aemiliane, vocatur,
dicatur quare non Taratalla mihi.   (1.50)

(If your cook, Aemilianus, is called Mistyllus, why should
not Taratalla be the name for mine?)

Here the Homeric line μίστυλλόν τ' ἄρα τἆλλα καὶ ἀμφ'ὀβελοῖσιν
ἔπειραν (Iliad, 1.465) is remembered. He may also achieve this
unexpectedness by saying the direct opposite of what is expected,
as in the famous poem where he says that, angry because of the
rarity of his patron's invitations, he will punish the patron, when
next invited, by coming (VI.51).

Mention has already been made of Martial's using in an epigram
the inanimate object, a purple mantle, to represent a proud
wearer of such a garment (v.8). For the benefit of a friend who by
demanding security for a loan put more trust in Martial's
farm than in his old comrade Martial, the farm is made human:

'Carus has informed against you: let my farm appear for you in court. You ask for a companion in exile—let my farm go with you': *agellus eat* (XII.25).

When Boswell dogged the footsteps of Johnson in the interests of posterity, and was slightingly referred to by an onlooker as a cur, another said 'He is not a cur, he is a burr.' Some of Martial's epigrams make their point in a similar way. A divorce procured by a wife who feared her husband would lose money soon is called 'not divorce, but good business': *lucrum est* (x.41). An ill-used slave who rescued his cruel master from death was giving him 'not life, but life-long shame': *non vita sed invidia* (III.21). A father who leaves his fortune to a spendthrift son is disinheriting him (III.10). The man who sells a slave and uses the proceeds to buy a mullet is eating not a fish but a man (x.31).

In his descriptive poetry Martial could capture the beauty of landscape and seascape, as when he describes with much realism the view from the Janiculum, whence may be seen the distant coaches moving along the Salarian road, too far away for their wheels to be heard (IV.64); or the glimpse from the Formian villa of the painted shallop gliding over the calm sea in the faint breeze (x.30).

In verbal music Martial is no Virgil, no 'wielder of the stateliest measure ever moulded by the lips of man'; he is not even perhaps a Tennyson. But in one poem of Martial's, according to a critic, the despised limping iambic approaches the sublime.[10] To have attained sublimity with a metre much resembling that of 'Mademoiselle of Armentières' is no negligible achievement. The poem was written in honour of the temple built by Domitian to the glory of the Gens Flavia, but if the reader transfers it to that other 'towering glory of the Flavian race', the Colosseum, he will not be committing the unforgivable:

> dum Ianus hiemes, Domitianus autumnos,
> Augustus annis commodabit aestates,
> dum grande famuli nomen adseret Rheni
> Germanicarum magna lux Kalendarum,
> Tarpeia summi saxa dum patris stabunt,
> dum voce supplex dumque ture placabit
> matrona divae dulce Iuliae numen,
> manebit altum Flaviae decus gentis

cum sole et astris cumque luce Romana.
invicta quidquid condidit manus caeli est.   (IX.2)

(While Janus shall lend winters to the year,
Domitian autumns, and Augustus summers;
While the great day of the Germanic Kalends
Shall claim a mighty name from vanquished Rhine;
While rock Tarpeian of high Jove shall stand;
While, suppliant with prayer and incense, matrons
Propitiate fair Julia, now divine;
The towering glory of the Flavian race
Shall co-eternal with the sun and stars
Endure, and with the light that shines on Rome.
Whatever work foundation has received
From arm unconquerable, is of Heaven.)

Martial sometimes used hyperbole to make his point in an epigram. He completes one in adulation of Nerva with the couplet:

ipse quoque infernis revocatus Ditis ab umbris
si Cato reddatur, Caesarianus erit.   (XI.5)

(Cato, too, himself, were he called back to return from the
nether shades of Dis, will be Caesar's partisan.)

This produces much the same effect as if an admirer of President Kennedy had said that the distinguished foe of the American Revolution,

Samuel Johnson, Tory Englishman,
Would join Whig rebels, be American

to honour Kennedy.

An epigram dealing with his wanton verses and stressing their readability ends:

erubuit posuitque meum Lucretia librum,
sed coram Bruto; Brute, recede: leget.   (XI.16)

(Lucretia blushed and laid down my volume; but Brutus was present. Brutus, go away: she will read it.)

The *nequitiae*, the prurient epigrams of Martial, were part of the epigrammatic tradition. Martial quotes from obscene efforts in the realm of epigram by Lucan and even by Augustus (unlike his *Ajax*, these did not fall on the sponge). Augustus banished Ovid. Martial pleaded epigrammatic tradition in excuse, and was more fortunate with the stern censor Domitian (1.4). He claimed that his lewd writings were quite separate from his private life.

His gross flatteries of Domitian have also been censured, and while such adulation was also following the tradition of Imperial times, he has helped to accuse himself by condemning, after Domitian's death, his own flattery of that emperor (x.72).

The desire to flatter would seem to have warped Martial's keen judgment as a literary critic when he praises Silius Italicus, the writer of 'the worst epic ever written', the *Punica*, as a great author (ix.86; vii.63), or when he makes Pliny the equal of Cicero (x.19). But these men were Martial's patrons. When he speaks generally of the frivolity of the epics attempted by his contemporaries, he can be more candid:

> ille magis ludit qui scribit prandia saevi
> Tereos aut cenam, crude Thyeste, tuam,
> aut puero liquidas aptantem Daedalon alas,
> pascentem Siculas aut Polyphemon ovis.
> a nostris procul est omnis vesica libellis,
> Musa nec insano syrmate nostra tumet.   (iv.50)

(He is more frivolous who writes of the meal of savage
Tereus or of thy banquet, dyspeptic Thyestes, or of Daedalus
fitting to his own son melting wings, or of Polyphemus
pasturing Sicilian sheep. Far from poems of mine is all
turgescence, nor does my Muse swell with frenzied tragic
train.)

He again returns to the plea for a simpler literary taste in x.4:

> quid te vana iuvant miserae ludibria chartae?
> hoc lege, quod possit dicere vita 'Meum est'.
> non hic Centauros, non Gorgona Harpyiasque
> invenies: hominem pagina nostra sapit.

(Vain twaddle, to vile scribbles known—
Such pastime put away!
Read rather this, for life can say
'It is my very own'.

No Centaur here, no Gorgon-rage,
No Harpy will you find.
Its savour is of human-kind,
The subject of my page.)

It would be unfair to leave Martial without mentioning one of his better qualities—his affection for his friends. Some of them were Spanish, like Decianus and Lucan; but it is to Quintus Ovid, his neighbour at Momentum, that Martial addresses his most charming lines of friendship. Writing on Ovid's birthday, he mentions his own, and says:

> felix utraque lux diesque nobis
> signandi melioribus lapillis!
> hic vitam tribuit, sed hic amicum.
> plus dant, Quinte, mihi tuae Kalendae.   (IX.52)

(Happy is either morn, and days are they to be marked by us with fairer stones. One gave me life, but the other a friend. Your Kalends, Quintus, gave me the more.)

Martial at his worst can be regrettably careless, trivial and graceless. But he can achieve the elegance of:

> ibis litoreas, Macer, Salonas;
> ibit rara fides amorque recti,
> et quae, cum comitem trahit pudorem,
> semper pauperior redit potestas.   (X.78)

(You will go, Macer, to Salonae by the sea; with you will go rare loyalty and love of right, and power, which, with moderation in its train, ever returns the poorer.)

He can write the simple and pathetic epitaph on the child Erotion (v.34) and produce the vivid character-sketch of the domineering manservant (XI.39), surely the literary ancestor of Jeeves. In him too, as in Virgil, *sunt lacrimae rerum*—in his lines on the house of Pompey (v.74), the consolation to Aratulla (VIII.32), and many of his epitaphs.

Martial himself would smile in disbelief if Landor's tribute to Catullus were extended to the most famous pupil of Catullus in the realm of epigram:

> In Thalia's laughing son
> Such stains there are, as when a Grace
> Sprinkles another's laughing face
> With nectar, and runs on.

For in Martial's work at its worst there is little to remind one of a Grace. Yet in his good epigrams, which are outnumbered, he says,

by his mediocre and bad ones, he displays such a love for his
native rustic scenery as Burns had for 'the streams and burnies' of
Kyle. Martial had the enquiring eye and love of life that Browning
possessed. He had some of the satirical skill in the portrayal of
character that Pope and Dryden displayed. He could also write at
times with an urbanity not unworthy of Horace. His epigram
about one of his admirers, Pompeius Auctus, would not—except
for its metre and perhaps the presence of the self-descriptive word
lasciva—be out of place in the first book of Horace's epistles,
whose charm Macaulay rated so highly. I conclude with the poem,
and hope that these few words with which '*lector studiosus*' has so
patiently borne thus far, will not prevent him becoming like
Pompeius Auctus, a 'fellow-servant' of the unpredictable Muse
of Martial:

> mercari nostras si te piget, Urbice, nugas
>   et lasciva tamen carmina nosse libet,
> Pompeium quaeres, et nosti forsitan, Auctum:
>   Ultoris prima Martis in aede sedet,
> iure madens varioque togae limatus in usu.
>   non lector meus hic, Urbice, sed liber est.
> sic tenet absentes nostros cantatque libellos
>   ut pereat chartis littera nulla meis;
> denique, si vellet, poterat scripsisse videri;
>   sed famae mavult ille favere meae.
> hunc licet a decima (neque enim satis ante vacabit)
>   sollicites, capiet cenula parva duos.
> ille leget, bibe tu; nolis licet, ille sonabit;
>   et cum 'iam satis est' dixeris, ille leget.   (VII.51)

(If you shrink from buying my trifles, Urbicus, and yet would
be acquainted with my wanton verses, you will seek out—
and perhaps you know him—Pompeius Auctus: he sits at
the entrance of Avenging Mars, steeped in law, and versed
in the many-sided practice of the gown. He is not a reader of
my books, Urbicus, but himself the book. He so remembers
my poems, though they are not before him, and declaims
them, that not a letter is lost from my pages; in fine, he
might, if he chose, have been counted their author; but he
chooses rather to support my fame. After the tenth hour—
for he will not be fully at leisure before—you may solicit

him: a small dinner will do for two; he will read: do you drink; although you may not wish it, he will mouth my verses; and when you have said 'Hold! enough!' he will go on reading.)

Notes

1 This is Byron's poetical rendering (*Childe Harold's Pilgrimage*, IV.145) of a quotation from Gibbon's *Decline and Fall of the Roman Empire*, ch. 61: 'The Flavian amphitheatre was contemplated with awe and admiration by the pilgrims of the North, and their rude enthusiasm broke forth in a sublime proverbial expression which is recorded in the eighth century in the fragments of the Venerable Bede: "As long as the Colosseum stands, Rome shall stand; when Rome falls, the world will fall."'

2 In A.D. 96, sixteen years after the opening of the Flavian amphitheatre, Martial could write: *dicitur et nostros cantare Britannia versus*. Professor A. C. Baugh (in *A History of the English Language*) writes that the statement was made 'possibly with some exaggeration'.

3 Byron in his *Occasional Pieces* not only has several poems with the heading 'Epigram', but has translated the first epigram of Martial's first book. We may also see traces of Martial in:

> Oh, Amos Cottle! Phoebus! What a name
> To fill the speaking trump of future fame!
> O, Amos Cottle! for a moment think
> What meagre profits spring from pen and ink!
>
> (English Bards and Scotch Reviewers)

and in

> 'Tis pity learned virgins ever wed
> With persons of no sort of education,
> Or gentlemen, who, though well born and bred
> Grow tired of scientific conversation;
> I don't choose to say much upon this head,
> I'm a plain man and in a single station,
> But—oh! ye lords of ladies intellectual,
> Inform us truly, have they not hen-pecked you all?
>
> (Don Juan, 1.22)

The corresponding passages in Martial are in IV.31, IV.376 and II.90. Byron's judgment on Martial is not flattering (he was equally discourteous to Horace but he still paraphrased *Ars Poetica*):

> And then what proper poet can be partial
> To all those nauseous epigrams of Martial?
>
> (Don Juan, 1.43)

Yet Byron performed the impossible feat of beginning a stanza with a couplet of Martial:

> 'Omnia vult *belle* Matho dicere—dic aliquando
> et *bene*, dic *neutrum*, dic aliquando *male*.'   (x.46)

The first is rather more than mortal can do,
The second may be sadly done, or gaily.   (xv.21)

The English poet overcame with ease the '*syllaba contumax*' (Martial, IX.11) of *male*, in a way that Martial (who cultivated a sterner Muse) would not have dared to attempt. But then, Byron did end his life as a Greek!

4 Such a nymph ('who cannot be above a span in stature') appears in the prose of R. L. Stevenson's *Memories and Portraits*, where in chapter vi he has a passage listing the 'incomparable' streams of Scotland rather as Martial does the beautiful scenes in Spain in IV.55: 'I may not forget Allan Water, nor birch-wetting Rogie, nor yet Almond; nor, in all its pollutions, that Water of Leith of the many and well-named mills—Bell's Mills and Canon Mills and Silver Mills; nor Redford Burn of pleasant memories; nor yet, for all its smallness, that nameless trickle that springs in the green bosom of Allemuir, and is fed from Halkerside with a perennial tea-cupful, and threads the moss under the Shearer's Knowe, and makes one pool there, overhung by a rock.'

5 Cf. in Catullus (one of Martial's avowed models: v. Preface to Book 1) the couplet:

> eripuisti. heu! heu! nostrae crudele venenum
> vitae! heu! heu! nostrae pestis amicitiae.   (77)

The '-ae -ae' of the pentameter stresses the 'heu! heu!'. Catullus is, so to speak, dropping a petal of 'the sanguine flower inscribed with woe' on the grave of friendship.

6 See note 5.

7 Four other epigrams on the same theme and in the same book as v.8 and v.14 can also be paired off similarly, in accordance with size. Each pair comprises a 'pompous' and a 'military' partner. Of the elegiac pair v.38 and 25, 38 is pompous and 25 military. Of the pair of short epigrams v.35 and 23, the former is pompous and the latter military. In v.38 the name Calliodorus is based on the Greek for 'more honourable'. The poem contains a reference to the divine sons of Leda; (their fraternal affection is described as *nobilis* in another poem, 1.36). The Latin is embellished with Greek phrases. Yet all this 'honour' is ironic. Calliodorus and his brother are pettily dishonest, like two theatre-goers who try to enter with one ticket. The Greek words are pedestrian. 'The Ledean stars so famed for love' are used 'to break a butterfly upon a wheel.'

In v.25 'Chaerestratus' denotes 'a farewell to arms' or perhaps 'one who rejoices in armies'. Plain military terms like *sta*, *fuge*, *curre*, *revocat* and *reducit* are used. Deflation is carried further, in that the pejorative word *caballus* is used for 'horse', and the Knights are represented by Scorpus the jockey.

Of the pair v.23 and 35, we find in 23 military terms like *iussit*, and *audit* (cf. *dicto audientes*). 'Bassus' is related in meaning to 'bathos'. In 35, the 'pompous' partner, the name Euclides denotes fame. He is *superbus*, *nobilis*, *locuples*. His descent is traceable to 'glorious Leda' (cf. v.38). Unlike the soldierly Bassus, whose not to reason why, Euclides argues against the order to depart. His honour is rooted in dishonour, too (cf. v.38): his famous name is also wickedly associated with κλείς, a janitor's key.

8 Further points of interest in 11.2 are: the third and fifth lines have rhyming halves, perhaps to denote accord—the enforced accord of Germany with the emperor's rule, and the voluntary accord of Titus and Vespasian in sharing the Jewish laurels. The last line falls into neither pattern, but eschews both V-form and rhyme. It carries this refusal to be governed by the poem's rules yet further: unlike regular pentameters it seems to end in a dissyllable. It is *sui generis* and, like Domitian's victory, entirely his own. A similar bending of the line can be created in the word-order of the third couplet of x.48—if the names are considered:

> Stella, Nepos, Cani, Cerealis, Flacce, venitis?
> septem sigma capit. sex sumus, adde Lupum.

The names, if written in alphabetical order thus:

> Stella,   Lupum
>   Nepos,   Flacce,
>   Cani, Cerealis,

present the appearance of a 'sigma' or crescent-shaped couch.

9
> Καὶ κραναᾶς Βαβυλῶνος ἐπίδρομον ἅρμασι τεῖχος
> καὶ τὸν ἐπ' Ἀλφειῷ Ζᾶνα κατηυγασάμην,
> κάπων τ' αἰώρημα, καὶ Ἡελίοιο κολοσσόν,
> καὶ μέγαν αἰπεινᾶν πυραμίδων κάματον.
> μνᾶμά τε Μαυσωλοῖο πελώριον· ἀλλ' ὅτ' ἐσεῖδον
> Ἀρτέμιδος νεφέων ἄχρι θέοντα δόμον,
> κεῖνα μὲν ἡμαύρωτο καὶ ἦν, ἴδε, νόσφιν Ὀλύμπου
> Ἅλιος οὐδέν πω τοῖον ἐπηυγάσατο.

G.A., IX.58

(I have set eyes on the wall of lofty Babylon on which is a road for four chariots, and the statue of Zeus by the Alpheus, and the hanging gardens, and the colossus of the Sun, and the huge labour of the high pyramids, and the vast tomb of Mausolus; but when I saw the house of Artemis that mounted to the clouds, those other marvels lost their brilliancy, and I said 'Lo, apart from Olympus, the Sun never looked on ought so grand'.)

10 The scazon 'is convenient only for light work (Martial, 1.67; III.58, etc.) but in Catullus approaches pathos, and in Martial is once at least magnificent (IX.2)'. A. W. Verrall, article on 'Metre', in *Companion to Latin Studies*.

Subject Index

271

Name Index